PERCEPTIONS OF THE PAST

IN THE EARLY MIDDLE AGES

MEDIEVAL INSTITUTE

University of Notre Dame

The Conway Lectures in Medieval Studies

2004

The Medieval Institute gratefully acknowledges the generosity of Robert M. Conway and his support for the lecture series and publications resulting from it.

PREVIOUS TITLES IN THIS SERIES:

Paul Strohm
Politique: Languages of Statecraft between Chaucer and Shakespeare (2005)

Ulrich Horst, O.P.
The Dominicans and the Pope: Papal Teaching Authority in the Medieval and Early Modern Thomist Tradition (2006)

PERCEPTIONS OF THE PAST IN THE EARLY MIDDLE AGES

Rosamond McKitterick

University of Notre Dame Press

Notre Dame, Indiana

Library of Congress Cataloging in-Publication Data

McKitterick, Rosamond.
Perceptions of the past in the Early Middle Ages / Rosamond McKitterick.
p. cm. — (The Conway lectures in medieval studies)
Based on lectures the author delivered at the Medieval Institute of the University of Notre
Dame in Sept. 2004.
Includes bibliographical references and index.
ISBN-13: 978-0-268-03500-6 (pbk. : alk. paper)
ISBN-10: 0-268-03500-8 (pbk. : alk. paper)
1. Historiography—Europe—History—To 1500.   2. History—Philosophy—History—
To 1500.   I. University of Notre Dame. Medieval Institute.   II. Title.
D13.5.E85M43   2006
930.072'04—dc22

2006023893

Contents

Illustrations

FIGURE 7. *Annales nazariani,* Vat., pal. lat. 966, fols. 56v–57r   **85**

FIGURE 8. "Lorsch Annals," Sankt Paul in Lavanttal, Stiftsarchiv,
Cod. 8/1, fol. 1r   **93**

I am very grateful for permission to reproduce these manuscript pages to the following individuals and institutions: Doctor Julia Walworth and the master and fellows of Merton College, Oxford; Doctor André Bouwman and the Special Collections of Leiden Universiteitsbibliotheek; the Bayerische Staatsbibliothek, Munich; the Medieval Institute, University of Notre Dame, and the Biblioteca Ambrosiana in Milan; the Stiftsarchiv, Sankt Gallen; the Biblioteca Apostolica Vaticana; and Professor Doctor Rudolf Freisitzer and the Stiftsarchiv, Sankt Paul in Lavanttal. Doctor André Bouwman of the Universiteitsbibliotheek, Leiden, also kindly granted permission to reproduce the page from MS Scaligar 28, fols. 17v–18r, on the cover of this book, and I am particularly grateful to the Universiteitsbibliotheek for waiving the reproduction fee.

Preface

This book is based on the Robert Conway Lectures I delivered in the Medieval Institute of the University of Notre Dame, Indiana, in September 2004. It complements and extends some of the themes I began to explore in *History and Memory in the Carolingian World* (Cambridge, 2004). My first thanks are due to Tom Noble for inviting me to give these lectures, to the University of Notre Dame Press for publishing them in this extended form, and to all those in the institute who made my ten-day sojourn on the campus of the University of Notre Dame so enjoyable, productive, and memorable. I am particularly indebted to Roberta Baranowski for all her organization and help, quite apart from introducing me to the sacred rites of a Notre Dame football game. I am also grateful to Linda Major and Marina Smyth in the Theodore M. Hesburgh Library, who helped me to use the library's excellent resources, not least the Biblioteca Ambrosiana microfilm collection, and who produced material from elsewhere as if by magic. Special thanks are also due to the faculty, research fellows, and research students of the institute, whose lively discussions (many conducted in walks around the lake), assistance with finding books and articles, and questions, were a constant stimulus.

Earlier versions of sections of this book were also presented, in the months between the presentation at Notre Dame and completion of the book, at the Forschungsstelle für Geschichte des Mittelalters (now the Institut für Mittelalter-forschung) in Vienna, the École Française in Rome, the Centre d'Études Supérieures de Civilisation Médiévale in Poitiers, and the Moscow State University. I should like to thank my hosts and my audiences in these places (especially Meta Niederkorn-Bruck and Max Diesenberger, François Bougard, Geneviève Buhrer-Thierry and Régine Le Jan, Wojciech Falkowski, Yves Sassier and Eric Palazzo, and Igor Filippov) as well as in Notre Dame for their contributions and suggestions, of all of which I have tried to take account in the following pages. Helmut Reimitz kindly read the entire text and offered very helpful comments. I am grateful also to Tom Noble and the anonymous reader for the University of Notre Dame Press for additional advice. The final stages of the book's progress through the press were completed in the idyllic working conditions provided for fellows-in-residence at the Netherlands Institute for Advanced Study in the Humanities and Social Sciences in Wassenaar, and warm thanks are due to the Rector, Wim Blockmans, and to all the staff and fellows at the institute, especially Mayke de Jong, Jan Ziolkowski, and Arjo Vanderjagt, for their support. I am very grateful too to Anneke Vrins and Yves de Roo at NIAS and to Peter Erhard, Christine Ottowitz, Helmut Reimitz, and Jonathan Smith for their help with the illustrations. I am indebted to the staff of the University of Notre Dame Press for all the work they have put into producing this book, and particularly to Helena Tomko for her meticulous copyediting.

As ever I have benefitted from the resources and the expertise of the staff of Cambridge University Library, but in addition I wish to thank the staff of the manuscript rooms at the Bibliotheek der Rijksuniversiteit in Leiden, the Bayerische Staatsbibliothek in Munich, the Biblioteca Apostolica Vaticana in Rome, and the Stiftsarchiv and Stiftsbibliothek in Sankt Gallen for their kind assistance on my visits to their collections in relation to codices discussed in this book. I also acknowledge with gratitude the continued support of the Principal and Fellows of Newnham College, Cambridge, and the generosity of Sarah Foot, Yitzhak Hen, Matthew Innes, Christina Pössel, and Elina Screen, as well as of current research students, especially Emma Beddoe, Tom Faulkner, Julian Hendrix, Paul Hilliard, Tom Kitchen, Sally Lamb, David Till, and Charles West, with whom I discussed aspects of the topics addressed in this book. My daughter Lucy and my husband David have helped me in many practical and intellectual ways, and my lasting, if inadequate, thanks, as always, are to them both.

Abbreviations

BnF	Paris, Bibliothèque nationale de France
Clm	Codices latini monacenses
fol.	folio
MGH	Monumenta Germaniae Historica
MS	manuscript
ÖNB	Vienna, Österreichische Nationalbibliothek
Patrologia Latina	J.-P. Migne, ed., *Patrologiae Cursus Completus: Series Latina*, 221 vols. (Paris, 1844–65)
trans.	translation
Vat.	Rome, Biblioteca Apostolica Vaticana

Introduction

My general context for a consideration of perceptions of the past in the early middle ages is the migration of ideas by written as well as by oral means within early medieval culture. Any examination of the exchange of ideas by written means, however, has to take into account the currency of particular methods and genres of writing and attitudes towards them. Thus within my general interest in literacy, and in the role of texts in the exertion of cultural influence, I have become particularly concerned with historiography. One outcome of this interest is my recent book on history and memory in the Carolingian world.[1] In this, my focus was the writing and reading of history in the Frankish kingdoms in the eighth and ninth centuries. I considered what is meant by history books, the Franks' knowledge of historical texts, and the ways in which the Franks constructed and understood their past. Although my study was by no means comprehensive, it became clear from the texts I examined that for the Franks an understanding of the past worked at several levels and was manifested to them in a number of different textual contexts. A sense of the past could express both local, and much more general, cultural affiliations and identities.

Within the general theme of perceptions of the past in the early middle ages, therefore, a sense of time and chronology played a crucial role in both local and more general cultural affinities.[2] With the notion of perceptions, moreover, I am conflating the German *Geschichtsbild*, or concept of history, and *Geschichtsbewußtsein*, or historical consciousness, which Franz-Josef Schmale has done so much to elucidate. I am also drawing on the observations made by Paul Magdalino that "the perception of the past included, but is not identical with, the writing and reading of history" and that it is also more than memory, "for it embraces the recognition that a thing remembered is past and not part of an undifferentiated eternal present."[3] I should also like to emphasize the importance of my choice of the plural "perceptions" rather than the composite "perception." As a methodological principle it is necessary for historians to look at the particular and the individual in order to establish how feasible or valid generalization might be. In the case of perceptions of the past, this is especially crucial, but we need nevertheless to explore the extent to which a variety of perceptions may be interdependent.

I shall focus on the areas incorporated into the Frankish realm by the Carolingian family in the eighth and ninth centuries. A major justification for this is the extraordinary concentration of new text production and older text reproduction in this area and period that has to be accounted for, and whose influence is still being investigated and established.

Historical writing in its many manifestations in late antiquity and the early middle ages was once regarded merely as a potential, if dubious, source for facts. Historical texts which drew on earlier sources were regarded as too derivative to be of value, unless by chance they yielded a piece of information not in their sources. A classic statement of such an attitude is provided by the second edition of the *New Catholic Encyclopedia:* "In general it may be said that all these works take on real historical value only as they approach periods contemporary with or immediately preceding those of their own writers."[4] Anyone who uses the folio volumes of the MGH Scriptores, the quarto-format Auctores Antiquissimi, and the octavo-format Scriptores rerum germanicarum in usum scholarum will be familiar with the editorial practice of printing any sections of text regarded as derived from an earlier source in small print, if they are included at all, and thereby signalling that they can simply be ignored (fig. 1). Even new information provided

A.

Greg. II, 12. maris utiliorem te cognovissem, ipsum expetissem[a] atque eum[b] 'copulassem'. Illeque[c] gaudens, eam ad coniugium suum copulavit. Illa vero concipiens ex eo, peperit filium vocavitque[f] nomen eius 'Chlodovechum. Hic[g] fuit rex magnus super omnes reges Francorum et 'pugnator fortissimus.

8. In illis diebus coeperunt Franci Agripinam[†, 1] civitatem super[a] Renum vocaveruntque[b] eam Coloniam[c], quasi 'coloni inhabitarent in eam[d]. Multo 'populo Romanorum[e] a parte Egidii illic 'interfecerunt; ipse Egidius fugiens evasit. Vene-

Greg. II, 9. runt itaque 'Treveris civitatem[f] super Mosellam[g] fluvium, vastantes terras[h] illas, et 'ipsam succendentes coepe-

ib. II, 18. runt. Post haec igitur mortuus est Egidius Romanorum rex. Siagrius enim, filius eius, in regnum eius[n] resedit[o]; con-

ib. II, 27. stituit 'sedem regni sui in Suessionis

ib. II, 18. civitate. Tunc Childericus rex commovit 'maximo exercitu hostium[s] Francorum, usque[t] Aurilianis civitate 'pervenit, terras quoque illas vastavit. Adovacrius Saxonorum dux cum navale hoste per 'mare usque Andegavis[v] civitate venit illaque 'terra succendit; magna tunc cede in[w] 'illa fecit. Redeunte igitur Ado-

B.

'adque[a] cum eo habitassem'. At ille g., e.[d] sibi ad[e] c. c. Post haec igitur concipiens　　　　　　　　　　　　　　　5 'Chlodoveo[g].

'F., p. bellicosissimus adque egregius.

　　　　　　　　　　　　　　　　　　　10 'q. c. i. i. e. *om.* 'Multoque[d] p. 'Eg. occiderunt ibi; Egidiusque exinde per fugam lapsus, evasit. 'V. autem T.　　　　　　　　　　　15

'illas; ipsam[i] urbem succ. c.[††] Nam antea a Chunis fuerat derupta[k] et[l] adflicta[2]. Eo tempore mortuus est E.[m] R. tirannus. S., f.　　　　　　　　　　　20 'res. habitavitque[p] in S. civitatem, ubi[q] et sedem regni[r] tenebat. Tunc. Ch. 'commoto magno exercitu h., usque 'perrexit[u]

　　　　　　　　　　　　　　　25

'per m. u. *om.* 'illaque t. succ. *om.* 'cede populo vastavit. Adovacrius itaque de Andegavis[x] vel de aliis civitatibus　30 obsedes accepit. Redeunte quoque A.

---

†) Ubi Franci ceperunt Agrippinam, quam et Coloniam vocaverunt *in marg. add. B 1a.*
††) Ubi Treverim Franci ceperunt *in marg. add. B 1a.*

Capp. 7. 8.　*A* 1*a*. *b.* 2. 3*a*[1]. *b.* β[1]. *β*[2]. *B* 1*a*. *b.* 2*a*[1, 2]. *b*[1, 2*], *c*[1].

Cap. 7.　a) expectissem *B* 1*b*; expectassem *B* 2*b*[2**]; atque c. eo h. *om.* *B* 2*b*[2**].　b) mihi *add.* 35 *A* 1*b*; atque ei me c. *A* 3*a*[1]. *b.* β[1]. *β*[2].　c) que *om.* *A* 1*a*. *b*. *c*; At ille *Greg. et B.*　d) eam suscepit sibique *B* 2*c*[1].　e) *om.* *B* 2*a*[1]; in *B* 2*a*[2], *c*[1] *cum Greg.*　f) vocavique ei *B* 1*b*.　g) Clodoeus (Hlodiveinm *B* 1*b*; Choldobeus *B* 2*b*[2**]), fuitque r. *B* 1*a*. *b.*

Cap. 8.　a) fluvium *add.* *B* 1*a*; supra (n *postea add.*) R. fluvium *B* 1*b*.　b) que *om.* *A* 3*a*[1]. c) Colonicam *B* 1*a.*　d) ea multos (que *add.* *A* 3*a*[1]) populos *A* 3*a*[1]. *b*; ea multos (vero *add.* *A* 3 *β*[2]) 40 Romanorum a *A* 3β[1]. *β*[2]; Multum quoque populum *B* 1*b.*　e) Alanorum *B* 1*a*. *b.*　f) civitate *A* 2. *B* 2*b*[1]; s. M. f. T. c. *B* 2*c*[1].　g) f. M. *B* 1*a*. *b*; Musellam *B* 2*a*[2].　h) terram illam *B* 1*a.*　i) ipsamque u. *B* 1*a*. *b.*　k) deruta *B* 2*a*[1] *(non B* 2*a*[2]*)*; dirupta *B* 2*b*[1]; diruta *B* 2*c*[1].　l) adque *B* 1*a.* m) dux *add.* *B* 2*a*[2] (?).　n) *om.* *B* 2*a*[2].　o) eius successit constituitque *A* 3β[1]. *β*[2].　p) habitabitque *B* 1*a*; habitabatque *B* 1*b*; ibi *add.* *B* 1*a*. *b.*　q) ibi et *B* 2*b*[1]. *c*[1]; et *om.* *B* 2*a*[1, 2]. *b*[2**]. 45 r) s. retinebat *B* 2*c*[1].　s) hostiliter *B* 2*b*[1].　t) u. A. c. p. *om.* *A* 3β[1]. *β*[2], *qui pergunt* et partes quoque illas v.　u) perrexerunt *B* 1*b*; pervenit *B* 2*b*[2**] *cum. A.*　v) Andegavos *A* 2; Andecavis *B* 1*a.*　w) cede illa (*corr. eadem m.* cedes illic) fuit *A* 3*a*[1].　x) Angavis *B* 2*a*[1]; vel (et *B* 1*b*) de — Andegavis *om.* *B* 2*b*[2**].

---

1) *Cf. Greg. II, 9.*　2) *Cf. supra c. 5.*　　　　　　　　　　　　　　　　　　　　50

Fig. 1.　"Original" and "borrowed" text in an MGH edition: an example from the *Liber historiae francorum,* ed. Bruno Krusch, MGH Scriptores rerum merovingicarum 2 (Hannover, 1888), p. 250

by early medieval writers has been assessed grudgingly, as if tainted by the author's general dependence on other written texts. Many older studies of historical writing, with displays of great erudition and virtuosity, identified the sources on which historical writers drew, emphasized whatever usefulness the text might possess as a source of independent information, and validated this information in relation to other sources. But they stopped there, their work done, at least to their authors' satisfaction.

As many, though not all, historians have realized more recently, of course, establishing on what sources a particular writer drew is only the first and essential step in assessing the implications of the selection, rearrangement, incorporation, and new emphases accorded those same sources in their new contexts. Yet I wish in this book to go one step farther even than this. The entire text of each history needs to be assessed, for it is this that can best offer insights into the intellectual world of the early medieval historical writers and compilers and their perspective on, and knowledge of, the past. The text created can help us to understand the motives for the selection of particular themes and information. It can reveal the consequent varying perceptions of the past.

Further, the use of other sources witnesses to what I have referred to elsewhere as "communication with the past" and what Joyce Hill has recently described as "intertextual dialogue."[5] The mode of composition depended on textual interaction. It created a frame of reference that was effective in varying degrees, depending on the prior knowledge of the reader. It reflects, as we shall see, particular attitudes towards what that past offered in terms of authority. Thus I am not so much concerned with the old issue of what was drawn from past texts, or even the newer concern of how past texts were drawn on. My concern is more why those texts in particular were selected, what new texts they create, and the implications of the ways in which particular texts provided a solid foundation for an understanding of the past in the early middle ages.

It is also necessary to examine the common understanding of medieval historiography as narrative representations of the past, for in some of the texts I shall be looking at in the course of this book, the narrative elements are subordinate to other considerations.[6] Indeed, there is a danger in current understandings of medieval historiography of allowing what is understood about the historical writing of the high middle ages, that is, the period from the later eleventh to the thirteenth century, to provide a benchmark for, or to represent, all medieval historical writing.[7] This certainly does not work for late antiquity and the earlier middle ages.

A case in point is the *Chronicon* of Eusebius-Jerome, at whose influence I shall look in the first chapter, and thus at the implications of the reception and composition of so-called universal history in the ninth and early tenth centuries. The way in which such "universal histories" were composed, and the various perceptions of the past they reflect, raise two further questions which I shall then explore in the remaining two chapters, namely, Carolingian perceptions of the Roman past and eighth- and ninth-century perceptions of the local past in the Frankish realm within the wider contexts of Christian and national history.

ONE

Chronology and Empire

GENESIS AND "WORLD CHRONICLES"

Let me begin with beginnings, from the first chapter of the Book of Genesis and the Gospel of St John respectively:

> In the beginning God made heaven and earth.
> *In principio creavit deus caelum et terram.*
>
> (Gn 1:1)

and

> In the beginning was the word.
> *In principio erat verbum.*
>
> (Jn 1:1)

Early Christian thinkers associated these two beginnings. Athanasius (296–373), in his tract on the Incarnation, for example, wrote:

> But as we proceed in our exposition of the Incarnation of the word, we must first speak about the Creation of the universe and its creator, God, so that in this way we may consider as fitting that its renewal was effected by the Word who created it in the beginning.[1]

Origen (185–254) also, in his *Homiliae in Genesim* (Homilies on Genesis), stated:

In the beginning therefore, that is, in his Word, God made heaven and earth, as the evangelist John also says at the beginning of his Gospel, in the beginning was the word.[2]

In hoc ergo principio, hoc est in verbo suo deus coelum et terram fecit, sicut et evangelista iohannes in initio evangelii sui ait dicens, in principio erat verbum.[3]

So too, Jerome (345–420), creator by both correction and translation of much of the Vulgate Bible, spelt out the connection between the first words of the Book of Genesis and of Saint John's Gospel.[4] In his tractate *Libri Hebraicarum Quaestionum in Genesim* (Hebrew Questions on Genesis), a work written between 391 and 393 and designed to communicate Jewish scholarship both on its own terms and in the form of investigations of Hebrew teachings, he commented that the connection

could be applied to Christ more in respect of its intention than following its literal translation: to Christ who is proved to be founder of heaven and earth both at the very front of Genesis which is the head of all the books and also at the beginning of John the Evangelist's work.

Magis itaque secundum verbi translationem de Christo accipi potest qui tam in ipsa fronte Geneseos, quae caput librorum omnium est, quae etiam in principio Joannis Evangelistae, coeli et terrae conditor approbatur.[5]

Quite apart from the parallelism in Christian thinking about the Creation and Fall, Adam and Christ, Eve and Mary, the two Biblical phrases about "the beginning" express an essentially Christian understanding both of the physical creation of the world in time, and of divine eternity in the past and future. The beginning of history had both a practical and a spiritual dimension. Patristic and early medieval commentators on Genesis and Saint John's Gospel, whether from a literal or an allegorical point of view, presented interpretations of the creation of the world and Christ as the Word which were propagated in the schools and among scholars. They were also communicated to the general population by means of the liturgical readings at Easter and Pentecost (Gn 1) and Christmas (Jn 1).[6]

Given the Franks' deep engagement with the past it is hardly surprising that there was such a wide interest in the Carolingian period in commentaries on Genesis and the other historical books of the Bible.[7] Indeed, it is no accident that so many Carolingian commentaries on both Genesis and Saint John's Gospel were produced, not least Eriugena's *Periphyseon* (*De divisione naturae*, or The division of nature).[8] In particular, the literal exposition of Genesis attributed to Wigbod and the commentary on Saint John by Alcuin are closely associated with the court circle of Charlemagne.[9]

I should like to suggest that these two phrases from the Vulgate, expressing in effect an understanding of human and divine time, provide the fundamental underlay for perceptions of the past in the early medieval west. It was not simply that these "*in principio*" phrases were, with the story of Adam and the Fall, among the most familiar to every Christian from their liturgical repetition at Christmas, Easter, and Pentecost and thus part of every Christian's understanding of the world. This liturgical repetition of Biblical narrative and Gospel story created a fundamental orientation of attitude and perspective as well as being common currency. The beginnings of Genesis and Saint John's Gospel, which themselves begin crucial historical narratives of the fortunes of the Jews and of Christ's birth, ministry, and passion, serve to highlight the theme of the precise role played by the historical writing contained in the Old and New Testaments in forming perceptions of the past in the early middle ages, especially in the Frankish kingdoms of the eighth and ninth centuries.

The most dramatic indication of this is that it is the Creation which is the beginning point of most late antique and early medieval chronicles. All but two of the thirty-two major "world chronicles" written between the third and the tenth centuries within a Christian milieu, and tabulated by Dorothea von den Brincken, start with the Creation.[10] The exceptions are the chronicle of Eusebius and its continuation by Jerome (which von den Brincken counts as two). The six days of Creation and the forming of Adam in God's image, the Fall, the formation of human society outside paradise and the struggle for survival in a world where sin and crime spread, the punishment for human wickedness in the form of the Flood, the rainbow and God's covenant with Noah, and, lastly, the break-up of human solidarity into diverse peoples symbolized by the Tower of Babel, are included in most Christian histories, even if only in very brief and allusive form.[11] Orosius in his *Historiarum adversus paganos libri septem* (Seven books of history against the pagans), written ca. 430, provides the fullest explanation of why he started at the beginning (though, like many historians since, he rather exaggerates the novelty of what he is doing as well as the extent of alternative practice):

> Nearly all writers of history (Greek as well as Latin) who have perpetuated in their various works the deeds of kings and peoples for the sake of form-

ing an enduring record have commenced their histories with Ninus, the son of Belus and king of the Assyrians. Indeed, these historians with their very limited insight would have us believe that the origin of the world and the creation of man was without beginning; yet they definitely state that kingdoms and wars began with Ninus, as if forsooth the human race had existed up to that time in the manner of beasts and then, as though shaken and aroused, it awoke for the first time to a wisdom previously unknown to it. For my part, however, I have determined to date the beginning of man's misery from the beginning of his sin . . . From Adam, the first man, to Ninus . . . in whose time Abraham was born, 3,184 years have elapsed, a period that all historians have either disregarded or have not known.

I. *Et quoniam omnes propemodum tam apud Graecos quam apud Latinos studiosi ad scribendum viri, qui res gestas regum populorumque ob diuturnam memoriam uerbis propagauerunt, initium scribendi a Nino Beli filio, rege Assyriorum fecere.*

II. *qui cum opinione caeca mundi originem creaturamque hominum sine initio credi uelint, coepisse tamen ab hoc regna bellaque definiunt*

III. *quasi uero eatenus humanum genus ritu pecudum uixerit et tunc primum ueluti ad nouam prudentiam concussum suscitatumque uigilarit*

IV. *ego initium miseriae hominum ab initio peccati hominis docere institui, paucis dumtaxat isdemque breuiter delibatis*

V. *Sunt autem ab Adam primo homine usque ad Ninum "magnum" ut dicunt regem, quando natus est Abraham, anni IIICLXXXIIII qui ab omnibus historiographis vel omissi vel ignorati sunt.*[12]

Orosius enhanced and reinforced his beginning with the Creation with his famous geographical description of the world created; his approach had its followers.[13] Yet the *Chronicon* of Eusebius translated by Jerome, the most influential "world history" of all, started at the point Orosius so strongly criticized, that is, with the divided world into which Abraham was born among the Chaldeans in the reign of Ninus. So, incidentally, did the Old English version of Orosius, though this did at least include Orosius's geographical chapter.[14] The account that follows in Eusebius-Jerome's *Chronicon* is essentially that of the fortunes of the Hebrews.[15] Jerome, however, at the end of his continuation to Eusebius's *Chronicon*, which covers the years from 327 to 378, provides the following summary of the chronology in reverse. This includes a reckoning from Adam, and complements the brief sketch of the descent of man from Adam and the peoples of the world from the three sons of Noah in Jerome's prefatory material before Eusebius's *canones* begin. Thus Jerome wanted his readers to think in terms of the history of the world from the Creation:

All the years down to the sixth consulship of Valens and the second of the Emperor Valentinian are reckoned here.

From the fifteenth year of Tiberius and the preaching of our Lord Jesus Christ, 351 years. From the second year of Darius, king of Persia at which time the temple was restored 899 years. From the first Olympiad in which age Isaiah was prophesying among the Hebrews, 1,155 years. From Solomon and the first construction of the temple, 1,411 years. From the downfall of Troy, at which time Samson was among the Hebrews, 1,561 years. From Moses and Cecrops the first king of Attica 1,890 years. From Abraham and the reign of Ninus and Semiramis 2,395 years.

All the list from Abraham down to the time written above which contains 2,395 years. From the Flood, moreover, to Abraham, the years are estimated to be 942 years. From Adam to the Flood, 2,242 years. From Adam down to the fourteenth year of Valens, that is, to his sixth consulship and the second of Valentinian, all the years that elapsed were 5,579 years.

Colliguntur omnes anni usque in consulatum Valentis. VI. et Valentiniani iunioris iterum Augusti:

a XV Tiberii anno et praedicatione domini nostri Iesu Christi anni CCCLI

a secundo anno Darii regis Persarum quo tempore templum Hierosolymis instauratum est anni DCCCXCVIIII

ab olympiade prima qua aetate apud Hebraeos Isaias prophetabat anni MCLV

a Solomone et prima aedificatione templi anni MCCCCXI

a capitivate Troiae quo tempore Sampson apud Hebraeos erat anni MDLXI

a Moyse et Cecrope primo rege Atticae anni MDCCCXC

ab Abraham et regno Nini et Semiramidis anni IICCCXCV

Continet omnis canon ab Abraham usque ad tempus supra scriptum ann. MMCCXVC

a diluvio autem usque ad Abraham supputantur anni DCCCCXLII

Et ab Adam usque ad diluvium anni IICCXLII

Fiunt ab Adam usque ad XIIII Valentis annum, id est usque ad consulatum eius VI et Valentiniani iterum omnes anni VDLXXVIIII [16]

Jerome also explained in his preface that he had added "certain things which appeared to us to have been allowed to slip, particularly in the Roman history, which Eusebius, the author of this book, as it seems to me only glanced at; not so much because of ignorance, for he was a learned man as because, writing in Greek, he thought them of slight importance to his countrymen" (*et nonnulla quae mihi intermissa videbantur adieci, in Romana maxime historia, quam Eusebius huius conditor libri, non tam ignorasse ut eruditus sed ut Graece scribens parum suis necessariam perstrinxisse mihi videtur).*[17]

A further principle of organization introduced by some authors was that of the Six Ages, most clearly explained by Bede in chapter 66 of his *De temporum ratione* (On the reckoning of time) and again harking back to the first verses of Genesis:

> We have mentioned a few things about the Six Ages of this world, and about the Seventh and Eighth [Ages] of peace and heavenly life above (chapter 10), by way of comparison to the first week, in which the world was adorned. Here I shall discuss the same subject somewhat more extensively, comparing it to the ages of man, whom the philosophers are accustomed to call "microcosm" in Greek, that is, "small universe". The First Age of this world, then, is from Adam to Noah, containing 1,656 years according to the Hebrew truth and 2,242 according to the Septuagint and ten generations according to both versions . . .
>
> The Second Age from Noah to Abraham comprises ten generations and 292 years according to the Hebrew authority, but according to the Septuagint 272 years and eleven generations . . .
>
> The Third from Abraham to David, contains fourteen generations and 942 years according to both authorities . . .
>
> The Fourth, from David up to the exile to Babylon has 473 years according to the Hebrew truth, twelve more according to the Septuagint, and seventeen generations according to both texts. . . . From this age—youth, so to speak—the era of the kings began among the people of God, for this age in man is normally apt for governing a kingdom.
>
> The Fifth Age—maturity if you will—from the exile into Babylon until the coming of our Lord and Saviour in the flesh, extends for fourteen generations and 589 years . . .
>
> The Sixth Age, which is now in progress, is not fixed according to any sequence of generations or times, but like senility this [Age] will come to an end in the death of the whole world.

By a happy death, everyone will overcome these Ages of the world and when they have been received into the Seventh Age of perennial Sabbath, they look forward to the Eighth Age of the blessed Resurrection, in which they will reign forever with the Lord.

De sex huius mundi aetatibus ac septima vel octava quietis vitaeque caelestis et supra in conparatione primae ebdomadis, in qua mundus ornatus est, aliquanta perstrinximus, et nunc in conparatione aevi unus hominis, qui microcosmos Grecae a philosophis, hoc est minor mundus solet nuncupari, de eisdem aliquanto latius exponemus.

Prima est ergo mundi huius aetas ab Adam usque ad Noe, continens, annos iuxta Hebraicam veritatem mille DCLVI, iuxta LXX interpretes IICCXLII, generationes iuxta utramque editionem numero X . . .

Secunda aetas a Noe usque ad Abraham generationes iuxta Hebraicam auctoritatem conplexa X, annos autem CCXCII, porro iuxta LXX interpretes ann. CCLXXII, generationes vero XI . . .

Tertia ab Abraham usque ad David generationes iuxta utramque auctoritatem XIIII, annos vero DCCCCXLII conplectens . . .

Quarta a David usque ad transmigrationem Babylonis, habens annos iuxta Hebraicam veritatem CCCCLXXIII, iuxta LXX translationem XII amplius, generationes iuxta utrosque codices XVII . . .

A qua velut iuuenali aetate in populo dei regum tempora coeperunt, haec namque in hominibus aetas apta gubernando solet existere regno.

Quinta quasi senilis aetas a transmigratione Babylonis usque in adventum domini salvatoris in carnem, generationibus et ipsa XIIII, porro annis DLXXXVIIII extenta . . .

Sexta, que nunc agitur, aetas, nulla generationum vel temporum serie certa, sed ut aetas decrepita ipsa totius saeculi morte consumenda.

Has erumnosas plenasque laboribus mundi aetates quique felici morte vicerunt; septima iam sabbati perennis aetate suscepti, octavam beatae resurrectionis aetatem, in qua semper cum domino regnent, exspectant.[18]

Von den Brincken's seminal study of the group of texts lumped together as the genre *Weltchronik* (world chronicle) argued that universal history was sacred history, that histories which traced the rise and fall of empires from the time of Abraham were by implication directed conceptually towards the Last Judgement and the working out of God's providence in time. Brian Croke, moreover, has demonstrated in his discussion of Count Marcellinus's chronicle how the nar-

rative presents the Roman empire as part of universal history. In Count Marcellinus's text, non-Roman nations were integrated into the political entity at
the centre of which was the church, whose doctrinal unity and integrity were
stressed.[19] Yet von den Brincken herself also pointed out that many historians
in the middle ages sought to identify or define the position of their own times in
relation to this larger scheme of events. Many of those who have studied the
Chronicon of Eusebius-Jerome have commented on the achievement of the history
in demonstrating how local or national history could be placed in the context of
God's time and how patterns emerge in such a way that the detail is less important.[20] Yet they have also seen it primarily as a story of four "universal empires"—
Assyrian, Persian, Greek, Roman—each succeeding the other in world dominance. This is far too simplistic, for it merely focusses on the framework within
which the detail is offered.

Eusebius-Jerome did not tell the Hebrew story alone, for the fortunes of
Jews and Christians are intertwined with the histories of the Assyrians, Persians,
Greeks, Romans, and others. Eusebius set the pattern of secular involvement by
demonstrating the intertwining of the fortunes of secular rulers with religious
events and ideas. To see these histories solely, or even primarily, as schematic sacred history is to underestimate them. The *Chronicon* is not just about the succession of empires. In this curious and disjointed text, chronological tables are
constructed from Abraham to the twentieth year of the reign of the emperor
Constantine I. Olympiads are cited alongside the years since Abraham by way
of chronological orientation, as are, where appropriate, the regnal years of kings,
judges, archons, and emperors. Columns are provided, at first spread across two-
page openings and afterwards confined to one page once the story becomes concerned mostly with the area ruled by the Romans. These columns are separately
labelled and even on occasion colour-coded in the earliest manuscripts to indicate
events under the headings of Medes, Persians, Athenians, Romans, Hebrews, and
Macedonians. One or two columns are filled with notes of events and other columns are taken up with the various dates, such as the the career of Moses, the
reign of Jereboam in Israel, the birth of Romulus and Remus, and the founding of
Rome, of Nicomedia, and of Byzantium (later Constantinople).[21] The importance
of Eusebius's synchronization of world history needs to be emphasized, for the
juxtapositions, such as the fall of Troy and the downfall of Samson, or the careers
of Homer and Solomon, or Deborah and King Midas, in the various pasts Eusebius documented are to be understood fully only in relation to Christian history.[22]

These columns create their own chronological and thematic juxtapositions (fig. 2). The earliest manuscripts, moreover, presented a series of marginal glosses, abstracts of selected entries, and chronological notes apparently copied in from an even earlier exemplar. The page illustrated in Franz Steffens's palaeographical handbook from the famous Oxford manuscript of Eusebius-Jerome from the fifth/sixth century, for example, provides a sense of what this text looks like. On this page the *Chronicon* records Herodotus, and a sloping uncial hand highlights the same words in the margin. Later copyists reproduced this lay-out as best they could, as can be seen from the Carolingian example illustrated here with an opening from Oxford, Merton College, MS Coxe 315, fols. 42v and 43r, where the columns are black, red, and green.[23]

Jerome continued Eusebius from 327 to 378. His work was written, as Benoît Jeanjean and Bertrand Lançon argue, between the Spring of 379 and November 380, though a date before 28 February 380 is conceivable.[24] Jerome's continuations anchored heresy, and especially that of the Arians, in his narrative.[25] Despite the dominance of the Arian theme, it is not just sacred history that Jerome communicates, but also a series of short, pithy, and highly opinionated comments about a great variety of events, rulers, and politics, about the construction of churches, and about the careers of famous scholars, such as Arnobius.[26] Jerome injects his personal scorn into the account of AD 362, for example, in noting the emperor Julian's conversion to paganism. Jerome comments that a "mild persecution was alluring rather than compelling Christians to sacrifice. In this persecution many of our people fell into ruin willingly." (*Iuliano ad idolorum cultum converso blanda persecutio fuit inliciens magis quam inpellens ad sacrificandum in qua multi ex nostris voluntate propria corruerunt.*)[27] In the following year Jerome also notes that there was a law forbidding Christians to teach the liberal arts.[28] Under AD 369 Jerome notes that Athanaric, king of the Goths, "killed a great number of Christians when he had incited a persecution. He also drove a great many people from their own settlements into Roman territory." (*Athanaricus rex Gothorum in Christianos persecutione commota plurimos interficit et de propriis sedibus in Romanum solum expellit.*)[29]

Let us look in more detail at the jumble of elements under AD 373. First of all there is a reference to Eunomius (from whom the Eunomian heresy derives), followed in the other columns by references to the Saxons who were cut to pieces at Deuso in the territory of the Franks; the descent of eighty-thousand Burgundians on the Rhine; the aqueduct built by Clearchus in Constantinople; and the

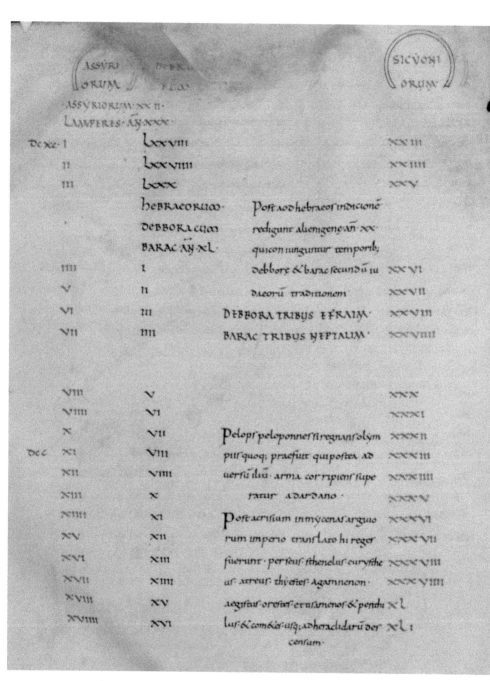

Fig. 2. Eusebius-Jerome, *Chronicon*. The page lay-out of the text from the ninth-century copy in Oxford, Merton College Library, Coxe 315, fols. 42v and 43r

ARGIYO
RUM·

ATHENI
ENSIUM·

AEGYPTI
ORUO·

ARGIYORUM	ATHENIENSIUM		AEGYPTIORUM
XVII	XXI	Amphion thebis regnauit quem	XLVIII
XVIII	XXII	ferunt cantu citharae saxa mouis	L
XVIIII	XXIII	se fuerunt au duro corde & uitia	LI
		dica saxei quidam auditores·	
XX	XXIIII		LII
XXI	XXV		LIII
XXII	XXVI		LIIII
XXIII	XXVII	Secundu quosda thebis regnauit	LV
		cadmus	AEGYPTI·RAM SES·AN·LXVI·
			I
XXIIII	XXVIII		
XXV	XXVIIII	Europa a cretensibus rapta est	II
XXVI	XXX	naui cuius fuit insigne taurus·	III
XXVII	XXXI	Ea quae desparus memorantur qr	IIII
XXVIII	XXXII	palefatus scribit cu proximaru essent	V
XXVIIII	XXXIII	regionu aduersu cadmu subito consu	VI
XXX	XXXIIII	tusse & propter repentinos quasde	VII
XXXI	XXXV	terra contractus & ex omni parte	VIII
ARGIYORU REGES DEFICER QUI IMPERAUER AN·DXLIIII·VSQ· AD PELOPEM QUI REGNAUIT AN· LVIII·	XXXVI	confluentes sparsos uocatos·	VIIII
	XXXVII	Mida regnauit in frygia·	X
	XXXVIII		XI
	XXXVIIII		XII

consecration of Petrus as bishop of Alexandria with the comment: "he was so easy about accepting heretics after the death of Valens that he aroused in some the suspicion that money was involved." (*Qui post Valentis interitum tam facilis in recipiendis haereticis fuit ut nonnullis suspicionem acceptae pecuniae intulerit.*)[30] Many of the remarks seem pointed in relation to Jerome's own career and personal knowledge. Why else would Jerome single out the journey of the widow Melania to Jerusalem or the election of Ambrose as bishop and tell his readers (under 374) that the "clergy of Aquileia were regarded as if they were a choir of the blessed"? (*Aquileienses clerici quasi chorus beatorum habentur.*)[31]

This is a history about Christian communities, and about individuals, organized within the framework of a host of general comments about political events across the Roman and Persian empires. Those who initiated heresies are catalogued tersely. Only the Arians and their pernicious doings are reported in greater detail. Occasionally natural disasters or events such as earthquakes and eclipses of the sun are also inserted. Jerome, writing in 380 or 381, chose to stop with the battle of Adrianople, the resounding defeat of the Roman army by a Gothic army, and the death of the emperor Valens.

A reader of Eusebius-Jerome would have met an apparently superficial set of bulletins, with the progress of the Arians as the principal theme. In other words the function of this text's sacred history is subordinated to a personalized summary of practical events within the Christian church against a more general backdrop of a succession of emperors and their campaigns. As already observed in relation to Eusebius's portion, the presentation is certainly interesting for the chronological juxtaposition of quite a lot of miscellaneous information delivered in a primarily telegraphic kind of style. There is a recurrence of particular topics, such as natural portents or events, the movement of different opponents to Rome—Huns, Goths, Sarmatians, Persians, and the like—and the nefarious activities of the Arians in many guises and with offshoots as other kinds of heretics. Yet this is not purely secular history, nor is it ecclesiastical history. Indeed, the constant reiteration of the secular chronology of Olympiads and secular consuls would belie the sacred framework.

Eusebius's chronological notes, his record of details such as those concerning the historian Herodotus, and the character of Jerome's additions, may serve as sufficient indications to us that what we have in this text is not so much world history and the rise and fall of empires as the moral of the fate of human vainglory. More important is the cultural and historical map this chronicle provides for the

reader. Visually and succinctly it sets out and locates in time the relationship between the various elements of an educated Christian's universe. For Eusebius this
was for those educated within the Romano-Greek tradition who were now also required to relate their own world to a new middle-eastern history and to appreci-
ate simultaneous events within the worlds of the Hebrews, Assyrians, Egyptians,
and others. For continuators from Jerome onwards, and for subsequent Christian
readers, the chronicle continued to serve primarily as an historical map, orienting
a reader in particular ways and providing a summary of basic historical land-
marks in an intellectual landscape that encompassed nearly all of human time.[32]
The authors presented readers with a framework of knowledge and a series of
connections and synchronizations, as well as a kind of chronological genealogy.
Yet the central strand in all these chronicles is the steady progression towards the
Christian people, who form the principal subject of the end part of the story, even
if the method of comparative synchronization is maintained throughout the text.
The focus on Christian people is echoed in Eusebius's *Historia ecclesiastica* (Ecclesiastical history), known in the Latin west in the Latin translation by Rufinus, especially in Eusebius's preface to book 5. Here the proper subjects of Christian
history, as against those of "pagan" historiography, are the champions of true religion, the martyrs, monks, ascetics, and virgins, and the wars against the devil.[33]
The combined effect of Eusebius's historical work was to engage all Christian
people, great and small, in the narrative.

EARLY MEDIEVAL CONTINUATORS OF EUSEBIUS-JEROME

Among the early medieval continuators of Eusebius-Jerome,[34] perhaps the
most influential world chronicle was that of Bede, included as chapter 66 of his
massive book on chronology, the *De temporum ratione*, and completed ca. 725.[35]
Working within the Eusebian-Hieronymian tradition, Bede coloured his historical map in a distinctively different way. As Paul Hilliard has established, Bede
relates his narrative even more emphatically than either Eusebius or Jerome had
done to the Old and New Testaments, in such a way as to be clearly the work of
the man who had written commentaries on the Books of Genesis and Kings, the
Gospel of Luke, and the Acts of the Apostles. His chronicle indicates, as that of
Eusebius-Jerome did, that Christian and Hebrew history was even older than
Greek mythology.[36]

Bede conducts his narrative in large steps. At first he is content to summarize the Book of Genesis, but he contributes a comment on the division of languages and families of Latin, Punic, African, and Babylonian attributed to Arnobius's commentary on Psalm 104.[37] As his text proceeds, more comparative detail from other regions and peoples besides the Hebrews is inserted, with close attention paid throughout the text to the chronology of and different authorities about both the length of time of things and particular details. Joshua's reign, for instance, lasted twenty-six years: "as Josephus teaches, for Scripture is silent on the number of years of his leadership" (*ut docet Iosephus, in scriptura enim sancta quamdiu praefuerit minime patet*).[38] There is a far greater proportion of information about the Hebrews and, subsequently, about the Christians than about the other peoples in Bede's text. At the year 4175, for example, he notes:

Marcus Aurelius Antoninus [Elagabulus] [ruled for] 4 years.

In Palestine the city of Nicopolis, previously called Emmaeus, was [re]-founded; Julius Africanus, a writer of Chronicles, received the commission to carry this out. This is the Emmaeus which the Lord deigned to sanctify by going there after his Resurrection, as Luke records.

Bishop Hippolytus, the author of many works, brought his book *The Canon of History* up to this point [in time]. His discovery of the sixteen-year Easter cycle gave Eusebius the opportunity to compose a nineteen-year cycle based on it.

IIIICLXXV. Marcus Aurelius Antoninus an. IIII.

In Palestina Nicopolis qui prius Emmaus vocabatur, urbs condita est, legationis industriam pro ea suscipiente Iulio Africano scriptore temporum. Haec est Emmaus, quam dominus post resurrectionem suo ingressu, sicut Lucas narrat, sanctificare dignatus est.

Hyppolitus episcopus, multorum conditor opusculorum. Temporum Canonem quem scripsit hucusque perduxit. Qui etiam sedecennalem paschae circulum repperiens Eusebio, qui super eodem pascha[-lem?] decennovennalem circulum composuit, occasionem dedit.[39]

The year 4444 mentions in sequence the rule of the emperor Zeno, the finding of the body of the apostle Barnabas, and the supposed autograph of the Gospel of Matthew, the rule of Odoacer in Rome, the Goths in Macedonia, Constantinople, and Italy, the persecution of the Catholic bishops of Africa by the Vandal king

Huneric, Ambrosius Aurelianus's leadership of the Britons against the Saxons, and the latter's eventual takeover of the island of Britain.[40]

The year 4518 shows a similar jumble of information, but again with events in Christian history predominating:

> Justinian, nephew by a sister of Justin [ruled for] 38 years.
>
> The patrician Belisarius, sent by Africa to Justinian, exterminated the Vandals. Carthage was recovered in the ninety-sixth year after its loss. The Vandals were defeated and expelled, and their king Gelimer was sent as a captive to Constantinople.
>
> The body of Anthony the monk, discovered by divine revelation, was brought to Alexandria, and buried in the church of the blessed John the Baptist.
>
> Dionysius wrote Paschal tables beginning in the 532nd year from the Lord's Incarnation, which is the 248th year after Diocletian.
>
> After [came] the consulship of Lampadius and Orestes, and in this year the Code of Justinian was promulgated to the world.
>
> Victor of Capua wrote a book about Easter, criticizing the errors of Victorius.
>
> *IIIIDXVIII. Justinianus Iustini ex sorore nepos an. XXXVIII.*
>
> *Bilizarius patricius a Iustiniano in Africam missus Vandalorum gentem delevit. Carthago quoque anno excessionis suae XCVI recepta est pulsis deuictis que Vandalis et Gelismero rege eorum capto Constantinopolim misso.*
>
> *Corpus sancti Antoni monachi divina revelatione repertum Alexandriam defertur et in ecclesia beati baptistae Iohannis humatur.*
>
> *Dionisius paschales scribit circulos, incipiens ab anno dominicae incarnationis DXXXII, qui est annus Dioclitiani CCXLVIII.*
>
> *Post consolatum Lampadii et Orestis, quo anno Codex Iustinianus orbi promulgatus est.*
>
> *Victor quoque Capuanus episcopus librum de Pascha scribens Victorii arguit errores.*[41]

The *Chronicon* of Eusebius-Jerome is one of the few patristic texts with a continuous transmission history, in terms of its manuscript, from the fifth to the tenth centuries. No fewer than twenty-eight manuscript copies are extant spanning this period, with eight from before the later eighth century. These include the Oxford copy from the middle of the fifth century, a fifth-century set of fragments of Fleury provenance, and four seventh-century copies from Corbie, Fleury, Oviedo, and Saint Amand.[42] The remainder, with the exception of the excerpts in Lucca, Biblioteca Capitolare, 490 (of ca. 800), and fragments in Munich, Bayerische Staatsbibliothek, Clm 6315 + 29022 + 29022e, possibly from Bobbio, were copied in Francia between the late eighth century and the middle of the tenth century in such centres as Reichenau, Tours, Micy, Corbie, Saint-Germain-des-Prés, Sankt Gallen, and Trier. Carolingian knowledge of the early codices is suggested by the use made at ninth-century Saint Amand of Eusebius-Jerome and the copy of the ancient Fleury codex made at Saint Mesmin, Orléans, in ca. 840. In some cases, such as Leiden, Universiteitsbibliotheek, MS Scaliger 14, London, British Library, Add. 16974, Oxford, Merton College, MS Coxe 315, and Paris, BnF, lat. 4860, the chronicle was extended with other texts, such as the continuations by Prosper, Marius of Avenches, or others mentioned above.[43]

Even without taking excerpts into account, such as those in the famous Verona miscellany,[44] there is thus ample evidence of a wide dissemination of the Eusebius-Jerome *Chronicon* within the Frankish kingdoms in the Carolingian period.[45] Similarly, copies of Bede's *De temporum ratione*, which included the world chronicle in chapter 66, were also widely dispersed in the Frankish kingdoms, with almost half of the over one hundred extant manuscripts of *De temporum ratione* dating from before the middle of the ninth century. Although a handful of the Frankish copies omit Bede's chronicle itself, others include only the chronicle chapter. To these should be added the Carolingian chronicles which incorporated sections of Bede's chronicle as parts of new and larger works,[46] as well as those influenced by both Eusebius-Jerome and Bede in their perceptions both of the past and of the relationship between human and divine time.

CAROLINGIAN "WORLD CHRONICLES"

So far we have seen that the perception of the past as springing from the beginning of the world, including all human time, painted on a worldwide canvas, and embracing one's own history, was established by Eusebius-Jerome and disseminated through both direct knowledge of that text and through his emulators, most especially Bede in chapter 66 of the *De temporum ratione*. Let us look in more detail at three examples of what the Franks in the Carolingian period made of this presentation of the past. As we shall see, a number of Carolingian chroniclers appear to have realized the concept of an historical map thus transmitted, though they also incorporated distinctively Carolingian developments in historical writing in the form of contemporary Frankish annals. Of these, the chronicle of Freculf of Lisieux, written in two parts in the late 820s and designed for the education of Charles the Bald, was certainly the largest enterprise. It is now accessible in Michael Allen's splendid new edition.[47] Freculf provides a clear instance of the continuity of a perception of the past oriented from Genesis, for his essentially Augustinian conception of history depends greatly, as Nikolaus Staubach has established, on the Carolingian scholar Claudius of Turin's commentary on Genesis.[48] Claudius, incidentally, was himself the author of a chronicle.[49] Freculf provides an explanation of his intentions in the dedicatory letter of part 2 of the history; he decided to stop his history at the point where he considered the Franks and the Lombards to have succeeded Roman officials and Goths as the rulers of Gaul and Italy.[50]

The Chronicle of 741

My first example of a Carolingian emulator of Eusebius-Jerome and Bede is the author of the *Chronicon universale—741* (Universal chronicle of 741), to which Georg Waitz, Bernhard von Simson, and Friedrich Kurze, and after them Wilhelm Wattenbach, Wilhelm Levison, and von den Brincken, long ago drew attention, and which predates Freculf by some decades.[51] This work runs from Adam to 741, when Charles Martel, the Frankish mayor of the palace, died and was succeeded by his two sons Pippin and Carloman. The sons divided their father's territory between them, so that Carloman received Austrasia, Alamannia, and Thuringia and Pippin's portion comprised Burgundy, Neustria, and Provence. The chronicle is thought to have been composed after ca. 768, though I have found no clear argument or evidence to support this supposition; the narrative was subsequently continued to 811. The part running to 741 is extant in two ninth-century manuscripts: Munich, Bayerische Staatsbibliothek, Clm 246, s. IX med. from Weltenburg in the diocese of Regensburg; and Leiden, Universiteitsbibliotheek, MS Scaliger 28, written at Flavigny ca. 816, fols. 43v–138 (fig 3).[52] The Scaliger codex includes Easter tables and Bede's *De temporum ratione*. Earlier parts of the text, as Philip Jaffé established, were also incorporated into the *Chronicon Moissiacense* (Chronicle of Moissac) (Paris, BnF, lat. 4886).[53] Theodor Mommsen also reports a sister manuscript to Scaliger 28 containing Bede's

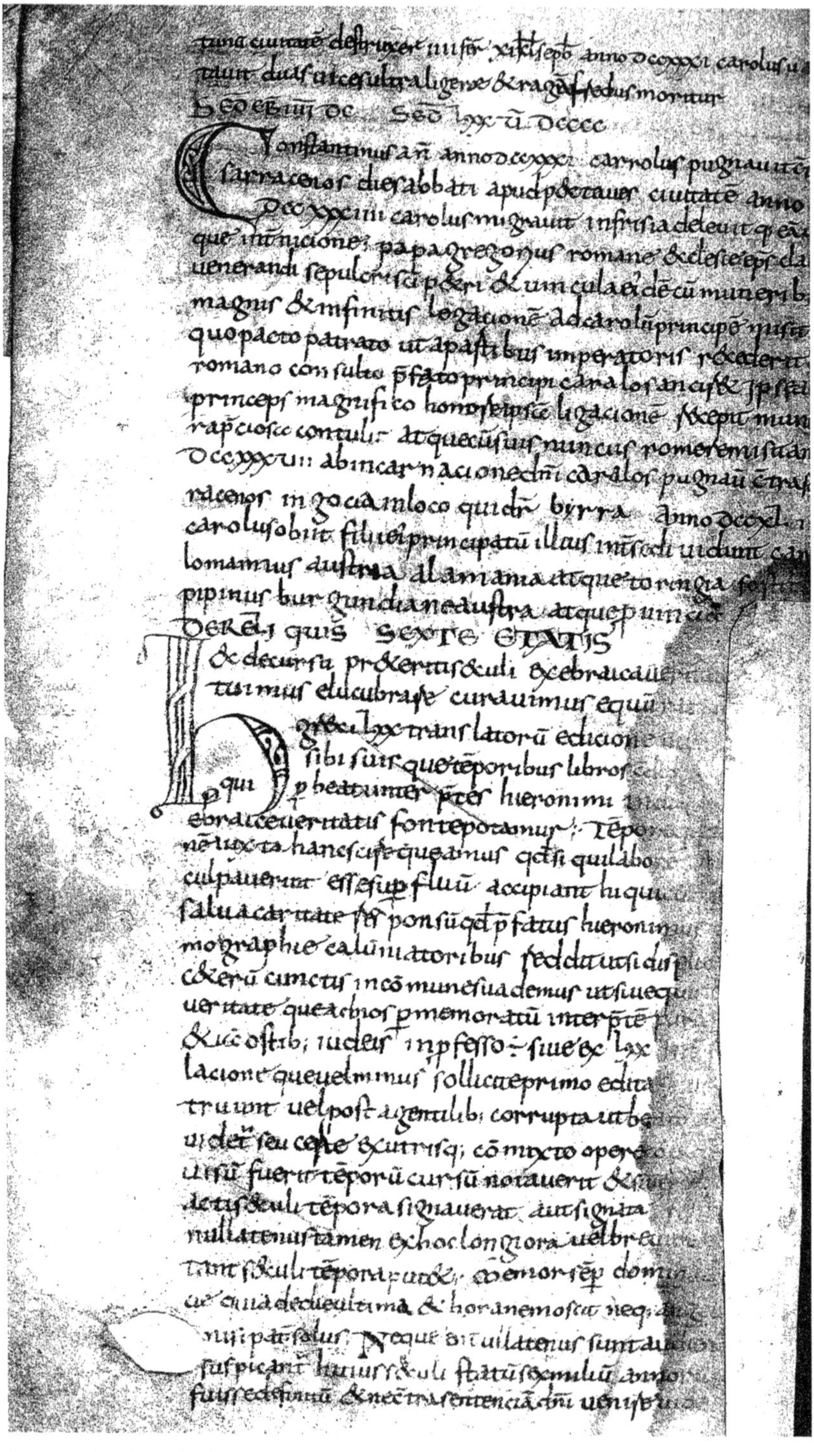

Fig. 3. *The Chronicle of 741,* Leiden, Universiteitsbibliotheek, MS Scaliger 28, fols. 134v–135r

carolus uac...

... bicesimo mostalibus quoto anno septem millenarie pasce uenit
... russit dies iudicii cuius iam aduentus maxime expectari unum
septem millenarii debeatis perari. Aquib, si quis uel ubi sit expu...
... randa uel credenda legerim mox stomacantes quod aliud ...
... spondere non libent annon legistis inquiunt in genesi quod sex
diebus mundus et cuncta in eo mento credebit cum pluriu...
... similibus annorum esse statuam. Et quod grauius fuere quippe septimu
die in quo sequentur a b operibus suis sperasent post sex annorum milia sortis
laboris in hac uita mostalib, septimo mille annorum cuius seculo eos post
resurrectione in hac ipsa uita immortales induituis et multa beatitudi
ne secuturos et cum xpo uerum his quia hereticam et friuola funditus
omissis intellegamus sincere et catolice sex illos dies inquib, mun...
diluuii ornamentum perficiendis et septimum inquo a bonis operibus suis re
quieuit que ob id ppetue qui dei benedicatione sanctificauit non sex annorum
milia sed laborans et septimum segni beatoru intellex et cum xpo sed
et xpo cuius et dies significare munet labentis inquib, sanctam laboraut
in hac uita ppopo et septimam ppetue qui dei malia uita quae solute
corporis pcipiunt animes et cum xpo. Quod animaru sabbatum tunc
recedit cum prima xpi mastyrum carne occasus a fratribus mox
... rantes latos in sequie. Tunc autem perficietur cum
... tione anime et eius corpora incorrupta sceperint
... quinqi pterraru mille annis aeta sexppera sed
... alie paucaoter habuere neque ulla alteri similem
... norum testatur par modo hec quoq quem agnu
... habeat sue longitudinis statum soli aui illi cognitu
... accenctis lumbis lucernis que ardentib, ut gilase poeg
... nib, expectantib, dum suu quo to seuestat anup cuis.

... IN OPINACIONE fidelium QUANDO UENIAT DOMINUS
... quidem aduentus horam certo scientis diligunt et cu
... desiderant. Sed periculose satis agunt si quibus hanc
... longe sit ptaset pdicase psuntum, un dequi cerissime
... ustinus remoto illo seruo nequa quid dic in corde suo
... mr uenire. Iste quippe per culdubio dominu suu dic aduen
... plu detrib, seruus optimus aduentu eius sitienter desi
... uigilant exp octant ib, fidelis amantib, quoru
... uigilem et osten quia cicius uenturus dominus. Alter
... osten quia breuis et incesta uita quam uis te cer
... dicit tercius dicit uigilem et osten quia et ipse
... incesta istaui ta et certe incertepus quo uenturus sit
... si boc ficuis fuera quod dixerat prophm gaudebunt eu
... dicuntur. Si autem ficuis fuerit mokuendum neqtur
... licet credideram et incipiant aduentu domini nram
... sed nulla quam te credimus quod dies sed ci tardius

De temporum ratione, namely Paris, BnF, n.a. lat. 1615 [Libri 90]. This was dated ca. 820 by Wesley Stevens with a suggested provenance of Fleury and ca. 830 by Charles. W. Jones, who posited Auxerre. Mommsen suggested that the Paris copy was based on the same earlier original as Scaliger 28.[54] The Munich version was certainly copied from another exemplar, for it has a number of indications of page-by-page copying. Further, an eighteenth-century copy of the chronicle of 741 in Brussels, Bibliothèque royale, 17351, adds the *Annales maximiani* of Trier as a continuation of the chronicle.[55] These various manuscripts appear to indicate a number of independent, albeit closely related, elaborations and adjustments to the base text provided by Bede's chronicle in chapter 66 of the *De temporum ratione*. They witness, therefore, to the wider reception of this particular presentation of the past.

It is typical of the MGH Scriptores editors that they omitted the first twenty-one folios (forty-two pages) of the manuscript text in Munich, Bayerische Staatsbibliothek, Clm 246, before the paragraph about Aeneas and Frigas on fol. 21v, and thus created a totally erroneous impression of the character of the history (fig. 4).[56] The Munich copy is in a generously proportioned codex but has suffered damage so that one or two leaves of text appear to be missing. The existing text starts with a bald statement: *Adam annorum cxxx genuit Seth* . . . The two ninth-century versions in the Munich and Leiden manuscripts in fact differ quite substantially. There is a greater departure from Bede's text in the latter, as the analysis by Simson makes clear.[57] Although the chronicle of 741 makes use of the Hebrew and Septuagint pairs of dates which we find in Bede to structure the narrative, and draws extensively on chapter 66 of Bede's *De temporum ratione*, its compiler displays even greater freedom in his selection from earlier historical works such as Eusebius-Jerome, Orosius, Isidore of Seville, and the *Liber Pontificalis* (Book of the pontiffs) than Fredegar does in his chronicle. The compiler of the chronicle of 741 effectively constructs a new chronicle. After beginning with Adam, as noted earlier, the Munich version inserts a series of prefaces, from the chronicles of Eusebius-Jerome, Bede, and Isidore, and starts the chronological sequence with Adam afresh, though this time the historical material is interspersed with exegetical commentary. It is possible that the version in Paris, BnF, n.a. lat. 1615, represents a further and possibly independent extension of Bede's chronicle text.

What is most striking about the text, however, is that it thoroughly incorporates the history of the Franks into the narrative from the destruction of Troy onwards. The brothers Aeneas and Frigas left Troy together, and it was from one part

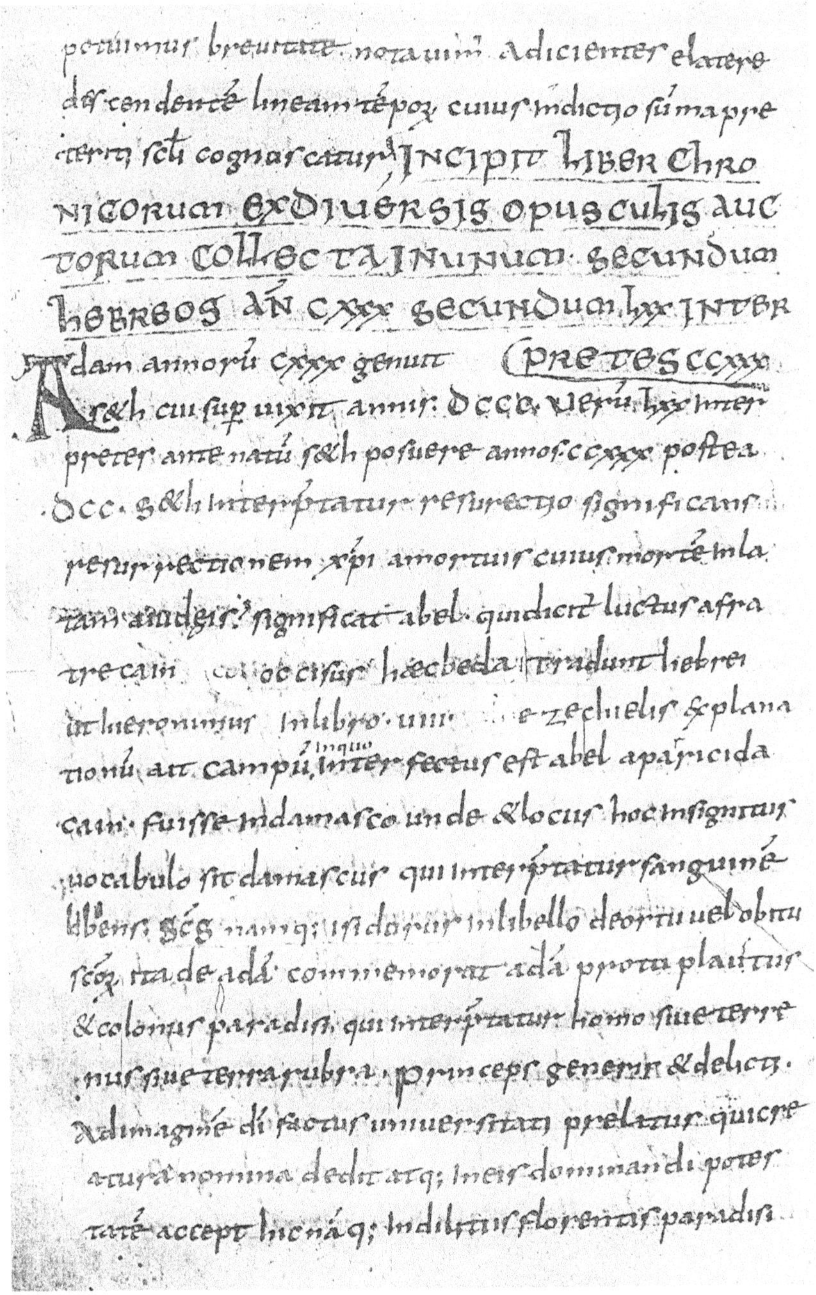

ponimus breuitate notauim adicienter elatere
descendente lineam tempor cuius indicio si ma ppre
iertn scti cognaretur INCIPIT LIBER CHRO
NICORUM EXDIVERSIS OPUSCULIS AUC
TORUM COLLECTA INUNUM SECUNDUM
hEBREOS AN CXXX SECUNDUM LXX INTER
dam annoru cxxx genuit (PRETES CCXXX
Aræl cui sup uixit annis DCCC ueru lxx inter
pretes ante natu sæl posuere annos ccxxx postea
DCC sæl interpretatur resurrectio significans
resurrectionem xpi amortuis cuius morte in la
cani audent significat abel qui dicit luctus afra
trecain cuius occisus hæc beda tradunt liebrei
ut hieronimur inlibro uni e zechielis & plana
tionu ait campu inter interfectus est abel apa ricida
cain fuisse in damasco unde & locus hoc insignitur
uocabulo sit damascus qui interpretatur sanguine
libens seg namq; inda datur inlibello deortu uel obitu
seog ita de ada commemorat ada prota plautur
& colonur paradisi qui interpretatur homo siue terre
nur siue terra rubra princeps generis & delicti
Ad imagine di factus uniuersitati prelatur quiere
aturá nomina dedit atq; in ter dominandi poter
tate accept lnenáq; in dilitur florentis parndisi

Fig. 4. *The Chronicle of 741*, Munich, Bayerische Staatsbibliothek, Clm 246, fol. 4v

of Frigas's descendants that the Franks emerged. They gradually moved west until they found their home between the Rhine and the Danube around the time of the emperor Valentinian. The end point of this chronology at least is in accord with the version of the Trojan origins and adventures of the Franks offered in the earlier *Liber historiae francorum* (The book of the history of the Franks), written ca. 727. It also shares some of the details to be found in Fredegar's chronicle written in the seventh century.[58] This claim of descent from Trojans, seen within the context of the knowledge of the Romans' descent from Trojans, of course makes the Franks brothers of the Romans.[59] It also indicates an attentive reading of earlier Frankish history on the part of the chronicle compiler and a clear attempt to make sense of different details within the story. As the chronicle of 741 proceeds, however, it offers a series of chronological connections, earnestly discussed with reference to all the authorities the author could find. The story weaves, in a somewhat telegraphic and erratic style, in and out of the fortunes of the Goths in the Balkans and in Italy, the Vandals in Spain and Africa, the Visigoths in Spain, the Burgundians and Merovingian Franks in Gaul, the Britons and Saxons in the British Isles, the Roman emperors in the west and in Byzantium, the Huns, the Lombards in Italy, attacks by the Saracens, and the popes in Rome. These references are interspersed with occasional short accounts of the discovery of sacred relics, such as the tunic of Christ or the head of John the Baptist and their transfer, respectively, to great basilicas in Alexandria and Jerusalem; the compositions of major theologians, such as Gregory the Great's *Dialogi* (Dialogues); the sending of missionaries to England; and the emergence and condemnation of various heresies. It is skilfully constructed so that the fortunes of the English and the Franks appear to come together towards the end of the text. Even the consecration of Willibrord as missionary to the Frisians by Pope Sergius and the death of Abbot Ceolfrid of Wearmouth-Jarrow on his way to Rome, as well as the fact that he had taken with him the great pandect we now know as the Codex Amiatinus, recorded in Bede's *De temporum ratione*, are taken over into this text.[60] The chronicler contrives to present the Carolingian mayors of the palace as the natural conclusion to this complicated progression of history. He does so by devoting the last few lines, immediately after the account of the transfer of Augustine's relics from Sardinia to the Lombard kingdom in the time of King Liutprand (also to be found in Paul the Deacon's *Historia langobardorum* [History of the Lombards] and in Bede's *De temporum ratione*), entirely to the career of Charles Martel.

Ado of Vienne

Ado of Vienne, my second example, took a rather different approach to writing history. His object in his *Chronicon*, which runs from the Creation to AD 870, was to call attention to the moral and spiritual implications of the progression of history through the Six Ages of the World.[61] Ado had been a young monk at Ferrières and possibly a pupil of Lupus of Ferrières. He had spent some time at Prüm and at Lyon before becoming archbishop of Vienne in 859/60. He was an ally of Pope Nicholas I in the case of the divorce of King Lothar II.[62] Ado dwells briefly on the six days of creation and the genealogies to Noah, and makes a point of calculating all the numbers of years involved. His work is divided into six sections, and at the end of each he stops to spell out for the Frankish Christian the implications of the story he has recounted. In the earlier sections these implications are more predictable, such as the importance of man being made in the image of God and Cain and Abel being made to symbolize Jews and Christians. Throughout these interpretative additions, Ado's purpose was to draw attention to a standard range of Old and New Testament exegetical parallels, not least that of the Tower of Babel as indicating the loss of unity in faith. He is able to sustain this Christian perspective throughout his narrative, even through the *Aetas Quinta*, which is packed full of the history of the Greeks and Romans. With *Aetas Sexta* he is able to interweave the history of Christ and the early church with that of the late Roman empire. It is in this section, moreover, that he contrives to place the history of Gaul and of Vienne itself. Thus it is to Vienne that Herod and Pontius Pilate are exiled, and a considerable amount of information about the bishops of Vienne is also woven into his narrative.

Of further importance for the distinctive historical map Ado provides, within the framework of a history since the Creation, is the emphasis on Christian martyrs, saints, and scholars. He even makes Symmachus and Boethius martyrs for the Catholic faith.[63] He is able to augment the basic chronicle narrative by drawing on such texts as Jerome-Gennadius's *De viris illustribus* (On illustrious men)[64] and his own historical martyrology, which he had completed before 859/60.[65] These all provide the foundation for the latter part of his history, which he brings up to his own day. By this means Ado incorporates the history of the Franks into his view of the past, but in a very different way from that of the chronicler of 741. He charts the genealogy of the Carolingian family and provides a laconic summary of the conquests and successes, the engagement of the Franks in major theological disputes, especially that of the *filioque* phrase in the Creed, which culminated in 809,[66] and the disputes between the sons and grandsons of Louis the Pious.[67] Although Ado has been accused of muddle and error at all points of his narrative, the overall effect is again to link the Franks securely to a progression of human history from the Creation to his own day, with a distinct emphasis on orthodox faith and securing orthodoxy in the face of all opposition.

Regino of Prüm

An alternative approach is provided by a younger contemporary of Ado's who is also connected to Prüm, namely Regino of Prüm. He is my third and final example of a Carolingian "world chronicler." Regino (d. 915), dedicated his *Chronicon* to Adalbero, bishop of Augsburg (887–909), in 908. He states that he was moved to write his history in order to provide a history for the Franks, just as the Hebrews, Greeks, and Romans all had their own histories. He explains that from the year 1 to 813 he had put together his account from other authors, but from 813 the narrative is in his own words, even though he draws on other texts for information. Incidentally, Reinhold Rau's reworking of Kurze's edition, in keeping with the common assumption about sections of text worth reproducing, omits all the entries before 813 apart from the preface addressed to Bishop Adalbero. Regino divided his work into two books: book 1 is the *Libellus de temporibus dominicae incarnationis* (The little book on the era of the Incarnation of our Lord); and book 2 is the *Liber de gestis regum francorum* (The book on the deeds of the kings of the Franks), which runs from 741 to 906.[68] His history was subsequently continued to 967 by Adalbert of Trier.[69] The work does not survive in the original manuscript. There are extant a number of tenth-century copies which are judged to be closely related to the supposed original, but Wolf-Rüdiger Schleidgen has insisted that the weaknesses of Kurze's MGH edition make it difficult to be certain about what Regino himself actually wrote. Schleidgen claims that Kurze's edition was based on an inadequate assessment of the manuscripts, for he used only seven out of the twenty-six copies available and never explained why he thought the "B" group was descended from an autograph of Regino's.[70]

Unlike all the other authors we have considered in this chapter, Regino chose to start his history with the birth of Christ in the forty-second year of the emperor Augustus and thereafter uses AD dating, accompanied by a statement about the then-reigning Roman emperors, as his chronological framework. His chronology is awry and is many years out by faulty calculation, but the sequence of events is correctly maintained and the chronology rights itself by 741.[71] By this simple means Regino imposes the connection between Christian and Roman history firmly on his audience's memory. He greatly augments the focus on Christian history throughout his narrative. Events such as the death of John the Baptist, the passion of Christ, the stoning of the first martyr Stephen, the careers of Saints Peter and Paul, the finding of the True Cross, Jerome's production of the Vulgate, the writing of Gregory the Great's *Moralia in Job* (Ethical lessons from Job), the conversion of the English to Christianity, the conversion of the Visigothic king Reccared to Catholicism, the Synod of Toledo in the time of the Visigothic kings Chintila and Sisenand, the Visigothic affirmation of the Catholic faith, and the witnesses to that faith provided by a succession of martyrs in Rome and elsewhere are all highlighted in his narrative. These accounts are interwoven with the succession of Roman emperors, attacks by Huns, the transfer of political control of former Roman provinces to Ostrogoths, Visigoths, Vandals, Saxons, Lombards, and Franks, the emergence of Arnulf of Metz and Pippin I, mayor of the palace, on the Frankish political scene in the seventh century, and the rise of the Carolingians. To reinforce the emphasis of his account he includes at the end of book 1 a list of popes from Peter to Zacharias. The close interweaving of secular and ecclesiastical matters is maintained throughout the second book.

Hitherto Regino's work has been judged more important for the comments it provides about Frankish politics of the late ninth and early tenth centuries. Simultaneously it has been seen as an end point in the development of Frankish historical writing and the starting point for new developments in the writing of universal history.[72] Certainly the dissemination of Regino's *Chronicon* was concentrated in Lotharingia and upper Alemannia; it is no accident that the most important world chronicles of the eleventh and twelfth centuries by Hermann of Reichenau, Sigibert of Gembloux, and Marianus Scotus are all closely connected with centres associated with surviving manuscripts of Regino. Yet the significance of the work as a whole has not been adequately appreciated.

In the spirit of the traditional approach to early medieval historical writing, moreover, Hubert Ermisch published in 1872 his identification of Regino's "promiscuous" use of sources for the section ending with 813.[73] Charges of promiscuity aside, Regino's choice of sources to construct his *Chronicon* is in fact highly revealing of his particular perception of the past; his choice reflects, even more dramatically than Ado's selection does, the wide historical knowledge of a man who deliberately constructed a narrative of the past with the emphases he desired. It is not just the actual events that are significant but what Regino's choices expose about his assumptions of their importance for his own audience in Lotharingia at the beginning of the tenth century. What he took over from his sources, what he jettisoned as not germane to his purpose, how he put his quotations together, and his working methods, are all indicative of his concept of history. Certainly in terms of his working methods it is fascinating to see how he could adapt information into other contexts. Thus, for example, in his account of the year 888–89 he puts to service the comments about Scythians and Goths in Justinus and Paul the Deacon to describe the Magyars.[74]

Regino was certainly inspired by Bede's exposition of the Six Ages incorporated into the *De temporum ratione*. He drew extensively on the Vulgate Bible, both Old and New Testaments and particularly the Acts of the Apostles, and made substantial use of the martyrology of Ado of Vienne, the *Liber Pontificalis,* and the *Collectio Hispana* (The Spanish collection) of canon law,[75] as well as a large selection of saints' lives, mostly those associated with the north of France and lower Lotharingia. In addition Regino drew on such eighth- and ninth-century Frankish histories as the *Liber historiae francorum*, the *Gesta Dagoberti* (The deeds of Dagobert), Paul the Deacon's *Historia langobardorum,* and a set of Frankish "minor" annals, most probably those known as the *Annales sancti Amandi* (Annals of Saint Amand), but the use of the so-called *Annales prumienses* (Annals of Prüm) has also been examined.[76] Regino's personal knowledge, derived from his own connections and contacts, has not yet been fully investigated.[77]

— The concept of the historical and chronological map, and the laying out of a mosaic of historical knowledge on the Eusebius-Jerome model, are maintained in Regino's chronicle. Yet what Regino and, indeed, Ado of Vienne construct from their range of sources is of an entirely different character from earlier "universal" histories. It was determined by their very choice of sources in which the *Liber Pontificalis* and martyrologies are of central importance. The contrast revolves around the presentation of Rome.

For the Carolingian chroniclers, and especially for the author of the chronicle of 741, Ado, and Regino, Rome and Roman imperial and sacred history assume enormous prominence at a number of levels. It is to the significance of Rome in Carolingian perceptions of the past, therefore, that I shall turn in my next chapter, before going on to consider the place of the Franks in Carolingian perceptions of the past in my final chapter.

TWO

The Franks and Rome

In the previous chapter, I argued that the perception of the past as springing from the beginning of the world, painted on a worldwide canvas which offered chronological synchronization and revealing juxtapositions, and embracing one's own history, was established by Eusebius-Jerome. It was disseminated both through direct knowledge of that text and by its emulators, most especially Bede in chapter 66 of the *De temporum ratione*. I then discussed how this concept was received and adapted by some Carolingian writers, though they also incorporated distinctively Carolingian elements. One of these elements is the extraordinary attention accorded Rome: the Roman imperial past, interwoven with the history of the Christian church, appears to assume enormous prominence. In this chapter, therefore, I want to explore further the significance of Rome in Carolingian perceptions of the past.

If we ask what image of Rome emerges from the chronicle of Eusebius-Jerome, it is primarily as the locus of old imperial power. Rome is mentioned only occasionally in order to record the reign of a particular fourth-century pope, such as Marcus, Julius, Felix, Liberius, and Damasus. Liberius's exile and the dispute about Ursinus's candidacy are also mentioned.[1] Other events are occasionally noted (all dates were provided by Jerome from the Creation and are given here in Helm's calculations of the equivalent AD dates), such as the destruction of the pagan temples, an earthquake that shook Rome in 346, and local factions in Rome in 350 and 371.[2] Rome was central to the careers of Peter and Minervius, the rhetoricians who taught at Rome in 336 and 353 respectively; of Gennadius, who was famous as an orator in Rome; and of the rhetorician Victorinus and grammarian Donatus, who taught in Rome in 354.[3] Occasionally events important for the religious history of Rome are reported, such as the reception in 357 of the relics of Andrew and Luke from the people of Constantinople. "Romans"— usually meaning Roman soldiers under the leadership of an emperor—are also occasionally mentioned fighting Goths, Huns, and others. The reign of Julian (362–63), as noted in chapter 1, is registered in rather more detail than that of the other emperors.[4]

In Bede's *De temporum ratione*, Rome becomes far more prominent than in Eusebius-Jerome. Bede draws many details out of the Acts of the Apostles, the *Historia ecclesiastica* of Eusebius-Rufinus, and the *Liber Pontificalis* to augment the Christian dimension to his story, albeit in a highly compressed manner. He makes passing references to the persecutions of Nero and Diocletian.[5] In the short section on Constantine, for example, Bede provides a very brief summary of Constantine's career and refers to the building of certain basilicas in Rome (fig. 5).[6] Bede's approach, as well as the plethora of small details in his text, may certainly have provided one source of inspiration for later compilers and historians. We have observed this already in relation to the chronicles of 741, Ado of Vienne, and Regino of Prüm; Freculf of Lisieux also drew on Bede.[7] Bede's *De temporum ratione* incorporating the world chronicle in chapter 66 was widely disseminated throughout the Frankish realms, either by itself or in combination with other texts, mostly those to do with computus and Easter reckoning, such as Leiden, Universiteitsbibliotheek, MS Scaliger 28, discussed in the previous chapter.[8] Another example is a copy with a calendar indicating connections with the monasteries of Lobbes and Herford and written ca. 866, now in the Biblioteca Ambrosiana in Milan.[9] It is a palimpsest of a late seventh- or eighth-century Gallican sacramentary or mass book. Bede's text is written partly in Tironian notes; this may suggest that the scribes had had some connection with the royal chancery, though knowledge of Tironian notes could be independent of the royal-chancery context.[10] The underneath text is a Gallican sacramentary, which was

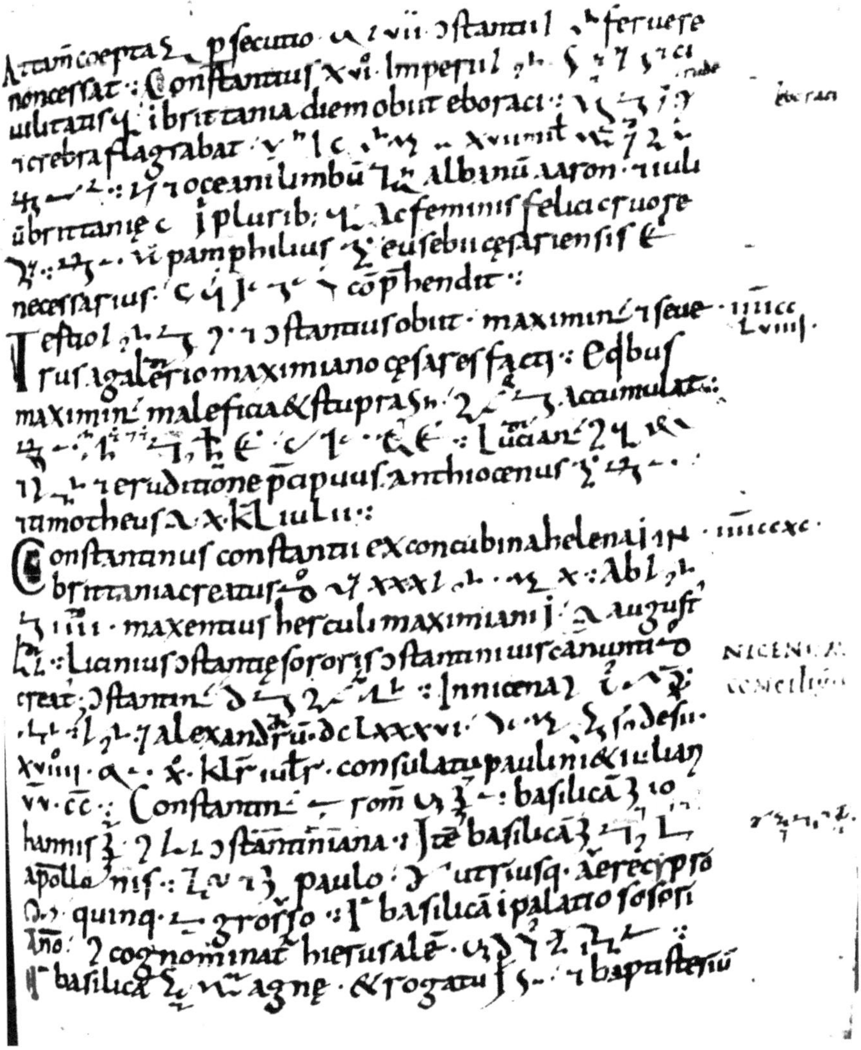

Fig. 5. Bede, *De temporum ratione*, ca. 66, Milan, Biblioteca Ambrosiana, M12 sup. fol. 179r

presumably regarded as superseded by the time this copy was made at Herford. The other texts in the volume are a calendar, Bede's *De temporibus* (On times) and Hyginus's *De astronomia* (On astronomy). Bede's text, therefore, would have given its many readers and users many fleeting glimpses of Rome and Roman history. If we turn to the Carolingian histories, the references to Rome are markedly different.

The Image of Rome in Carolingian Chronicles

Rome is present to a considerable degree, as we have seen, in the chronicle of 741, but it is a constant presence in the chronicles of Ado of Vienne and Regino of Prüm. Ado stretches the chronology of the bishops of Vienne, for example, to make the first bishop a disciple of Saint Paul and thus establish Vienne as of virtually apostolic origin.[11] Such a claim to apostolic origins was not new in Francia: Paul the Deacon in his *Gesta episcoporum mettensium* (The deeds of the bishops of Metz), commissioned by Bishop Angilram of Metz and written ca. 784, traces the history of Metz from its first bishop, Clement, sent from Rome by Saint Peter.[12] Claims were advanced in the *Actus pontificum* of Le Mans (The acts of the bishops of Le Mans) that Le Mans had been founded by Julian, allegedly one of the "72 disciples" of Christ.[13] Flodoard of Rheims, too, traced the history of the bishops of Rheims from Sixtus, the first bishop of Rheims, who was allegedly sent by Saint Peter.[14] Flodoard also augmented the city's secular Roman associations with a discussion of the *vulgata opinio* that the city had been founded by Remus, brother of Romulus. Flodoard doubted this story and drew on his knowledge of Livy's *Ab urbe condita* (From the founding of the city [of Rome]) to support him.[15] He acknowledged that the ancient Roman foundations of the city were clearly attested by the Roman Triumphal Arch of Mars and suggested that Rheims might have been founded by members of Remus's military retinue.[16] Rome, according to Regino, was especially esteemed "because of the presence of the apostles Peter and Paul, and which had once been called mistress of the world on account of the unconquered might of the Roman name" (*propter presentiam apostolorum Petri et Pauli speciali quodam veneratur privilegio et quondam propter Romani nominis invictam potentiam orbis terrarum domina dicta fuerat*).[17]

Let me give a few further examples from the chronicles of Ado and Regino. In the *Aetas Sexta* of his work, Ado provided a systematic survey of the Roman emperors, with, on the one hand, never an opportunity lost to bring Gaul, and especially Vienne, into the story. On the other hand, he inserts the fortunes of Christian communities into the story. There is, for example, a full list of those martyred under the emperor Diocletian. Yet Ado is also concerned to cram his narrative with biographical details about emperors (who give way to the Frankish rulers in the course of the eighth century), heretics, and especially bishops, such as Hilary of Poitiers and Avitus of Vienne.[18]

For his part, Regino managed from the beginning of his text to enhance the relevance of events in the Holy Land and in Rome for the Franks. He does so first of all in his preface, which he insisted everyone must read before they proceeded to the rest of his text. Secondly, by the bald information that in the reign of Augustus, Archelaus, son of Herod, had been exiled to Gaul, he contrives to mark the physical presence of Gaul in the history of Rome, the Jews, and the Christians.[19] He is able to do it again in the process of cataloguing martyrs by mentioning the death of Irenaeus of Lyon.[20] Somehow or other, moreover, all the principal saints of the liturgical calendar are recorded in terms of the reigning emperor; the places of their deaths are thus chronologically located. The record of the martyrdom of Apollinaris in Ravenna, for example, is mentioned alongside the destruction of Jerusalem by Titus. John the Apostle's exile to Patmos, the exile of Flavia Domitilla, and Pope Anacletus (the third pope) receiving the martyrs' crown are all mentioned together.[21] Regino records that John the Apostle wrote his Gospel at Ephesus. Martyrs elsewhere are also noted, such as Mark in Alexandria, Nazarius, Celsus, Gervasius, and Protasius in Milan, and Hermagoras and Fortunatus in Aquileia. The listings of the martyrs are interspersed with references to the teaching or scholarly writing of the major theologians of the early church, such as Origen.[22]

Above all, however, it is Christian Rome, from the arrival of Saints Peter and Paul onwards, which emerges so strongly in Regino's text. Instead of the brief chronological notes on the persecutions of Nero and Diocletian that we observed in Bede's *De temporum ratione*, Regino offers a long list of the Roman martyrs in the persecutions of Nero in AD 72, which is then echoed in the catalogue of martyrs under nearly every section of the narrative during the reigns of the emperors Domitian, Nerva, Trajan, Decius, Gallienus, Aurelian, and, above all, Diocletian. In the latter reign men and women received the martyr's crown throughout the Roman empire—in Spoleto, Antioch, Spain, Sirmium, Smyrna, Illyria, Aquileia, Sicily, Britain, Rhaetia, Africa, Scythia, Nicaea, Bithynia, Palestine, Naples, Augsburg, Gaul, Cologne, and Soissons—as well as in Rome itself.[23] With the conversion of Constantine the story becomes one of successions of bishops, of the disputes between Christians and emergence of heretics, of the major writers and historians of the church, such as Jerome, Eusebius, Arator, Cassiodorus, Venantius Fortunatus, Theodore of Canterbury, Willibrord of Frisia, Cuthbert of Lindisfarne, and Boniface of Mainz, all interspersed with the fortunes of the secular rulers (not least the campaigns of Belisarius and the deeds of the Lombard rulers) and the development of the kingdom of the Franks. Of further note are the references to the translation of particular relics and to the founding of particular churches, such as the finding of the True Cross during the reign of Constantine and the consecration of the Pantheon in Rome as a church dedicated to the Virgin in the time of Pope Boniface IV (608–15).[24] Regino's preface explains his emphases and also indicates his awareness of a critical and sensitive contemporary audience for his text:

> It seems to me to be a shameful thing that although histories of what the Hebrews, Greeks, Romans, and other nations did in their time have been written for our enlightenment, about our own times—long distant from these, granted—there is such a silence that one might suppose either that in these days of ours human activity has ceased, or that nothing has been done which may be considered worthy of recording, or that, if things worthy of being committed to memory have been done, it has not been thought worthwhile setting anything down on paper because of the laziness and negligence of the scribes. For this reason I have not allowed our own time and those of our fathers to go by untouched by all, but have undertaken to set down a few of the things which have come to pass, restraining my pen when I came to the present lest I cause offence to persons still living and leaving these matters to be followed up in greater detail by posterity.
>
> *Indignum etenim mihi visum est, ut, cum Hebreorum, Grecorum et Romanorum aliarumque gentium historiographi res in diebus suis gestas scriptis usque ad nostram notitiam transmiserint, de nostris quamquam longe inferioribus temporibus ita perpetuum silentium sit, ut quasi in diebus nostris aut hominum actio cessaverit aut fortassis nil dignum, quod memoriae fuerit commendandum, egerint aut, si res dignae memoratu gestae sunt, nullus ad haec litteris mandanda idoneus inventus fuerit, notariis per incuriam otio torpentibus. Hac itaque de causa non passus sum tempora patrum nostrorum et nostra per omnia intacta preterire, sed ex multis pauca notare curavi et, ubi ad presentia tempora ventum est, stilo temperavi propter quorundam offensam, qui adhuc sunt superstites, latius haec posteris exequenda relinquens.*

Likewise, at the end of book 1 he writes:

> Taking therefore as the beginning of my narrative the year of our Lord's Incarnation, I have brought it up to the present time, so that, just as my little book begins with the events of the years of our Lord's life, so in whatever time or place and under whatever ruler a thing happens is summarily de-

scribed and the victories also of the holy martyrs and confessors, in whatever place and under whatever kings they receive their crown, appear in all their details.

Haec idcirco ab ipso incarnationis Domini anno exordium capientes usque huc perduximus, ut quia sequens libellus a nostra parvitate editus per eiusdem incarnationis dominicae annos tempora principum et gesta declarat, iste nihilominus, quo tempore, quo in loco vel quid sub unoquoque principe actum sit, summatim demonstret, triumphos quoque sanctorum martyrum et confessorum, quibus in locis vel sub quibus regibus coronam gloriae perceperunt, nominatim aperiat. Igitur ubi iste finitur, ille consequenter initium capiat et, ubi ille incipit, iste finem sortiatur.[25]

Ado of Vienne and Regino provide a distinctive and well-developed Roman theme in their narratives. They accommodate a chronology based upon the martyrs and orchestrated according to political events in Rome. It may be that we should take Regino's claims to novelty in his emphasis on martyrs and confessors rather more seriously and ask whether the chronicles of Ado and Regino were unusual among Carolingian historical works in this respect, or whether they reflect the culmination of the development of a more general perception of the Roman past in the Carolingian period.

Certainly both Ado and Regino were drawing on a deep familiarity with many aspects of the Roman past, in terms both of texts, and of the Carolingians' own increasing interaction with Rome and the popes from the middle of the eighth century onwards that Tom Noble has done so much to elucidate.[26] Yet it is not sufficient to point out that much of the information Ado and Regino use is provided in the sources on which they appear to have drawn. This begs the questions of how and when the Carolingian authors came to be in a position to draw on particular texts, why they did so, why they chose to impose the particular emphases we have observed, and whether we need to distinguish between sources of information about Rome and a more general understanding of the significance of the city in history from the Franks' perspective.

Much has been achieved by scholars already in investigating relations between the Carolingian kings and the popes from the middle of the eighth century onwards.[27] This has precipitated the examination of a large number of other issues over the past two centuries of historical scholarship. These include the degree to which the Frankish kings emulated Roman emperors in their legislation,[28] the ideology of Rome and the Roman empire in Carolingian political aspirations,[29] and the identification of Nero's Rome as the harlot Babylon in early medieval commentaries on the Apocalypse, which of course echoed Augustine's comparison of Rome and Babylon in *De civitate dei* (City of God).[30] The extent to which the architecture of (some) Carolingian churches was a conscious emulation of early Christian Roman architecture,[31] the promotion of what was claimed or understood to be Roman liturgy[32] and liturgical chant,[33] or the recovery and reinterpretation of Rome's early Christian past in missionary contexts in Germany have also been debated.[34] So too, the recovery and dissemination of classical Roman texts have been extensively and intensively investigated,[35] and I have myself suggested that the promotion and distribution of Roman history books—Livy, Tacitus, Suetonius, Ammianus Marcellinus, the *Historia Augusta* (Augustan history), and others—can be linked with the Carolingian court itself as well as with certain royal monasteries.[36] It is also necessary to ascertain whether a distinction is to be drawn between the attitude of the Carolingian rulers to Rome and the perceptions among Frankish writers more generally and whether, as has sometimes been claimed, Rome is simply, or even only, envisaged as the city of Saint Peter and the martyrs.[37]

However necessary and important all these topics are, I suggest that what Rome meant to the Franks is to be understood above all as an integral element in their understanding of the past as a whole. It is an idea, moreover, that we should attempt to chart in its development. To do so it is necessary to cast the net far wider than will be possible in the compass of this chapter, but I hope at least to make a beginning.

THE SACRED TOPOGRAPHY OF ROME

Let me start with a Frankish codex compiled at the end of the eighth century and now in Vienna, ÖNB, lat. 795.[38] It includes two texts about the sacred topography of Rome known as the *Notitia ecclesiarum urbis Romae* (An account of the churches of the city of Rome) and *De locis sanctis martyrum quae sunt foris civitatis Romae* (Concerning the holy places of the martyrs outside the city of Rome).[39] The *Notitia ecclesiarum urbis Romae* starts with a reference to the great Basilica of Saints John and Paul (Santi Giovanni e Paolo) on the Caelian Hill, one of the earliest *tituli* to be converted into a Christian church. Thereafter it proceeds in an orderly sequence from the Via Flaminia, where Saint Valentine the martyr rests in a basilica restored by Pope Honorius (625–38),[40] to the Via Salaria Vetus and the church of Saint John the Martyr and the martyrs Boniface, Festus, [Blaise], John, and Longinus, to the Via Salaria Nova, and to the Via Nomentana with the Church of Saint Agnes. This had at an earlier stage been restored by Constantia and by Pope Symmachus (498–514) and reconstructed by Pope Honorius, so the author of the text notes.[41] Thereafter the text proceeds to the Via Tiburtina, Via Labicana, Via Latina, Via Appia, Via Ardeatina, Via Ostiensis, Via Portuensis and Via Aurelia. The route culminates in the Basilica of Saint Peter, where the *Notitia* provides a full account of the various saints within that church. The second text starts at Saint Peter's and goes in the opposite direction anticlockwise until it arrives at the Via Flaminia. It is a slightly different presentation of similar information. The map provided by the editors shows how this sequence of roads works, and that for the most part this is a progressive itinerary to shrines and churches outside the walls of Rome.[42] Indeed, that is what the heading for the second of these itineraries states at the outset: *De locis sanctis martyrum quae sunt foris civitatis Romae*.[43]

The two texts might be interpreted as belonging to the genre of pilgrim narratives and sylloges. Pilgrim narratives, which include the descriptions of those who travelled to the Holy Land as well as to Rome, long predate the Carolingian period.[44] The most famous of these are Egeria's entertaining and far from gullible account of her visit to Old and New Testament sites in the eastern Mediterranean in the fourth century and the *Hodoeporicon* of Willibald (The itinerary of Saint Willibald), written by Hugeburc of Heidenheim, which recounts the travels of the Englishman Willibald from Northumbria to the Holy Land via Sicily and back to Italy and Germany via Constantinople in the eighth century.[45]

The sylloges, on the other hand, appear to be a ninth-century phenomenon. They comprise the notes of Christian and ancient Roman monuments, especially those of Rome itself, and sometimes they include the texts of monumental inscriptions which took a visitor's fancy. These are set out somewhat like a modern walking tour of a city in a guide book. That is, the sylloges are arranged in a sequence following the route of a pedestrian and appear to be the consequence of a pilgrim or visitor recording the monuments he saw and occasionally copying down the inscriptions. The better known of these sylloges, namely that from Einsiedeln and the collection of papal epitaphs from Lorsch, primarily record inscriptions. As well as monuments concerning war-making and imperial expansion, the Einsiedeln compiler, sometime between 817 and 824, noted the inscriptions of a few major sacred sites, such as the resting place of Nereus and Achilleus, the grave of Saint Felix, and the Basilica of Saint Sebastian (San Sebastiano). He made a faithful transcription of inscriptions on Trajan's Column, the Baths of Diocletian, the Triumphal Arches of Titus, Arcadius, Honorius, and Theodosius, the record of the renovation of the Pons Salarius under Narses, the inscription on the grave of the legionary legate C. Dillius Vocula, whose career is mentioned by Tacitus, and many other inscriptions from graves, temples, and monuments from the pre-Constantinian period, including the epitaph for Domitia Faustina, the daughter of Marcus Aurelius.[46] He did so in a manner that indicates he fully understood what he was transcribing. The Einsiedeln codex appends an itinerary to the sylloge. This walks the reader from Saint Peter's and the Tiburtine Bridge into the city to Trajan's Column, the Baths of Diocletian, and the Palatine Forum. With the compiler one walks over many bridges and under many arches, including the Triumphal Arches of Constantine and Severus. The visitor also made a point of seeing the library where Pope Gregory I had written the *Dialogues*.[47] His interest is thus in both imperial and Christian Rome.

The Lorsch visitor, by contrast, recorded the epitaphs of no fewer than thirteen of the early Roman popes and notes, among the early saints, those in memory of Anastasia, John, Laurence, and Peter, as well as the fine epitaph written in Francia for Pope Hadrian (still visible in Saint Peter's in Rome, though now in the portico rather than on the back west wall of the south transept in Hadrian's burial chapel, as it was in Old Saint Peter's).[48] These epitaphs are extant in Vat., pal. lat. 833;[49] it is no accident that a related early tenth-century text that appears to be a Lorsch adaptation of Bede's martyrology, with many Gallo-Roman and Merovingian-Frankish saints added, was bound in with the epitaph collection. This perception of the association of martyrs with particular locations was nourished by a range of texts which recorded the names of the martyrs and their resting places. They thereby created a topography of sanctity in Rome itself.

Thus what we see in the sylloges and itinerary evidence is the response of visitors, some of whom, such as Sigeric of Canterbury, related what they saw to their own knowledge.[50] These visitors may well have been on voyages of discovery, but the itineraries in particular give the distinct impression of visits being paid to the "usual" places that every one visited. The texts in the Vienna codex, however, have a rather different character. Although also organized as if on a walking tour, the principal concern of the author appears to be to provide a checklist of all the early Roman saints and martyrs who can be associated with the churches he mentions.

If we look at what else is in the Vienna codex, the inclusion of these Roman itineraries begins to make more sense. The Vienna codex is a book more famous now for containing the largest single collection of the letters of the Northumbrian scholar Alcuin of York, who had spent some years at the Carolingian court and who retired to Tours, where he died in 804.[51] The collection is associated with Alcuin's friend, the Bavarian bishop Arn of Salzburg, who had also served as abbot of Saint Amand in northern Francia. The letter collection was formed by 799 and the compilation of the book completed by 801.[52] The topographical texts are in a self-contained quire but nevertheless are fully integrated into the book in terms of its scribes and codicology. They also contribute further to an underlying theme of the compilation as a whole. In addition to the Alcuin letters, the book contains some school texts, such as Alcuin's *De orthographia* (On orthography). Greek, Runic, and Gothic alphabets were also added. A persuasive case has been made that this is a compilation on the theme of missions to the heathen and is linked with Arn's interest in the conversion of the Avars.[53] The bulk of the book, however, also represents a preoccupation with Rome, not only a "concerted attempt to imagine the reconstruction of Rome,"[54] but a book which places Christian Rome in the foreground of evangelization. There are many exegetical works on Paul's Epistle to the Romans which would merit further study. Paul's letter itself, moreover, was addressed "to all that be in Rome, beloved of God and called to be saints" (Rom 1:7). The commentaries in the Vienna codex are by Augustine and Pseudo-Jerome. There is also a collection of extracts from the various fathers who had discussed the Epistle to the Romans, including Origen in Rufinus's translation, Jerome on Galatians and Romans, and Jerome's letter 120 with its discussion of twelve points from the Gospels and Epistles. In addition there are discussions of Matthew and Luke, Alcuin on Paul's Epistle to the Corinthians, and an unknown commentator on the Letters to the Ephesians, Titus, and Hebrews.

The letters of Alcuin also include many referring to Rome, not least one to Arn enquiring about Pope Leo III, the verse epistle addressed to Candidus concerning the latter's visit to Rome and urging him to bring Alcuin news about Rome, to pray at the shrines of Saints Peter and Paul, and to ask the pope for relics of the saints. There is also a general letter of recommendation for messengers to Rome.[55] There seems little doubt that the texts in Vienna, ÖNB, lat. 795, arise out of Arn's own interest in Rome. He had been there in 787 on an embassy with Abbot Hunric of Mondsee to try and get the pope to intercede in the dispute between Charlemagne and Tassilo.[56] He had gone to Rome again in 798, this time to receive the pallium, and in 799 in connection with the attack on Pope Leo III.[57] It has been speculated that Arn found the exemplar of some of the Alcuin letters in Francia and that the handbook was compiled at Saint Amand, for some of the texts included in this collection, such as the additional letters by Alcuin, were not addressed to him.[58] But the Roman topography was corrected and extended in Salzburg by the Salzburg scribe Baldo, who supplemented the text in the early ninth century with phrases not found in any other source.[59] These look as if they were based on Baldo's personal knowledge as he read through the texts. Baldo may even have taken the manuscript with him to Rome. Given the interest of the Carolingian clergy, not least Arn himself, in acquiring relics, these texts, with their topographical description and the detailed itemization of saints buried in particular churches and cemeteries, could also be accorded the status of "shopping lists" for relics. Although the two topographies may date to as early as the seventh century, as Giovanni de Rossi proposed, it is just as likely that they reflect Arn's own record of the holy sites, possibly drawing on an earlier text and subsequently augmented by Baldo. Indeed, Conrad Leyser has remarked that while de Rossi's dating of the itinerary texts to the seventh century need not be doubted, Vienna, ÖNB, lat. 795, "leads more directly to the 'Rome in the mind' of Arno and his circle."[60] In that the itineraries record the resting places of saints in burial places outside the walls of Rome at about the time that many of them were moved to shrines within the city, they could represent an elegy for the past in themselves.[61] Yet these places were the sites of the original burial that formed an essential aspect of the memory of the saints that the Frankish or Bavarian compiler of this codex wished to preserve. If added to the knowledge of where these saints now rested, the knowledge of the original burial places could reinforce the links between memory, time, and place, and the delineation of a sacred topography, at a time when the translation of corporeal relics was either only just beginning or well under way. The notes in the *Notitia* concerning restorations of these suburban churches is one indication that these churches continued to be used.[62] Whatever the case, their inclusion in this codex represents a practical and devotional dimension to the understanding of Rome projected by other texts in the manuscript. The compiler of this codex nevertheless was drawing on both personal observation and textual knowledge which placed early Christian Rome in the foreground.

THE *LIBER PONTIFICALIS*

The most obvious source of textual knowledge of early Christian Rome was the *Liber Pontificalis*, which is indeed alluded to in the first topographical text in

Vienna, ÖNB, lat. 795, in relation to the documentation of successive restorations of particular Roman churches. The *Liber Pontificalis* was first produced, according to Louis Duchesne, in two different recensions in the sixth century and subsequently augmented on a life-by-life basis until the end of the ninth century.[63] The great majority of the extant manuscripts go no further than life 97, that is, Pope Hadrian I, and a further substantial group stops with life 94, that is, Stephen II. Only one late eleventh-century manuscript from central Italy continues to the end, life 112 (Stephen V). Thus hardly any extant manuscripts contain life 98 of Leo III with its list of the pope's gifts to 117 Roman churches and monasteries in 807.[64] Circulation of the later portions of the *Liber Pontificalis*, including the life of Leo III, therefore, appears to have been very limited, and only one ninth-century Frankish manuscript containing the life of Leo III is extant, namely, Paris, BnF, lat. 5516, written at Tours before 871.[65] In any case, the list's emphasis is more on the churches and monasteries and the ornaments given to them by Leo III than on the importance of the churches as the resting places of martyrs, though a section within the list notes the major martyrs' churches of Stephen (the first martyr), Apollinaris, Pancras, Valentine, Clement, Savina, Aquila and Prisca, Balbina, Laurence, and Xystus.[66] In other words, nearly every extant manuscript of the *Liber Pontificalis* stops at the end of the eighth century, and it was thus the earlier portion of the *Liber Pontificalis* which had the widest dissemination.

Any reader of this earlier portion of the *Liber Pontificalis* will be struck by the extraordinary emphasis on the martyrs, their deaths, and their burial places. In the pre-Constantinian era nearly all the popes were martyred; in the post-Constantinian era a steady succession of popes embellish, move, and provide for the care of tombs of the martyrs. All the details of the popes' very particular relationships with their martyred predecessors are provided in the *Liber Pontificalis*, just as the churches and the wondrous columns, porticoes, basilicas, golden vessels, mosaics, frescoes, silks, hangings, and towers added by various popes are described.[67] It is the *Liber Pontificalis* which tells us about the great number of members of the community of Christians in Rome, and Christians brought to Rome, who were martyred in the first three centuries of the Christian era. Secondly, the *Liber* describes how many more of the Christian population of Rome, in the periods before Christianity was accepted within the Roman empire, were buried in the cemeteries and catacombs of the city. The most famous of the martyrs are of course Saint Peter, who arrived in Rome AD 42, Saint Paul (AD 56–61), Saint Sebastian, and Saint Laurence, one of the archdeacons of Pope Xystus I who was martyred in AD 258. The relics of the True Cross were brought to Rome from the Holy Land by Helena, mother of the emperor Constantine.[68] As we have already learnt from Ado of Vienne and Regino of Prüm, there were hosts of martyrs associated with the excesses of Nero in AD 64, Domitian in AD 81–96, and the persecutions under Decius and Diocletian in 245–61 and 303, and their names are also included in the *Liber Pontificalis*.[69] Early popes, many of whom had also been martyred, such as Pope Marcellinus under Diocletian, were also revered as saints.[70] Indeed, of the thirty-three popes before Sylvester, twenty-three are recorded in the *Liber* as martyrs. In the late Ostrogothic period two further popes, John and Silverius, are noted as martyrs and Martin as a confessor.[71] With these popes died many priests and deacons. Under Xystus I, for example, six deacons, Laurence the Archdeacon (already mentioned), and five others perished.[72] When Urban I was pope, Valerian and his wife Caecilia and many others were killed for their faith.[73] All kinds of obscure members of Roman families were elevated to martyr and saint status. Some, such as St Pudentiana, were effectively invented by some creative historical identification.[74] This produced Pudentiana and Praxedes (Prassede) as the daughters of Pudens the Senator, in whose house Saint Peter had allegedly been lodged. Pudens himself was identified with the Pudens mentioned in 2 Tim 4:21. But the third-century house of Pudens which became the *titulus* (*ecclesia Pudentiana*) appears to be the sole basis on which Saint Pudentiana was created.[75] Similarly, the sanctity of Petronilla, as the *Liber Pontificalis* notes, was based on a romantic misinterpretation of an inscription of a grave slab that identified her as Saint Peter's daughter.[76] Cemeteries were dedicated to the early martyrs. Pope Callistus, for example, built another cemetery on the Via Appia between 217 and 222, where "many *sacerdotes* and martyrs lie at rest," though Callistus himself was buried in the cemetery of Calepodius on the Via Aurelia.[77] The cemetery of Nereus and Achilleus (where Petronilla had been buried) was restored by Pope John I in the sixth century.[78]

According to the *Liber Pontificalis* itself, the records of the martyrs' names and their deaths were carefully recorded by the popes and their officials. This may well be an indication of the degree of control particular popes wished to exert, or to be seen to be exerting, over martyr cults rather than a necessarily accurate witness to their devout record-keeping. Pope Anteros, for example, "sought out the acts of the martyrs and deposited them in the church." (*His gestas martyrum diligenter a notariis exquisivit et in ecclesia recondit.*)[79] Pope Fabian created seven subdeacons to watch over the seven notaries so that they would faithfully collect the complete acts of the martyrs.[80] Many popes actively promoted martyr cults, and perhaps no one more strategically than Pope Damasus, who appears to have used the public celebration of martyrs to promote concord and consensus within the Catholic community in Rome.[81]

At various stages particular saints were moved: Pope Cornelius (251–53), at the request of the widow Lucina, took up (exhumed) Peter and Paul from the catacombs at night.[82] Lucina took Paul to her estate on the Via Ostiensis close to where he was beheaded. Peter was taken close to where he was crucified, "among the bodies of the holy bishops at the temple of Apollo at Nero's palace." (*Beati Petri corpus accepit Cornelius episcopus et posuit iuxta locum ubi crucifixus est, inter corpora sanctorum episcoporum, in templum Apollonis, in monte Aureum, in Vaticanum palatii Neroniani.*)[83]

On these sites great basilicas were subsequently constructed, such as the Churches of Saint Laurence, Saint Peter, Saint Stephen in the Round (San Stefano Rotondo), and Saint Mary Major (Santa Maria Maggiore). Saint Paul's Outside the Walls (San Paolo fuori le mura), for example, built ca. 400, was the last of the great basilicas the emperor erected in Rome. From the fourth century onwards, and particularly between 760 and 860, the popes, especially Pope Paul I and Pope Hadrian I in the eighth century, took a leading role in the embellishment of churches in the city. Relics of saints discovered in Rome were established in new churches, or old churches were restored and richly decorated and furnished. As Richard Krautheimer stressed in his classic study, popes on coming to office would be expected to build a church, or else it was paid for by a wealthy parishioner or priest. Krautheimer cited the examples of Vestina, who paid for the construction of Saint Vitalis (San Vitale) under Pope Innocent, and Peter, the priest who was the benefactor of the magnificent Church of Saint Sabina built under Popes Celestine I and Xystus III. The Basilica of Saints John and Paul (Santi Giovanni e Paolo) was financed by Senator Pammachius in 410. Thus the pope might secure a benefactor, but it was left to him to organize the design of the building, dedicate it, or lay its foundation stone.[84] There are some exceptions to this pattern. Occasionally there was a benefaction from the emperor, and the building was constructed under his auspices. Saint Paul's Outside the Walls (San Paolo fuori le mura) was built as a result of the munificent donations the emperor made to Rome in this period. It is only in the case of imperial donations that the pope did not claim to be a founder; it was manifestly expensive to become a pope, and it helped if one came from a wealthy aristocratic Roman family. There was a building committee to finance and supervise the city's church building and construction and upkeep of the martyrs' shrines.[85]

A further development in Rome was the designation or, when necessary, construction of stational churches where the pope would celebrate mass on particular feasts of the liturgical year. On Christmas day, for example, it was the turn of Saint Peter's Basilica.[86] Yet it would be a mistake to see the place of martyrs in Rome, the celebration of their cults, and the pope's involvement as either uniform or straightforward, let alone free of political resonance and manipulation by factions.[87] The promotion and control of martyr shrines in Rome needs to be compared with their counterparts in Constantinople and the efforts to bring them under episcopal control. Such control, as Daniel Caner has demonstrated, was not simply about determining the credentials of a particular martyr or even exploiting the devotion to the cult. It was also an aspect of controlling the "Christian *demi-monde*" that clustered around martyrs' shrines and the potentially subversive monks who served as their custodians.[88] As far as Rome is concerned, the very fluency of the *Liber Pontificalis*, quite apart from its origin within the Lateran, is a warning about the text's possible preoccupations and its partisan nature. Thus the *Liber Pontificalis* needs to be augmented by other texts of papal and Roman origin.

At one level, even so, the *Liber Pontificalis* could be read as the fullest possible visitors' guide. At another it is a map of the sacred places and holy topography of Rome. At a third, and most fundamentally, it provides a particular perception of the Roman past of great importance and with lasting influence. I have stressed the information about martyrs and Christian sites in order to underline the link between the Vienna codex and the *Liber Pontificalis*. What should be added, however, is the narrative about current politics and papal factions of Rome, about liturgical and doctrinal disputes, and about the political relations between popes and secular rulers in Italy, Byzantium, and Francia. The *Liber Pontificalis* presents, in its own distinctive way, an intermingling of sacred and secular history.

Yet for such a presentation of the past to be effective it must reach an audience. I have already mentioned the concentration of manuscripts on the portion of the text running to the end of the eighth century. It also needs to be emphasized that with three, possibly four, exceptions every extant manuscript before the tenth century is Frankish, and that they come from major centres across the Frankish realm such as Laon, Cologne, Saint Amand, Saint-Germain-des-Prés, Auxerre, Saint Bertin, Beauvais, Tours, and Rheims.[89] The manuscript evidence is of course not the only indication of the circulation of the *Liber Pontificalis* text. Instalments appear to have been sent out from Rome from time to time, so that even Bede in far-off Northumbria had had access to an early portion of the text.[90] It is also precisely the sacred tombs and churches mentioned in the *Liber Pontificalis* which are incorporated into the sylloges and itineraries. The Churches of Saints Apollinaris and Formosus and the Claudian Aqueduct, for example, were all restored by Pope Hadrian I and recorded in detail in the *Liber Pontificalis*.[91] All are also mentioned in the Einsiedeln itinerary sylloge, though that visitor added a reference to the *Scola graecorum* near Saint Mary's in Cosmedin (Santa Maria in Cosmedin) which is not in the *Liber Pontificalis*.[92] As far as textual knowledge is concerned, the *Liber Pontificalis* could certainly serve to inspire potential visitors with a particular wish to see specific places. Once there they added other places, just as nowadays we, using a tourist guide, visit recommended sites but also make some special discoveries of our own. Yet the *Liber*'s insistence on papal history, contemporary politics, and authority, its catalogue of martyrs, and the precise location of crucial events in the history of the early Christian church, appear to have been its most lasting legacy.

We should also consider the unique means by which the particular idea of Rome as a resting place of martyrs and saints, and associated with momentous events in the history of the church and the Roman empire, was translated to other locales. In their new homes, the saints both connected a place with Rome and the Roman church and provided a particular identity for the community among whom the saint was placed. In addition they linked the new place with the past of the old and thereby extended the historical framework of the new place. The means for this were twofold, textual and physical. In other words, the *Liber Pontificalis* needs to be brought into conjunction with martyrologies and the cult of physical relics of saints. Both played distinctive roles in promoting a knowledge of Roman martyrs and thereby a very particular perception of the Roman past among the Franks.

Martyrologies and Relics

Martyrologies abound from the Carolingian period.[93] They comprise collections of brief accounts of a martyr's origins, engagement with the political authorities, an often grisly, and even, to modern eyes, gratuitously detailed, account of the sufferings of the martyr and mode of death, and an account of his or her burial. In some instances miracles related to the burial site might also be included. The texts are usually organized according to the calendar year.

The transmission of martyrologies creates problems for historians because so many of them are far later than their probable dates of composition. The principal line of development of martyrologies begins with the compilation of the Hieronymian martyrology in Greek in the fifth century and its subsequent translation into Latin and transmission through late sixth-century Auxerre.[94] Yet the process of the production of Bede's martyrology, the early ninth-century Lyon collection in Paris, BnF, lat. 3879, and the martyrologies of Usuard and Hraban Maur offer us a particular type of history book from the eighth and ninth centuries which has still not been adequately assessed.[95] It certainly does not extend sufficiently into the plethora of martyrologies which are loosely based on the more famous consolidated ones. A case in point is the small collection in the Vatican manuscript, Vat., pal. lat. 833, which also contains the Lorsch collection of papal epitaphs.[96] It is probably an early tenth-century abbreviation and adaptation of Bede's martyrology with other insertions relating to early popes and additional Gallo-Roman and Frankish saints. Even by the simple device of including more saints from particular regions, the compiler was thus able to portray a different saintly past from that provided in other martyrology compilations.

The question of martyrologies also brings us back to Ado of Vienne. Interesting light is thrown on Ado in a letter from Lupus of Ferrières, written in connection with Ado's candidacy for the see of Vienne:

> Ado, a monk and pupil of mine has never fled from our monastery but at the request of the late Marcward abbot of Prüm he was sent there for good reasons and remained with him for a considerable length of time where he avoided the snares of jealous men. And then, that he might devote himself to study and rest, he resided in the city of Lyon . . . He lived an exemplary life with us. The church needs him very much. He has a gift for teaching. He is supported by letters from his monastery and bishop. He has a noble ancestry. In the judgement of the aforesaid bishops with whom he lives [Remigius, archbishop of Lyon, 852–78, and Hebbo, bishop of Grenoble, 855–69] he is staunch in his devotion to the holy monastic life . . . What more remains except to accomplish that which God has inspired his prelates to recommend.

[M]onachum et discipulum meum Ad[onem] nunquam a nostro monasterio aufugisse, sed ad petitionem beatae memoriae Marc[wardi] abbatis ex Prumia aut Proneam a nobis eum honeste directum et cum illo aliquandiu conversatum quorundam invidiosorum vitasse insidias et inde discendi studio et quietis amore in urbe Lugdunensium constitisse, . . . Bene apud nos conversatus est; quo plurimum indiget ecclesia, idoneus est docendum; regularibus et pontificalibus fultus est epistolis; progenitorum nobilitate ornatur; in sancto proposito, iudicio praedictorum antistitum, inter quos degit, devote perdurat. Quid restat, nisi ut quod sanctis praesulibus Deus inspiraverit fiat?[97]

Ado, therefore, had been educated in one of the best centres of learning in the Carolingian empire, had been one of those sent to study under Marcward at Prüm, and had also studied in Lyon. He thereby would have had access to the resources at Prüm, Lyon, and Ferrières, if not Auxerre as well, with which, of course, Ferrières and Lupus had many close connections.[98] Ado's martyrology was one of a number of major historical martyrologies produced in the Carolingian period but was arguably the most influential, at least as a collection of material.[99] Ado himself drew on Bede's martyrology and the anonymous compilation made in stages at Lyon in the earlier part of the ninth century. Ado's, however, differed greatly from those of his predecessors. It was not really suitable for liturgical use, with the information about the saints divided into two sections. In any case it is also very long (it is 424 pages in the printed edition). It would nevertheless have provided material for public reading, such as that prescribed in the Aachen reform decrees of 816 and 817. This required readings from a martyrology or the Rule of Benedict at Prime in monasteries.[100]

Not only was Ado more prolix in the individual entries, but he also added a great amount that was simply not in the texts of Bede or the anonymous of Lyon. Lupus's letter quoted above indicates the possibility that Ado might have had access to the Lyon compilation when studying there. It should be noted that Ado had also spent time at Prüm, where Wandalbert later compiled his own martyrology.[101] The first recension of Ado's martyrology, made in 855, does not survive, but in the second Ado apparently added 197 entries and modified 188 of the original ones. He drew copiously on the New Testament, Eusebius-Rufinus's *Historia ecclesiastica*, Jerome-Gennadius's *De viris illustribus*, the *Liber Pontificalis*, Gregory of Tours's *In Gloria martyrum* (Glory of the Martyrs) and *In gloria confessorum* (Glory of the confessors), and Bede. Yet it is the Roman saints who abound in Ado's selection, with precise notes added about their burial places and cemeteries. This is the emphasis Ado chose to propagate in his martyrology; it is in complete accord with the strong focus on Rome in both his history and that of Regino.

Two things have tended to be omitted from the understanding and exposition of the martyrs' role but which the Carolingian martyrology compilers emphasize quite clearly. The first is the martyrs' representation in historical time. The second is their triple location, namely, the place where they were martyred, the place or places where their bodies or parts thereof now rest, and their place in heaven.[102] The location of the human life and suffering of a saint at a specific chronological moment and in a particular place was as important a means for the sympathy and devotion that the saint evokes as the holiness of his physical presence at the cult site at which she or he was later revered. A saint thus represents the coming together of past, present, and future time. The insistence on Rome in relation to the principal martyrs and their relics gives us the precise historical location. Although dead, they are still present and alive in memory. For the martyrs, their death in historical time is the qualifying characteristic for their becoming saints in the first place.

In other words, a sense of the past is built into the veneration of a saint. A relic brought from the Holy Land, Africa, or Rome, furthermore, carried with it associations of those places where, and of the time when, the saint had died. Thus when the relics of particular saints were brought across the Alps to Francia, as in the case of Saints Marcellinus and Petrus in the ninth century,[103] the Franks could be thought of as the people who offered protection to the saints' relics. As the extraordinary prologue to the eighth-century recension of the *Lex Salica* (Salic Law) put together under Pippin III, and reiterated in the *Lex Salica Karolina* (Caroline Salic Law) states:

> [T]he Franks, after the knowledge of baptism, having found the bodies of the blessed martyrs whom the Romans had mutilated with fire or sword, or thrown to wild animals to be torn to pieces, decorated them with gold and precious stones.
>
> *Romanorum iugum durissimum de suis ceruicibus excusserunt pugnando, atque post agnicionem baptismi sanctorum martyrum corpora, quem Romani igne cremauerunt vel ferro truncauerunt vel besteis lacerando proiecerunt, Franci [reperta] super eos aurum et lapides preciosos ornaverunt.*[104]

The primary evidence for such movement of relics, especially across the Alps to the kingdom of the Franks, survives in texts known as *translationes*.[105] A remarkable number of these from the ninth century record the passage of saints across the Alps. We also have many new *vitae* of saints composed for the first time in the ninth century in order to mark the arrival of relics of saints. These relics could take the form of the body itself or parts thereof, dust from the tomb, or objects associated with the saint, such as the chains of Saint Peter, or with Christ, such as a piece of the cross or the lance which pierced his side. The best known Carolingian *translationes* concern the *translatio* of Marcellinus and Petrus recorded by Einhard, the achievement of Hilduin of Saint Denis, who brought the relics of Sebastian and Gregory to Saint Médard of Soissons,[106] and the *translatio* of Saint Liborius.[107] We also know of the transport of relics from lists preserved in monastic and cathedral narratives, from treasure lists and inventories, and very occasionally from surviving relic labels.[108] The Jouarre list of the ninth century included Gallo-Roman saints and the Roman saints Felicitas and Sebastian, Vitus, Innocent, Laurence, Eufemia, Peter, and Paul.[109] Among Saint Riquier's relics recorded by Hariulf in the eleventh century is a list of the relics acquired by Angilbert at the beginning of the ninth century, possibly as a gift from Charlemagne. In an account preserved in 1192, Peter and Paul, Andrew, Cosma and Damian, and many more Roman martyrs and popes are recorded. The same account included Clemens, Crispin, and Crispian, Laurence, Sebastian, Petronilla, Anastasia, Paul, and a huge list of the relics of virgins and martyrs, many of whom are Roman.[110] At Sens between 879 and 992 relics were collected, including those acquired by Magnus, archbishop of Sens, some of which were a gift from Charlemagne.[111] There are also the many saints moved to Saxony from Rome.[112] Many came as gifts from Charlemagne and were part of a strategy of conquest. The Church of Saint Maria in Paderborn, for example, received the hair of the Virgin, and Osnabrück claimed to have received relics of Crispin and Crispian.[113]

These relics not only extended the perceptions of Rome's past; the time and place of the martyrdom of the Gallo-Roman saints, and the lives of Gallo-Roman, Frankish, and English saints, meant that the saints embodied an element of Christian history. Thus veneration of them incorporated a particular perception of the past. One might in consequence extend the notion for which Hedwig Röckelein coined the term "hagio-geo-graphy" to express the way in which relics and the miracles they wrought bound together a number of places. We might then end up with an albeit clumsy neologism like "hagiogeohistoriography" to embrace the notions of historical context, the place of the original martyrdom, and the place to which the primary corporeal remains were taken, as well as the subsequent resting places and cult networks of the saints promoted in part by written texts.[114]

THE SACRED PAST OF ROME

I began this chapter with the presentation of Rome's past which Ado of Vienne and Regino of Prüm integrated into their chronicles. From the evidence I have discussed above, it would appear that Ado and Regino were not offering a new perspective on Rome's past. On the contrary, the *Liber Pontificalis*, the itinerary texts, historical canon law collections, and historical martyrologies all insisted on the city of Rome's Christian past.[115] The latter two categories in particular represent chronologically ordered history books of a special kind, largely focussed on either the great councils and papal decisions of the church or the sequence of predominantly Roman martyrs, the manner of their deaths, and their places of burial. They shaped perceptions of the past by offering a history of the early Christian church and the Roman empire from very particular perspectives. In their turn, moreover, all the compilers of such texts had themselves inherited a strong understanding of the complexity and diversity of Rome's past in which religion played a crucial role. This is perhaps nowhere more clearly stated than by Livy. In his history *Ab urbe condita*, for example, Livy recounts how the general Camillus made the case that it was necessary for the ancient cults of Rome to be within the boundary of the city:

> We have a city founded by the auspices and augury; there is not a corner of it that is not full of our cults and our gods; our regular rituals have not only their appointed places, but also their appointed times.
> *Urbem auspicato inauguratoque conditam habemus; nullus locus in ea non religionum deorumque est plenus; sacrificiis sollemnibus non dies magis stati quam loca sunt, in quibus fiant.*[116]

Livy describes a topography of religious devotion supporting the political life of the city; Cicero and Horace also record much of the ancient topography of the city. The physical presence of the city under Augustus and his successors, with ambitious urban planning and monumental architecture, opulent decoration and costly materials, was magnificent. Observers well into the middle ages commented on the impressive statistics about the quantities of bricks, tiles, concrete, gems, textiles, marble, and sheer wealth manifest in the buildings.[117] Constantine and his successors did not diminish the importance of Rome but augmented it. Certainly the Christian basilicas and the subsequent elaborate building programmes of many of the popes reoriented the religious places and created many new locations and foci of religious devotion. Recent work on early medieval church buildings in Rome has revealed a history of transformation and new building work as well as places that simply ceased to be a central focus and were replaced by others.[118] Yet the uncovering of the late eighth-century villa in the forum of Nerva, in association with the papal jubilee excavations for 2000, suggests that the forum, despite the consecration and Christianization of many of the great buildings, and the rich decoration of such churches as Old Saint Mary's (Santa Maria Antiqua) and Saints Cosma and Damian's (Santi Cosma e Damiani) would nevertheless have retained much of the character and majesty it had possessed in late antiquity.[119] Rome itself—despite its being treated over the past sixteen hundred years as if it were a giant quarry, with many fine buildings despoiled or converted for alternative use, the marble burnt for lime for more building work, and the metal stripped off—continued to impress all who saw it and to inspire those wealthy enough to adorn it further in a constant process of renewal.

Livy's own expression of Rome's religious centrality may have exerted some influence in Francia and Italy. His work was known and copied, for there are echoes of his phrases in the Frankish annals and in surviving ninth- and tenth-century witnesses to the text in two main families from Corbie, Fulda, the Loire region, and elsewhere.[120] Moreover, a host of other texts from classical antiquity—all of which, as I have demonstrated elsewhere, were widely disseminated throughout the Carolingian world—offered similarly vivid reflections on Rome's physical structures, its religious cults, its history, and its role as a symbol of power.[121] The importance of place and the physical and symbolic resonance of Rome as a political and religious centre is thus as crucial for the Christian early middle ages as it was in the pagan ancient world.

The sense of the importance of Rome as a place of religious significance for Christians in the early middle ages arose directly from its status as the city of the apostles Peter and Paul and a host of martyrs. It was likely to have been derived primarily from texts other than Livy and most clearly from those that relate to the saints and sacred topography of the city itself. Rather than focus on more obvious and intensely studied texts such as Augustine's *De civitate dei* and Orosius's *Seven Books of History against the Pagans*,[122] I shall now turn to a rather less acknowledged text which could be taken as reflecting a more general and arguably more common understanding of Rome that was widespread within western Europe by the sixth century. I refer to Arator's *De actibus apostolorum* (On the Acts of the Apostles) which reinforces the idea of Rome as a city of the apostles. This idea is first of all to be found in the New Testament's Acts of the Apostles, commonly attributed to Saint Luke in the early middle ages.[123] Judging from the extensive Carolingian manuscript distribution of his poetic version of the Acts of the Apostles, Arator's poem was in a position to play a role in the formation of perceptions of Rome's past in the Frankish realms.[124] Indeed, Regino of Prüm mentions him.[125]

Arator had been trained in Milan, Pavia, and Ravenna during the reign of Theodoric the Ostrogoth. He composed his epic poem when a subdeacon in Rome, dedicated it to Pope Virgilius between 536 and 544, and gave it a public reading in the Church of Saint Peter in Chains (San Pietro in Vincoli) close to the Forum in April and May 544.[126] With the encores, and performed in instalments, the reading reputedly extended over four days.[127] In the absence of any patristic exegesis on Acts, Arator provided an account which spells out the spiritual and mystical meaning of the historical acts of the apostles in the earliest years of the formation of Christian communities. Indeed, characters and events are rather swamped in abstraction but his language is redolent of that of classical epics with a vocabulary associated with heroes, soldiers and athletes transferred to the *milites Christi*.[128] The opening twenty lines on Christ's descent into hell and the Resurrection reinforce Arator's didactic purpose, for they are not in Acts. The principal focus, however, emerges as the apostles Peter and Paul, and, above all, the city of Rome itself. Thus in the last section of the poem Arator describes how Paul came to the lofty pinnacles of Rome:

> The account begs [me] more profoundly to say that the two lights of the world [Peter and Paul] came together and from regions [far and] wide chose a single place, through which they, who make all lands bright with the virtues of truth, might unite their stars. . . . Peter rose to be leader in the body of the church; turret crowned, she [Rome] surrounded her head with the regions of the world; the greatest things were gathered to her [Rome] so that all the

[episcopal] sees might observe the secure heights of the mistress of the world. More justly present in this [place than in any other city] the preferred [city] which instructs the nation, Paul, chosen to be teacher for the gentiles forever, unleashes the power of his eloquence, and whatever he thunders there, the honour of the city compels the subject world to hear.

Altius ordo petit duo lumina dicere mundi
Convenisse simul tantisque e partibus unum
Delegisse locum, per quem sua sidera iungant
Omnia qui fidei virtutibus arva serenant.
Quae licet innumeris tendatur causa figuris,
Pauca referre volens isdem praestantibus edam
Petrus in ecclesiae surrexit corpore princeps;
Haec turrita caput mundi circumtulit oris;
Conveniunt maiora sibi, speculentur ut omnes
Terrarum dominae fundata cacumina sedes.
Gentibus electus Paulus sine fine magister
Aequius huic praesens oris diffundit habenas
Quae gentes praelata monet; quodque intonat istic
Urbis cogit honor, subiectus ut audiat orbis.[129]

An understanding of the political and religious implications of a particular site or location can be defined in terms of the perception of the space occupied physically, socially, intellectually, and spiritually by both place and ideas.[130] Hagiography and the extraordinary proliferation of saints' lives in the early middle ages indicate, as is well known, a perception of the past that was entwined with heaven and eternity. Yet that perception of the past is also dependent on a sense of place and its many connotations in terms of its history. The Rome of Livy, of Saint Peter and of Constantine, of Arator and of the *Liber Pontificalis* authors, are thus one and the same.

As we saw in the chronicles of Ado and Regino, however, the Christian past of Rome, which has such a long series of manifestations and reinforcements, is intertwined with that of the Roman empire. The Carolingian perception of the Roman past appears to have been one in which the sacred and the secular history of Rome and of the Roman empire were integrated. Virgil's *Aeneid* undoubtedly played a pivotal role,[131] but we also need to acknowledge the role of texts such as Suetonius's imperial biographies,[132] the compilation about later emperors known as the *Historia Augusta*,[133] as well as the *Factorum et dictorum memorabilium libri* (Memorable Doings and Sayings) by Valerius Maximus, the earliest manuscript of which is associated with Lupus of Ferrières.[134] It may be Valerius Maximus (rather than Aurelius Victor, as Ernst Dümmler surmised) which was produced in summary form for Charles the Bald by Lupus of Ferrières to provide the Frankish king with models to follow or avoid.[135] Valerius Maximus makes it clear that conventions of personal and public morality and conduct within public affairs were communicated through rhetorical examples. Yet Valerius Maximus also presents a concern for the excesses of civilization. He offers moral reflections on the very monuments, political symbols of power, statues, public buildings, and the ostentatious display of wealth in the form of marble, gold, and paintings that undoubtedly impressed so many visitors. His text could certainly provide historical examples and information, but with his perception of the past as a moral warning and set of historical precedents, Valerius Maximus provided a model for subsequent reinterpretations of the classical ideas of Rome and for perceptions of the past more generally.[136]

— I started this chapter by commenting on the significance of Rome in particular Carolingian presentations of the past. It should be evident that I have by no means fully explained that significance, but what I have tried to do is indicate, first of all, how we as historians might begin to identify and disentangle the various strands which witness to the Carolingian and Frankish perceptions of the Roman past. In highlighting the intertwining of Roman sacred and Roman secular and imperial history I have actually been reproducing the emphasis of the Carolingian texts. Even at the level of the sylloges, itineraries, and martyrologies, they reflect a perception of Rome that makes it integral to an understanding of both Christian and imperial history. By looking at a somewhat disparate selection of texts, moreover, I have been intent on demonstrating that perceptions of the past are indeed mirrored in a variety of texts produced for other, or additional, purposes than straightforwardly to record the past. The imperatives of the emulation of Rome, the religious function of ancient Rome, and the Christian memory of Rome in the Carolingian sources are very striking. Indeed, the preoccupation with Rome is far greater than the religious memory and knowledge of the Holy Land, though that remains an issue to be explored further.[137] Similarly, the perceptions of Constantinople as a "second Rome" could be investigated further, but these would need to be considered in the light of Frankish claims that Aachen was the "second" and "future" Rome.[138] Within my selection, a personal handbook like Vienna, ÖNB, lat. 795, has as much to tell us as individual presentations of the past in narrative form such as the chronicles of 741, Ado, or Regino. These same chroniclers drew on other authors. This intertextuality and dialogue with the past is a further dimension of a perception of a past peopled with a host of authorities who could provide enlightenment and information, not least the chronicle of Eusebius-Jerome, the *Historia ecclesiastica* of Eusebius-Rufinus, the *De viris illustribus* of Jerome-Gennadius, and the *Historia tripartita ecclesiastica* (Tripartite ecclesiastical history) of Cassiodorus-Epiphanius. As I have stressed elsewhere, the Christian past was emphatically one built on texts which created a cumulative network of understanding and knowledge.[139] These early Christian histories and guides to Christian authors played a key role in creating a context for the Franks' understanding both of the history of the Christian church and of the circumstances in which Scripture and the patristic writings were composed and disseminated. I have also stressed that physical and material relics of the past, whether buildings or bones of saints, played a crucial role in Frankish perceptions of the past and especially of the past of Rome.

It is important to emphasize the timing of the production as well as of the availability of the texts I have presented in this chapter. There seems little doubt that the papal interest in the expansion of the Frankish church into Frisia, Hesse, Thuringia, and Saxony from the reign of Pope Sergius I onwards, coupled with the papal alliance with the Carolingian rulers from the middle of the eighth century, and the conquest of the Lombard kingdom in 774, had far-reaching consequences in terms of expanding the horizons of Frankish perceptions of the past.

Yet for all the texts presenting a past in which the Rome of the apostles Peter and Paul and of the Roman emperors assumes great prominence, we still have to reckon with the fact that the chronicles of 741, Ado of Vienne, and Regino of Prüm, as well as the vast corpus of Frankish annals produced in the later eighth and the ninth centuries, also offered a Frankish dimension to perceptions of the past. The following chapter, therefore, addresses the question of the Franks and their own history in relation to universal history and the Roman past.

THREE

The Franks and Their History

In the previous two chapters I have examined perceptions of the past reflected in a range of historical writing, both that written in late antiquity and disseminated within the Carolingian empire and that composed by the Franks themselves. This historical writing maintains the concept of the historical and chronological map and the laying out of a mosaic of historical knowledge on the Eusebius-Jerome model. Yet what the chronicler of 741, Ado of Vienne, and Regino of Prüm constructed from their range of sources is of an entirely different character from that in earlier "universal histories." The contrast revolves, first of all, on the presentation of Rome nourished by their choice of sources, in which the *Liber Pontificalis* and historical martyrologies are of central importance. In the preceding chapter, therefore, I examined the perception of Rome and the Roman past in the Frankish world of the eighth and ninth centuries in greater detail. I highlighted the way in which the intertwining of Roman sacred and Roman secular and imperial history echoes the emphasis of the Carolingian texts. Even the sylloges, itineraries, and martyrologies reflect a perception of Rome as important for both Christian and imperial history. The imperatives of the emulation of Rome, the religious function of ancient Rome, and the Christian memory of Rome in the Carolingian sources are very striking. In offering an interpretation of Arn of Salzburg's handbook on Rome in the Vienna, ÖNB, lat. 795, codex, as well as of the individual presentations of Rome in Frankish narrative sources, I stressed textual knowledge. But I also emphasized the crucial role played by the physical and material relics of the past, whether buildings or bones of saints, in Frankish perceptions of the past.

Secondly, I noted in both the previous chapters how the Franks and local issues were integrated into their historical narratives by the chronicler of 741, Ado of Vienne, and Regino of Prüm. I also remarked, however, that in so doing these writers draw on already existing conventions of Frankish historical narrative, quite apart from drawing on existing Frankish annals.

Yet so far the Franks have been left to one side. I want in this chapter, therefore, to look more closely at Frankish history. I shall examine how local issues might have been seen against the wider canvas, not only of the "national" history of the *gens francorum* and the expansion of the Carolingian realm, but also the entire span of human and Christian history. In other words I shall explore both the extent to which the Franks place themselves and Frankish contemporary history on their historical and chronological "map" of the world and the interplay between written and oral exchanges of news, gossip, and knowledge in the writing of contemporary history.[1] This identification of the issues involved in perceptions of the Frankish past in the Carolingian period begins first of all in Saxony in 785.

— The year entry for 785 in the *Annales regni francorum* (Royal Frankish annals) contains an account of a campaign carried out by Charlemagne at the confluence of the Weser and Werre rivers. From thence, according to the narrative, Charlemagne retired to the Eresburg for the winter and summoned his wife Fastrada and sons and daughters to join him. He stayed there until Easter. While in residence, Charlemagne sent out *scarae* and captured many Saxon strongholds. He convened a general assembly at Paderborn and thereafter advanced through Saxony. In the Bardengau (in Westphalia) he met Widukind and Abbio, the Saxon leaders. The annalist says that Abbio and Widukind were summoned by the king and that the king "swore they would not escape unless they came to him in Francia."[2]

Abbio and Widukind secured a promise from Charlemagne that they would not be harmed. Subsequently Charlemagne sent his *missus* Amalwin with hostages. Abbio and Widukind brought hostages with them when they came to the villa of Attigny, and it was on this occasion that both Widukind and Abbio received baptism, together with all their companions. Subsequently or, we might suppose, consequently, "all" Saxony was subjugated. Again the annalist merely recorded a succession of events.

The baptism of Widukind marks the beginning of a famous lull, lasting about seven years, in the thirty-year process of the Saxon conquest by Charlemagne with which, in this entry as in many others, the *Annales regni francorum* are so preoccupied. The extraordinarily complex social upheavals within Saxony that the conquest and conversion to Christianity occasioned are not my principal concern.[3] Nevertheless, the Saxon conquest and the opportunities it afforded elite groups to consolidate their status, not least with respect to relations between the Saxon *edhilingui* and the lower status *frilingi* and *lazzi* in Saxon society, appear to be the context within which to consider both the opposition to Charlemagne's rule from other elite groups east of the Rhine and how any record of this might have been made and preserved.[4] The perception of the past mirrored in the *Annales regni francorum* was one in which the themes of successful Frankish and Carolingian conquest and consolidation are intertwined.[5] The annalist provides a central perspective and only hints at local responses. A dominant theme of this chapter, however, is how far it is possible to identify alternative or independent voices about the past and local perceptions of Carolingian rule. These voices and perceptions emerge out of narrative accounts associated with places other than the court.

FRANKISH ANNALS

The Carolingian period saw a veritable explosion of history writing, with all kinds of new genres developed and older forms reconfigured and adapted to record contemporary history. Not only are there the universal histories extended to embrace the Franks, the *gesta episcoporum* (deeds of bishops) and *gesta abbatum* (deeds of abbots) modelled on the *Liber Pontificalis*, secular biographies such as the *Vita Karoli* (Life of Charlemagne) by Einhard, historical epic poems such as Ermold the Black's poem in praise of Louis the Pious, political hagiographies such as the *Epitaphium Arsenii* (Life of Wala) and *Vita sancti Adalhardi* (Life of Saint Adalhard), personal presentations of politics such as Nithard's history of the quarrels between the sons of Louis the Pious and Notker Balbulus's *Gesta Karoli* (Deeds of Charlemagne), the historical martyrologies, and the historically organized collections of canon law and cartularies;[6] alongside these there is also a vast corpus of Frankish annals. These are texts ranging in character from sets of brief notes on the deaths of rulers, abbots, or bishops, political events, military campaigns and victories, eclipses, cold winters or famine, to full historical commentary. Their common feature is that they are organized in a year-by-year sequence and dated according to the year of the Incarnation.[7] This form of historical writing is a Frankish development in the eighth century. The extant examples are usually divided into groups according to a typology proposed by the earliest MGH and French editors.[8] First of all there are "major" annals such as the *Annales mettenses priores* (Prior Metz annals), the *Annales regni francorum,* and the continuations of these in the west and east Frankish kingdoms known as the *Annales Bertiniani* (Annals of Saint Bertin) and the *Annales fuldenses* (Annals of Fulda) respectively. Secondly there is the large and motley collection of so-called "minor" annals regarded as emanating from a number of different centres throughout the Frankish realm. The labels "major" and "minor" are in effect value judgements as distinct from usable categorizations.[9] They bear no relation to ninth-century references to annals. The word *annales* is not, to my knowledge, used as a heading in Carolingian manuscript copies of annals, and before the ninth century is more likely to be used with reference to the Easter tables. From the ninth century, however, and mostly from the second half of the ninth century, this type of history writing is sometimes referred to as *annales,* or *gesta,* or annals of kings. Hincmar of Rheims, for example, alluded to the reign of Charlemagne and Carloman *sicut in annali regum scriptum habemus* (as we find in the annals of the kings), a reference to the *Annales regni francorum.*[10] The titles of the works, it should thus be remembered, are a mixture of Carolingian designation and modern convention, as in the *Annales fuldenses.*

The manuscript tradition of all these annal texts is also notoriously complicated. Thus the *Annales regni francorum,* which run from 741 to 829, survive in four different recensions of the "original" version, labelled "A," "B," "C," and "D," as well as a revised or "E" version. All have a number of ninth-century manuscript witnesses disseminated right across the Frankish realm from Brittany to Bavaria, and the earliest extant is dated to the second quarter of the ninth century.[11] Many of the "minor" annals, however, survive essentially in single manuscripts, which can rarely be precisely located.

Past discussion has rather sterilely focussed on whether the "major" annals drew on information in the "minor" annals or whether the "minor" annals adapted the "major" annals. The role of the *Annales regni francorum* in supplying information seems clear and has provided one means of associating groups of annal texts, that is, several appear to use the same stem text of annal entries. Some scholars have also tried to group sets of annals in different manuscripts according to their stylistic features, though this has been notably inconclusive.[12] Grouping might be more usefully proposed on the basis of networks of information. Thus the use made by these "minor" annal compilers of the *Annales regni francorum* is supplemented by information drawn from alternative sources. These could include knowledge acquired by word of mouth at political or legal assemblies, in relation to the movement of armies, or disseminated by messengers and travellers.[13]

Stemmata of annal texts, based on perceived relationships or similarities between individual entries in them, have been constructed at the expense of focussing on the impact of the texts as a whole. Certainly, as Jennifer Davis has rightly pointed out, the use of the same stem text in the compilation of annals does not necessarily establish a connection among the later sections of the annals, though it does indicate the author's wish to situate his own narrative in a larger historical context.[14] Further, the use of the stem text indicates an acceptance of its chronological and political orientation and emphases and reflects, therefore, a particular perception of the past.

Of crucial significance in this respect, as well as generally, is the starting point of these annals. Most begin with key moments in the fortunes of the Carolingian family. Thus the *Annales regni francorum* start in 741 with the death of Charles Martel.[15] The *Annales fuldenses* start in 714 with the death of Pippin II and the beginning of Charles Martel's ultimately successful attempt to win control of the Frankish kingdom.[16] The *Annales mettenses priores* start in 687 with Pippin II's assumption of leadership in Austrasia.[17] Most of the "minor" annals take other points in Carolingian chronology as their starting point or make particular reference to events within it. One could cite the so-called Austrasian group of annals (including the *Annales sancti Amandi* and the *Annales Tiliani* [Annals from the manuscript of du Tillet]), which start with 708, the death of Drogo, son of Pippin II.[18] The so-called *Annales murbacenses* (Murbach annals) adopt the same starting point.[19] This may indicate a particular sympathy for Drogo's branch of the family.

It has also become an established view—so perhaps that is all the more reason to question it—that annals were derived from notes in Easter tables.[20] Quite apart from difficulties in dating the earliest annal texts in relation to the earliest surviving manuscripts of Easter tables with historical annotations, it is more productive to think of annals as at least a parallel development alongside Easter table annotations, and inspired by Dionysius Exiguus's insistence on dating according to the year of the Incarnation.[21] One instance of this is Paris, BnF, lat. 5543, of the late ninth century, in which the Easter tables occupy the top two-thirds of the page running from 532 to 1060, with marginal annotations beside some of the year dates here and there, while the bottom third of the page is filled with longer discursive entries after 854 which have been labelled the *Annales floriacenses* (Annals of Fleury).[22] Certainly, quite apart from its possibly being regarded as more convenient, a Christian era might have been thought the most fitting dating scheme for a triumphal narrative about the Christian Carolingian rulers, self-appointed promoters and protectors of the Christian faith. In the light of the fact that the Carolingian mayors of the palace were not yet kings when their story starts to be told, Christian-era dating could also have functioned as a politically neutral dating scheme at a time when the authors may not have wished to highlight the regnal years of the Merovingian kings.

Hardrad's Revolt

Let us now return to the year 785. The expansion of the Frankish realm in the last three decades of the eighth century undoubtedly caused considerable social upheaval and a major readjustment of political relations. War, in its many manifestations, is a prominent theme in the annals.[23] One might well label such readjustment a crisis for the elites at a local and regional level, if not for the population at large. Yet it is extraordinarily difficult to document such upheaval. This difficulty raises the question of the perceptions of such an immediate past within the social groups involved as well as that of the manner in which any historical commentary on any event might have been preserved. In this respect the textual context in which opposition to Carolingian rule is recorded may prove significant, for in the 780s and 790s at least, elite aristocratic insurgence is juxtaposed with Saxon rebellion in some annalistic accounts.

If we look at the revised version of the *Annales regni francorum* for the year 785, as distinct from the supposedly "original" version, for example, some interesting additional details emerge. It is not simply that there is a far more graphic account of the attacks on the Saxons during the "winter of discontent":

> [Charlemagne and his *duces*] ranged here, there and everywhere; they threw everything into disorder with killings and burnings. By ravaging in this fashion throughout the whole period of the winter, the king inflicted immense destruction on well nigh all the regions of the Saxons.
>
> *Inquietam satis hiemem ubique discurrendo et cuncta caedibus atque incendiis permiscendo tam per se ipsum quam per duces, quos miserat, Saxonibus reddidit. Cumque huiusmodi vastationibus per totum hiberni temporis spatium omnes fere Saxonum regiones ingenti clade adfecisset.*[24]

Yet, as we have seen, the account of the "original" annalist was not at all clear. It may be for this reason as much as any other that the so-called reviser of the annals altered the phrasing to explain that the hostages brought by Abbio and Widukind to Charlemagne were the king's confirmation of his agreement that the Saxon leaders should not come to any harm if they came to the king in Francia. The reviser also saw fit to add the gloss that Charlemagne's endeavour was not so much conquest as the conversion of the Saxons. Thus the approach to Widukind and Abbio is presented as part of an effort to convert them to Christianity, and the explanation offered is that the hostages were for their safety. Widukind and Abbio came with Amalwin, a dignitary of the palace whom the king had sent to escort the hostages to them.[25] The *Annales mosellani* (Moselle annals), incidentally, a text which takes as its starting point 703 and ends at 798, and which appears to offer contemporary comment for much of the decades between 768 and 798, claims a far more positive outcome from this same episode:

> After the Saxons had surrendered themselves to him they once again accepted Christianity, which they had long since cast off . . . and Widukind was baptised at Attigny (whither he had come with his companions) and was there baptised, and the lord king received him from the font and honoured him with magnificent gifts.

> *Cumque Saxones se illi dedissent, christianitatem quam pridem respuerant,*
> *iterum recipiunt . . . Widuchind tot malorum auctor ac perfidie incentor venit cum*
> *sociis suis ad Attinacho palacio, et ibidem baptizatus est, et domnus rex suscepit*
> *eum a fonte ac donis magnificis honoravit.*[26]

Further, the reviser extended the original narrative of the *Annales regni francorum* with an account of a political crisis and the rising of an elite *coniuratio*, a word (together with some other key words) which I highlight in the following paragraphs:

> This same year a sworn association, the work of Count Hardrad as was well known, and very extensive, was formed against the king across the Rhine among the eastern Franks. But intelligence of this was swiftly brought to the king who by his shrewdness soon laid this formidable conspiracy to rest, before any great danger had occurred. Some of its leaders were condemned to loss of their eyes, others to banishment or exile.
>
> *Facta est eodem anno trans Rhenum, apud orientales Francos adversus regem in-*
> *modica* coniuratio, *cuius auctorem Hardradum comitem fuisse constabat. Sed*
> *huius iudicium cito ad regem delatum est, eiusque sollertia tam valida* conspira-
> tio *citra ullum grande periculum in breve conquievit, auctoribus eius partim pri-*
> *vatione luminum partim exilii deportatione condemnatis.*[27]

The reviser is generally thought to have been working soon after 801, for that is the point at which the substantial alterations to the "original" *Annales regni francorum* cease. At least fifteen years after the event, therefore, the reviser wished this information to be included in the narrative. A further reference is made to the revolt in the *Annales regni francorum* for 817 in connection with the rebellion of Bernard of Italy. Here the leaders of the revolt are described; they included Reginhar, son of Count Meginhar, whose maternal grandfather Hardrad once conspired in Germany with many noblemen of the province against the emperor Charles: *Huius* coniurationis *principes fuere Eggideo, inter amicos regis primus, et Reginhardus camerarius eius et Reginharius Meginharii comitis filius, cuius maternus avus Hardradus olim in Germania cum multis ex ea provincia nobilibus contra Karo-lum imperatorem* coniuravit.[28]

It is not only the revised, or "E," version of the *Annales regni francorum* which records the Hardrad revolt, however. It is also included in the so-called "D" recension of the original version. This also specifies that the members of the *coniuratio* were Hardrad and east Franks, who conspired against the king and were punished by death or exile: Coniuratio *Hardradi et orientalium Francorum, qua contra regem conspiraverant, deprehensa est, et auctores eius partim morte partim exilio damnati sunt.*[29]

I shall return to the possible motives for including references to the Hardrad event in the *Annales regni francorum.* What I want to signal before I do so is the significance of the use of the word *coniuratio.*[30] This is the word used in the Carolingian capitularies from the late 770s onwards in relation to the possibility of organized armed insurgents and sworn associations against the Frankish ruler. Such *coniurationes* clearly caused Charlemagne and his advisers considerable anxiety. For example, the capitulary of Herstal in 779 warns against the formation of a military troupe and legislates against *coniurationes,* or "sworn associations":

> c. 14 That no one is to presume to form an armed following.
> *De truste faciendo nemo praesumat.*

> c. 16 Concerning the oaths of those who form sworn associations of brotherhood: that no one is to presume to make these. Although men may form brotherhoods concerning alms-giving or fire or shipwreck in other ways, no one is to presume to swear to these.
> *De sacramentis per gildonia invicem* coniurantibus, *ut nemo facere praesumat. Alia vero modo de illorum elemosinis aut de incendio aut de naufragio, quamvis convenentias faciant, nemo in hoc iurare praesumat.*[31]

Similarly, the Synod of Frankfurt in 794 is emphatic:

> c. 31 Concerning sworn associations and conspiracies: that these are not to take place; and where they are found let them be destroyed.
> *De* coniurationibus *et* conspirationibus: *ne fiant et, ubi sunt inventae, destruantur.*[32]

The capitulary of Thionville of 806, moreover, sets out penalties:

> c. 10 Concerning conspiracies, however: those presuming to engage in a conspiracy of any sort and sealing it with an oath are to have judgement passed on them in one of three fashions [details of the punishments—death, flog-

ging, cutting off the nose, cutting off the hair—according to the level of involvement follow]. And that no such conspiracy is henceforth to come to pass in our realm, either by means of an oath or without one.

De conspirationibus *vero, quicumque facie praesumerit et sacramento quam-cumque* conspirationem *firmaverint, ut triplici ratione iudicentur . . . Et ut de cetero in regno nostro nulla huiusmodi* conspiratio *fiat, nec per sacramentum nec sine sacramento.*[33]

Further, the insistence on oath swearing and loyalty to Charlemagne in 789, 793, and 802 should also be understood as part of an attempt to direct the loyalty of his elites. For example, an edict from Aachen, 23 March 789, states:

c. 18 As regards the matter of the oath of fidelity which men have to swear to us and our sons, that the declaration ought to be in the following words: "Thus I . . . promise my lord king Charles and his sons that I am faithful and shall be so all the days of my life, without fraud and evil design.'

De sacramentis fidelitatis causa, quod nobis et filiis nostris iurare debent, quod his verbis contestari debet: "sic promitto ego ille partibus domini mei Caroli regis et filiorum eius, quia fidelis sum et ero diebus vitae meae sine fraude et malo in-genio".[34]

The capitulary for the *missi* of 786 or 792/93, moreover, actually refers to a recent insurgence; it could be a reference either to the Hardrad revolt, to the rebellion of the Thuringians, or to that of Pippin the Hunchback in 792:

c. 1 As to why this oath is necessary, they have to explain, first that it derives from ancient custom and, second, that those unfaithful men recently plotted to cause great strife in the realm of the lord king Charles and conspired against his life and said, when questioned, that they had not sworn fidelity to him.

Quam ob rem istam sacramenta sunt necessaria, per ordine ex antiqua consuetu-dine explicare faciant, et quia modo isti infideles homines magnum conturbium in regnum domni Karoli regi voluerint terminare et in eius vita consiliati sunt et in-quisiti dixerunt, quod fidelitatem ei non iurasset.[35]

We can compare with this the oath accompanying the Aachen capitulary for the *missi* of March 802 and the capitulary of Thionville of 806:

c. 9 Concerning the oath: that fidelity is not to be promised by oath to anyone except to ourself and to each man's lord with a view to our advantage
and that of his lord. Excepted is that oath which is rightly due from one man
to another according to the law. And children previously unable to swear because of their tender years are now to promise fidelity to us.

De iuramento, ut nulli alteri per sacramentum fidelitas promittatur nisi nobis et
unicuique proprio seniori ad nostram utilitatem et sui senioris; excepto his sacra-
mentis quae iuste secundum legem alteri ab altero debetur. Et infantis, qui antea
non potuerunt propter iuvenalem aetatem iurare, modo fidelitatem nobis re-
promittant.[36]

This is not the place to consider fully the implications of all these admoni-
tions concerning fidelity and against sworn associations.[37] What I wish to stress
is that they hint at pockets of disaffection and the overturning of local hierarch-
ies, in the wake of Carolingian expansion, on a far wider scale than the well-
documented rebellions of the Saxon Widukind or the Friulan Rotgaud. With
these proscriptions of *coniurationes* as well as Saxon social and political upheaval
in mind, we can now focus on the narrative about Count Hardrad's revolt in 785,
for this is both a direct reflection of the instability hinted at in Carolingian legislation and an historical record of it. The textual context of these narratives, together with the reference made to the revolt in the original version of the *Annales*
regni francorum under 785, the reviser's subsequent insertion about it, and the
later allusion to it in the year entry for 817, raise issues about the memory of an
elite group, the possible oral transmission of such a memory from generation to
generation, the historical record made of it and subsequent reference made back
to it, and local perceptions of how local history fits into events in the Frankish
realm as a whole. In other words, an understanding of the composition of annals,
and especially the *Annales regni francorum*, is essential first of all for an assessment
of the reasons for the inclusion or omission of the story. Secondly, it is crucial for
any modern interpretation of the representation of elites and their efforts to secure or to maintain their social and political position within Carolingian society.
In short, the narratives of the Hardrad revolt have important implications for our
understanding of the forms memory and history could take in the Frankish empire and thus of Frankish perceptions of their own past. We can then consider
how such perceptions fitted into the Franks' wider conceptualization of the past
as I have characterized it in the preceding two chapters.

Little more information about the actual incident can be teased out of our sources than I have already provided. A consideration of the geography may nevertheless be instructive, given that the "original" *Annales regni francorum* and the reviser describe the Hardrad *coniuratio* as being among the east Franks across the Rhine. The sheer distances involved make it clear that Charlemagne had been more than usually energetic in the amount of ground covered.[38] The implication of the geographical location of the sojourn at the Eresburg, the encounter with Widukind, and the movement from royal camp to the assembly at Paderborn appears to be that these east Franks were based in the region between the Sieg and Lahn rivers, that is, south of the lands dominated by the Westphalian Saxons, or conceivably farther east in the territory of the Thuringians, south east of the confluence between the Werra and Weser rivers. Certainly Karl Brunner and others before him, despite the disparity in the narrative style and the details of the texts concerned, were inclined to identify the Hardrad incident with a quarrel between Thuringian nobles and Charlemagne, recorded at considerable length in the *Annales nazariani* (Annals from the manuscript of the monastery of Saint Nazarius) (Lorsch).[39] No names of the leaders of this group are provided by these annals, and it might more plausibly be regarded as an additional example of an elite group protest against Carolingian rule.[40] Elsewhere in the annals, the writers' distinctions between the many groups of people beyond the Rhine have a degree of precision which needs to be taken seriously. Documents such as the Saxon hostage list reflect a similar understanding of the particular configurations of local groups.[41]

The breakdown in aristocratic solidarity identified in relation to the Saxon nobles and the Frankish confiscation of lands along the Hellweg could well have destabilized the elites in the bordering lands as well.[42] Hardrad and his supporters, therefore, are not Saxons, nor, though this is far less certain, were they Thuringians; they appear to have been a local elite in eastern Austrasia attempting to take advantage of the political volatility of the time.

Why should the reviser have inserted this brief account of Hardrad? Why does the author of the *Annales regni francorum* entry for 817 recall the family tradition, on the maternal side, of revolt against the Frankish king? To answer these questions it may help to survey the references to the incident in other Frankish narratives from the ninth century. The issues of both dating and location of these sources is crucial, but it should be emphasized at once that in most cases they cannot be completely resolved.

The earliest reference to Hardrad is probably the "D" version of the *Annales regni francorum* already cited, if the traditional dating of the composition of the first section of the annals to 788 be accepted. The earliest manuscript of the complete "D" version dates, however, from almost a century later. This is the now well-known codex Vienna, ÖNB, lat. 473, which was written at Saint Amand and has been associated with Charles the Bald's coronation at Metz in 869 when he was endeavouring to expand his kingdom eastwards.[43] An earlier fragment of the "D" version, dated to the second quarter of the ninth century and extant in Leiden, Universiteitsbibliotheek, BPL 2391p, however, is from "west Germany."[44] Similarly, the next earliest reference to Hardrad would be the revised version, if this, again as is usually surmised, was completed soon after 801. This revised version apparently circulated from the Rhineland eastwards, though the majority of its extant manuscripts post-date the ninth century. Shortly after the supposed revision of the *Annales regni francorum* was completed there is a long report in the so-called *Annales laureshamenses* (Lorsch annals) under the year 786. It mentions no names, however:

> Certain counts and some nobles in Austrasia attempted to rebel. They formed a sworn association and compelled everyone they could to rise up against the lord king. Such a deed filled many with fear. And when they realised that they could not carry through their abominable enterprise and that the moment was inopportune, they were seized with sudden terror and sought out hiding places on all sides. When he learned of this, the lord king with his customary clemency, managing the whole affair in politic fashion, ordered them to come to him. And in due course, in August, he had a synod of bishops and a great general assembly gather at Worms, where he gave sentence that those convicted of being the principal figures in this sworn association should be deprived alike of *honores* and of eyes but in his mercy he allowed those innocently seduced into it to go free. Then he set forth and proceeded . . . to St Peter's Rome where he celebrated Easter.
>
> *Rebellare conati sunt quidam comites, nonnulli etiam nobilium in partibus Austriae ac coniurantes invicem coegerunt, quos poterant, ut contra domnum regem insurgerent. Quod factum multos exterruit. Cumque perspicerent quod opus nefandum implere non possent, neque oportunum tempus adesset, subito exterriti latebras undique quesivere. Quod compertum, domnus rex solita clementia omnia consilio regens, iussit eos ad se venisse. Procedente autem tempore in mense Au-*

*gusto apud Wormaciam sinodum episcoporum ac conventum magnificum coire
fecit; ubi decernens quod, hii qui potissime in hac* coniuratione *devicti sunt, hon-
ore simul ac luminibus privarentur; eos autem qui innoxii in hac* coniuratione
*seducti sunt, clementer absolvit. Inde proficiscens perrexit ad Romam, et inde
ad monasterium sancti Benedicti et inde perrexit ad Capuam. Et inde reversus est,
et pervenit ad sanctum Petrum apostolum et ibi celebravit pascha.*[45]

The revised version of the *Annales regni francorum* also records the 786 assembly at Worms. There, however, it is the Bretons who come and are judged. For
good measure the reviser also inserts a short account of the settlement of Brittany
by Britons at the time of the Saxon and Angle invasion of Britain.[46] This is presumably derived from Bede's *Historia ecclesiastica gentis angolorum* (Ecclesiastical
history of the English people), already known at the Frankish royal court at the
end of the eighth century,[47] but it forms a useful reminder that the author at least
took a long view of the contemporary events he described. Further, the annalist
wanted his audience to understand the origin of the Bretons in order to make the
point that they were relative newcomers in Francia.

The Worms Assembly was presumably one in which a number of cases could
have been heard, but local perceptions apparently noted only the one most rele-
vant to their own concerns. Unfortunately, no other record of the meeting is extant, and it is impossible now to determine whether it should be understood as an
assembly, synod, or judicial hearing.[48] The apparent gap in Charlemagne's legislation between 782 and the *Admonitio generalis* of 789 is usually attributed to his
preoccupation with the Saxon wars, but this does not take into account a possible
level of local dissidence or insurrection.

One extant text of the so-called Lorsch annals is the only surviving fragment
of any Frankish annals which has appeared to indicate a close connection between
the composition and the writing down of the text. In Vienna, ÖNB, lat. 515, a single gathering of eight leaves, written ca. 800 and containing the Lorsch annals
from midway between 794 and 803, four different scribes have been identified; all
were writing at the turn of the eighth century.[49] All wrote an Alemannian script
type whose precise origin has still not been satisfactorily established, though the
case for Lorsch itself is weak.[50] The scribes, moreover, appear to have been writing
from dictation, so the text cannot be regarded as autograph in any strict sense. As
I have explained elsewhere, much hinges on whether these year entries can be regarded as year-by-year entries, and therefore directly contemporary with the

events they describe.[51] If written year by year, then the Lorsch annal account for 786 would predate even the "original" version of the *Annales regni francorum*. The fragment of ca. 800 in Vienna, ÖNB, lat. 515, however, contains only the entries for 794–803. That it is part of a larger text is suggested by the copy made of it, with only a few textual variants, extant in Sankt Paul in Lavanttal, Stiftsarchiv, Cod. 8/1. It was made ca. 835 in Reichenau where the year-by-year annal section of the text runs from 703 to 803.[52]

There are indications in the transmission of the Lorsch annals, first of all, of a wider readership and use, which appears to extend from the upper to the middle Rhine region, after their initial production. Thus, for example, Heinrich Fichtenau suggested that both the Austrasian texts known as the *Annales mosellani* and the *Fragmentum Chesnii* (Chesnianum, or the Du Chesne fragment) were influenced up to 790 by the Lorsch annals.[53] Certainly up to 785 the entries for the Lorsch annals, the *Fragmentum Chesnii*, and the *Annales mosellani* are apparently based on the same set of annal entries for 768–785, but they diverge thereafter. Roger Collins has suggested important refinements to our understanding of the possible relationship between these texts. He suggests that all three made use of the "Lorsch annals of 785" (as he labels the stem from which the rest of the Lorsch annals arguably developed).[54] The use of a common source to at least 785, therefore, might be a further indication of the circulation and dissemination of sets of annals to, and their use in, different centres. Similarly, the "Murbach annals group," that is, the *Annales nazariani*, *Annales guelferbytani* (Annals in the Wolfenbüttel manuscript), and *Annales alemannici* (Alemannian annals), as Lendi has explained, are also related to each other, as well as to the Lorsch annals as far as 759 and to the *Annales regni francorum* for the span of years between 791 and 805. This may suggest both an earlier dissemination of a short narrative sequence of the events of the earlier part of the reign of Pippin III and further notice in a number of places being accorded the narrative offered by the *Annales regni francorum*.[55] Such use reinforces the impression of the wide and efficient early dissemination of sections of the *Annales regni francorum* at the end of the eighth century and in the early years of the ninth century. It witnesses, furthermore, to a dispersed local audience for contemporary Frankish history.

In other words, it looks as if copies of portions of the annals might have been circulated in batches of year entries before the entire narrative was completed.[56] The piecemeal circulation of annals as a form of news and comment might help to explain the overlapping and repetition of entries in annals from elsewhere.

Those who have worked closely on the text have suggested that it is only from 785 that the Lorsch annals offer an independent narrative, and that the contents of the annals were dependent on other resources up to then. This has led to the proposal that the Lorsch annals were begun in 785 and prefaced with a preliminary section comprising short entries for the years 703–84. It was thereafter updated each year until 803, and all its entries are from a single mind. The end point of 803 is the real conclusion of the text and suggests that its author departed or died thereafter.

Rather than accepting the customary view of the fragment as indicating year-by-year composition, at least from 785, I suggest that the Lorsch annals offer a text that is more likely to be an alternative and independent history of the Franks composed in 803 and circulated within the Rhineland region; the possibility of the annals' distribution in sections remains open. Given that Canisius's lost manuscript of the *Annales regni francorum* was allegedly from Lorsch and that the entries for the years 789–93 in that text closely resemble the Lorsch annals,[57] the Lorsch annals may actually be deliberately divergent and may have been conceived in reaction to the account offered in the royal *Annales*.

Above all, this little group of sources with references to the Hardrad revolt have one important thing in common. With the exception of the "D" version of the *Annales regni francorum*, all have associations with Austrasia or the regions east of the Rhine and cannot be described as west Frankish in emphasis. (Even Vienna, ÖNB, lat. 473, containing the "D"-version reference, has been linked with Charles the Bald's eastern pretensions.) It might be possible, therefore, to regard the preservation of the memory of the Hardrad revolt as important for the east Frankish elite and as an indication of an east Frankish audience.

There are also the later ninth-century allusions to the Hardrad story to be taken into account, such as that by Einhard:

Another powerful conspiracy against Charles had risen even earlier in Germany, but all its perpetrators were sent into exile; some blinded, others unharmed . . . [I]t is widely believed that the cruelty of Queen Fastrada was the cause and source of these conspiracies.

Facta est et alia prius contra eum in Germania valida coniuratio. *Cuius auctores partim luminibus orbati partim membris incolomes, omnes tamen exilio deportati sunt . . . Harum tamen* coniurationum *Fastradae reginae crudelitas causa et origo extitisse creditur.*[58]

As Matthew Innes and I have argued elsewhere, Einhard may have written his *Vita Karoli* as early as 817.[59] In his text the Hardrad revolt follows the account of the revolt of Pippin the Hunchback. Both revolts are mentioned immediately after the description of the king's family, and Einhard alleges, as if to reduce it to a more domestic level, that Queen Fastrada was to blame. Given the court offices of Hardrad's son Meginhar and grandson Reginhar, Einhard may indeed have perceived Hardrad's revolt as an essentially domestic or family affair. That is, Einhard presents it more as an uprising of an elite group associated with the royal household than as a regional uprising.[60]

Another east Frankish text is the section of the *Annales fuldenses* which includes the brief reference to the Hardrad revolt and refers to the group led by Hardrad as a *coniuratio*: "The conspiracy of the east Franks, which is called that of Hardrad, arose and was swiftly suppressed." (Coniuratio *orientalium francorum quae vocatur Hartrati contra regem exorta et cito conpressa est.*)[61] The *Annales fuldenses* have not been satisfactorily dated. It is generally accepted that the oldest manuscript, Leipzig, Universitätsbibliothek, Rep. II.4 129a, of s. IX/X, thought to be from Niederaltaich in Bavaria, originally contained the text of 714–901, with the entries judged to be autograph from 897, if not from 894. From 714 to 792 the *Annales fuldenses* is certainly a compilation with a clear indebtedness to other known historical narratives, such as the *Chronicon laurissense breve* (The short chronicle of Lorsch), the continuations of the chronicle of Fredegar, the "D" and revised "E" versions of the *Annales regni francorum*, and possibly also the *Annales laureshamenses*.[62] Nevertheless, the *Annales fuldenses* provide a distinctive east Frankish perspective. The text for the years 714–828, and possibly 828–38, was put together at the end of this period, conceivably as late as 838. They once formed, therefore, a free-standing text much like the *Annales regni francorum*. To explain the pause in 828 one might have to construct the same kind of scenario that Felix Grat proposed for the composition of the *Annales regni francorum*. Thus, divisions in the kingdom became sufficiently marked in the late 820s to prompt the production of an "east Frankish" version of the *Annales regni francorum*. Alternatively, the entire text for 714–838 could have been composed in 838 by Rudolf of Fulda, who drew on earlier accounts for the section to 828 at least to such an extent that the earlier portion does not look like his prose. Ironically enough, however, it is this early portion of the text that is usually ignored precisely because Kurze, its MGH editor, thought that it was so predominantly made up of extracts from other identifiable or hypothetical sources as to fail the test of an "original" work.[63] Rau did at least include 828–38 in his reprint of Kurze's edition with a German translation but omitted 714–828.[64] Even Timothy Reuter decided to start his translation at 838. He acknowledged that the section 830–38 was probably original but regarded the entries as too "thin and uninteresting" to be worth translating; he paid no attention to 714–828 at all.[65]

Lastly, the "Astronomer," probably writing under the auspices of Bishop Drogo of Metz in about 843, in his *Vita Hludowici* (Life of Louis), refers to one of the advisers sent to help Louis rule in Aquitaine, namely, "Meginhar who had been sent to [Louis] by his father [Charlemagne] and was a sensible and enterprising man, well aware of what was advantageous and fitting for the king." (*Habebat autem tunc temporis Meginarium secum, missum sibi a patre, virum sapientem et strenuum gnarumque utilitatis et honestatis regie.*)[66] This appears to be Hardrad's son. Further on in the Astronomer's narrative, the Astronomer explains, as in the *Annales regni francorum* for 817, that one of the conspirators in support of Bernard of Italy was Reginhar, formerly a count of the emperor's palace and a son of Count Meginhar.[67]

WRITING AND MEMORY

Discussions of past discrepancies between annal accounts, whether of this incident or others, have concentrated exclusively on whether they help to establish which version of a text was dependent on another. It would be more constructive to consider the implications of context and perspective that the variations might suggest concerning different formations of memory by means of historical writing, and thus different perceptions of the Frankish past. Certainly the largely east Frankish texts I have cited transmit and preserve the story of Hardrad's revolt. Why do they do so?

Given that a number of texts omit it, the retention of the story in the east Frankish sources assumes significance. The *Annales regni francorum*, whether in the "D" or "E" versions, could well have played a simple role as a transmitter of knowledge of the story. Thus Einhard, the author of the early section of the *Annales fuldenses*, and the Astronomer, all of whom appear to have had access to the "D" or "E" versions of the *Annales regni francorum* and draw on them to a greater or lesser extent in their own narratives, chose to preserve the memory of Hardrad's revolt. All might have learnt about it solely from this earlier historical text. This is not to say that they reported the revolt either positively or with any overt signs that they regarded it as a tragedy. They stress the punishment meted out to the rebels, which could be interpreted as either warning or lament. Nevertheless, the acknowledgement of the revolt is in itself important. It created at least a ripple on the smooth surface of the narrative of steady triumph over local elite groups, whether Saxon or east Frankish, on the part of Charlemagne and the Carolingians. The repetitions of the story, moreover, widespread as a consequence of the dissemination of the "D" and "E" versions of the *Annales regni francorum*—arguably shaped subsequent memories of Carolingian expansion and its impact on local communities.

Yet the apparently independent east Frankish record of another rebellion preserved in the Lorsch annals suggests a local and east Frankish memory that was not quenched, but rather transmitted in the form of a local historical record for a local audience. Every locally produced set of annals which appears to chart the political advance of the Carolingians, therefore, potentially indicates local elite attitudes to that advance. These annals were one of the means by which memory of Carolingian expansion at the expense, as well as sometimes to the advantage, of local elites was preserved.

LOCAL ANNALS

One of the issues affecting evaluation of annals as statements about, or records of, the past is whether one should envisage independent scribes or compilers, or designated record keepers in a particular institution, sitting down every Christmas Eve or Easter Eve to write up the year's events, even if only to write *Venit organa in Franciam* (757) or *Rex Pippinus venit Saxonia* (758).[68] Current assessments of the annals also appear to envisage these same scribes or compilers needing the prop of a set of annals from somewhere else to provide information, if not the actual text, for their own notes. These two scenarios may not be incompatible, or even too fanciful, but I find them difficult to accept. I have already explained that the Lorsch annals, once thought to be year-by-year entries, should more probably be envisaged as a complete history written as a retrospective account in or after the last year recorded. That a copy should be preserved from Reichenau also indicates that such an annal record could be circulated. It might indeed have been in a position to form perceptions of the immediate past in another centre as well as to provide material to build other larger histories. This does not, of course, address the problem of the origin of the elements common to two or more texts. Nor does it indicate whether the set of annals providing the basis for extension and extrapolation, such as we see in the Lorsch annals, the "Austrasian group," or the "Murbach group," was a central or even court-generated text deliberately disseminated as an official record of national history.

A look at the small group of annals labelled the Murbach annals by the MGH editors, due to their references here and there to abbots who can be associated with Murbach, nevertheless reinforces the importance of the local or regional circulation of sets of annals and their role in forming perceptions of the past. The *Annales guelferbytani* are members of the Murbach group and are extant in one manuscript in Wolfenbüttel, Herzog-August Bibliothek, Aug. 67.5 8°, a small-format *libellus* of fourteen leaves measuring 155 × 105 mm (120 × 75 mm), written by three or four hands in the early ninth century.[69] The *Annales alemannici*, however, survive in three copies. One of these is Monza, Biblioteca capitolare, f9/176, a west German manuscript of the third-quarter of the ninth century, containing astronomical and astrological works with, on fols. 2r–4v, the *Annales alemannici* for the years 709–912, written in a single hand of the beginning of the tenth century.

The earliest, and arguably the original, version of the *Annales alemannici* is the copy now in Sankt Gallen, Stiftsarchiv, Zürcher Abteilung, Nr. 1 (fig. 6).[70] This too, like the *libellus* in which the *Annales guelferbytani* survive, appears to be a self-contained and complete *libellus* of eight leaves only. The first section of this text originally ran only to 787 and was later continued by another scribe to 799, who also appears to have written out dates until 980, against which perfunctory notes were added from time to time by different scribes, probably in Sankt Gallen. The version now in Sankt Gallen, Stiftsarchiv (Lendi's Codex T), was regarded by Lendi as a copy of the Murbach annals made for Reichenau. Two hands shared the entries for the ninth century, with the section 802–76 being the work of a Reichenau-trained hand and the section 876/78–88 being by a Sankt Gallen–trained hand. The hand who wrote entries for 882–911 is either a Sankt Gallen– or Reichenau-trained scribe. Thus wherever it was originally written, it served as a form, as it were, for later scribes to fill in. Although affiliations between entries and manuscripts within this group are undoubtedly an important thing to establish, these annal accounts appear to shed more light on the process of accumulating news. The version in the Sankt Gallen Stiftsarchiv manuscript, fol. 2v, for

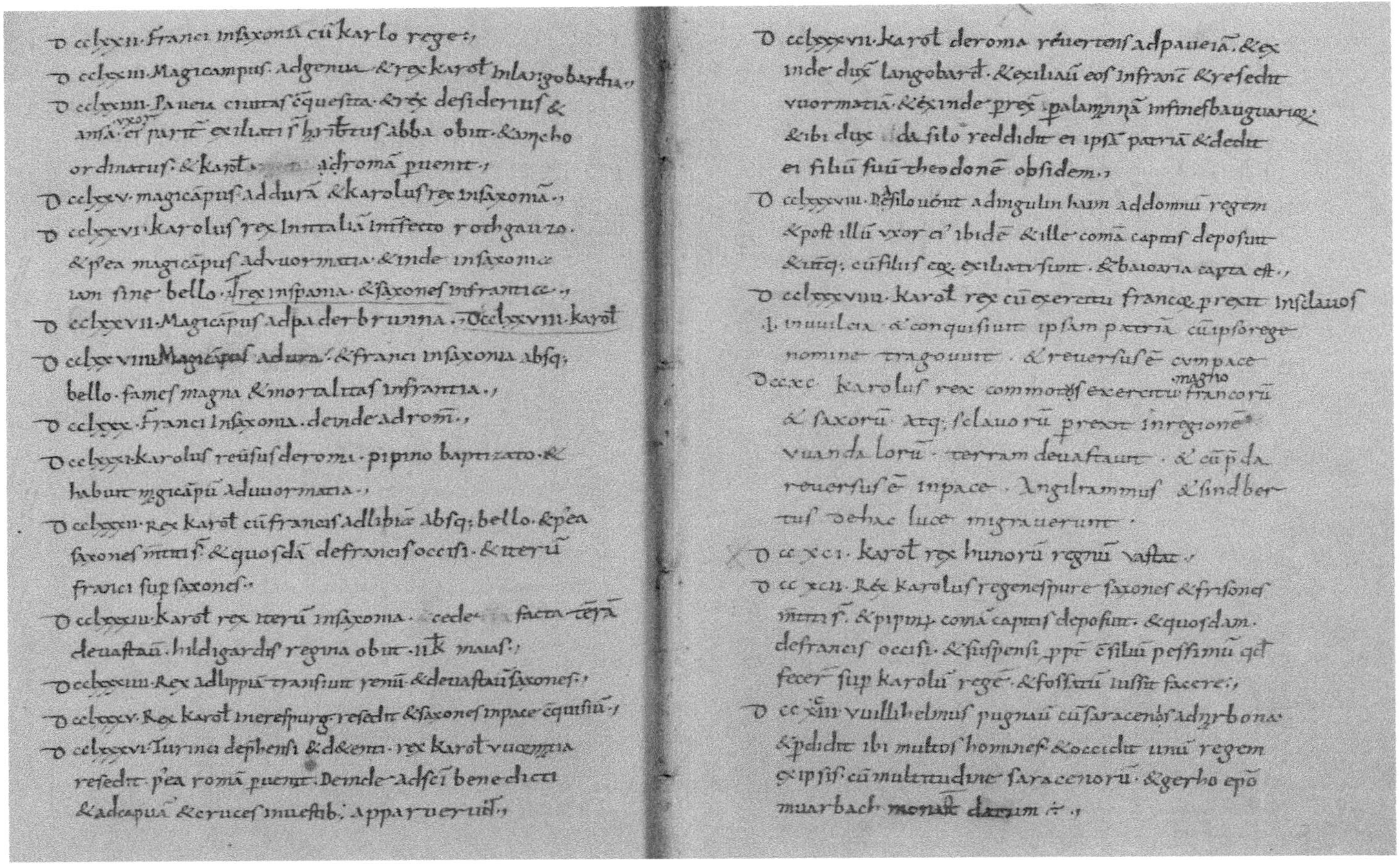

Fig. 6. *Annales alemannici*, Sankt Gallen, Stiftsarchiv, Zürcher Abteilung, Nr. 1, fols. 2v–3r

example, has a laconic note about the fate of the Thuringians under 786: *Thuringi deprehensi et detenti*. The *Annales guelferbytani* do not mention the Thuringians at all, and it is only in the so-called *Annales nazariani* that their story is told. This occupies fols. 53v–59v of Vat., pal. lat. 966, and is in the same hand as the earlier part of the manuscript which contains the *Liber historiae francorum*. The *Annales nazariani* carry on from the preceding text in mid-quire, as if to supplement it. The script is an early Caroline minuscule, dated by Elias Avery Lowe and Bernhard Bischoff to the late eighth century and located by Lowe to Lorsch and by Bischoff tentatively to Murbach, though he agrees on the Lorsch *Bibliotheksheimat*.[71] Quite apart from the entry for 786 it has many other details of interest, not least a handful of cursive additions noting events relating to the Lombard kingdom, such as the arrival of the daughter of Desiderius in Francia with Bertrada. There is also a lengthy passage under 788 concerning Tassilo of Bavaria and possibly significant gaps, such as that between 768 and 771. The 786 entry in the *Annales nazariani* is an extraordinary story and serves as a culminating illustration of the argument adduced so far. This story's preservation in only one contemporary manuscript is a salutary reminder both of the precariousness of source survival and of the local anxiety that this rebellion and its circumstances might otherwise be forgotten. Because this text is too often overlooked in general accounts of the inexorableness of Carolingian success, it is worthwhile to reproduce the entire text, as recorded in the late eighth-century manuscript, and a translation, as follows (see fig. 7):

> The Thuringians formed a plot to capture Charlemagne and kill him. If they were unable to perpetrate this sin and most abominable crime, then they desired at least to bring it about that they should not obey him or comply with his commands. This vile design could in no wise remain hidden from the king who, however, prudent and mild as he was, bore it with the most extreme patience. And so, after some time had elapsed the said king sent his legate to one of those Thuringians in the matter of his daughter who was betrothed to a Frank and known to have been betrothed according to the law of the Franks saying that he should hand the Frank's bride over to him at the appointed time. But the Thuringian, treating the king's commands with contempt, not only refused to promise to hand her over but also gathered almost all his Thuringian neighbours together and sought to defend himself from the king of the Franks.

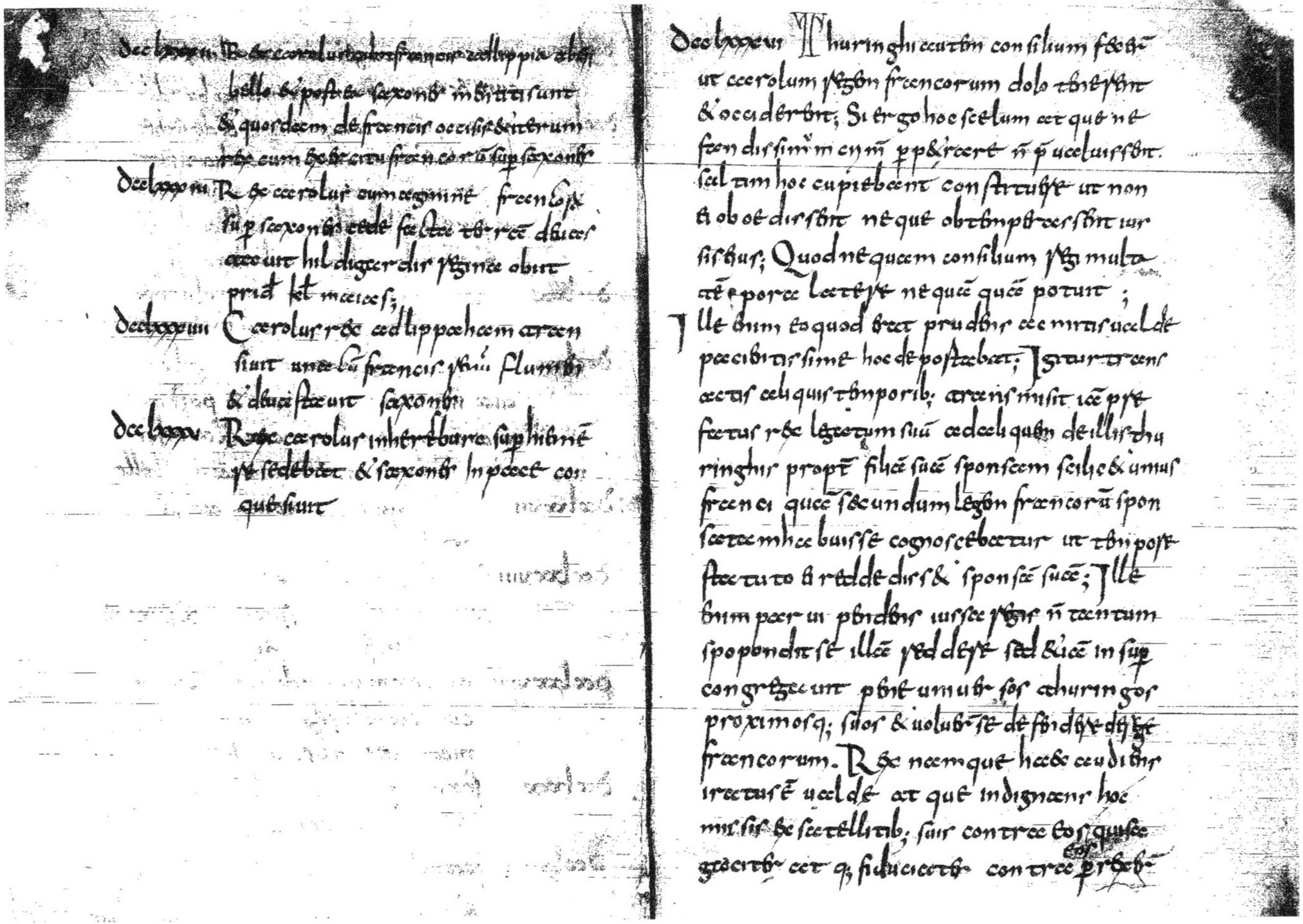

Fig. 7. *Annales nazariani,* Vat., pal. lat. 966, fols. 56v–57r

Now the king was mightily angered on hearing this and in his displeasure dispatched against them some of his satellites who proceeded against them with shrewdness and boldness devastating their estates and properties. Seized by fear, the Thuringians took refuge at the tomb of the blessed martyr Boniface that the king might, for veneration of this saint and through his merits, forgive them the injury, treachery and plots which they had attempted to set in train. Then the abbot [Baugulf] of that monastery gave them cheer with words of peace and sweet discourse and informed the king of everything through his messenger. The king therefore sent his legate to them that they should come to him in peace, and soon they journeyed to him and stood before him. The king for his part inquired of them whether what he had been informed about them, namely that they had intended his death and if unable to effect that to treat his commands with contempt, was true or false. And they could in no way deny it and disdained to do so. Indeed it is reported that one of them said to the king

"If my confederates and associates had proved to be of my sentiments, never again would you have been seen crossing to this side of the Rhine alive."

But the king since he was most mild and most wise, above all the kings who had preceded him in Francia, bore this most moderately.

After some days had passed therefore, the king sent those Thuringians off in the company of his *missi*, some into Italy and to St Peter and some into Neustria and Aquitaine, sending them to the tombs of the saints so that they might swear fidelity to the king and his children. And this they are attested to have done. Several of them were arrested on their return journey from these places. Their eyes are known to have been torn out. Some however reached the city of Worms and were arrested there and sent into exile and their eyes are known to have been torn out there. And all their possessions and estates are known to have been confiscated by the crown. The king remains unharmed and safe therefore, ruling the kingdom of the Franks and the Lombards and Romans most excellently inasmuch as the king of heaven is proved to be his protector. And the aforementioned king journeyed to Rome.

[fol. 57r] *DCCLXXXVI. Thuringhi autem consilium fecerunt, ut carolum regem francorum dolo tenerent et occiderent. Si ergo hoc scelum atque nefandissimum crimen perpetrare non praevaluissent, saltim hoc cupiebant constituere, ut non ei oboedissent neque obtemperassent iussis eius. Quod nequam consilium regi multa*

tempora latere nequamquam potuit. Ille enim eo, quod erat prudens ac mitis, valde
pacientissime hoc deportabat. Igitur transactis aliquis temporibus transmisit iam
prefatus rex legatum suum ad aliquem de illis Thuringhis propter filiam suam,
sponsam scilicet unius Franci, quam secundum legem Francorum sponsatam
habuisse cognoscebatur, ut tempore statuto ei reddedisset sponsam suam. Ille enim
parvi pendens iussa regis non tantum spopondit se illam reddere, sed etiam insu-
per congregavit pene universos Thuringos proximosque suos et voluerunt se defend-
ere de rege Francorum. Rex namque haec audiens iratus est valde atque indignans
hoc missis ex satellitibus suis contra eos, qui sagaciter atque fiduciater contra
eos perrexerunt [fol. 57v] *predia possessionesque eorum devastantes. Thuringhi*
namque timore perterriti ad corpus beati Bonifacii martyris confugierunt, ut per
merita venerationemque ipsius sancti rex relaxeretur illis noxam dolum insidi-
asque, quae praeparare conati fuerant. Porro pater monasterii illius consolabatur
eos verbis pacificis dulcisque sermonibus, per nuntiumque suum intimavit haec
omnia regi. Rex ergo distinavit ad eos legatum suum, ut ad se cum pace venirent.
Qui mox ad eum profecti sunt steteruntque coram rege. Rex nemphe sciscitabatur
ab eis, si verum an falsum fuisset, quod ei intimatum fuerat de illis. Scilicet ut de
morte eius cogitarent et si constituere nisi fuissent, ut parvipendissent mandata il-
lius. Illi enim nullo modo poterant neque condignaverunt hoc negare. Fertur namque
unum ex illis dixisse ad regem: "Si collige sociique mei mihi consentire conprobar-
entur, [fol. 58r] *tu numquam post modum citra Renum fluvium transire vivus cog-*
noscebaris." Rex vero, q[uo]n[iam][72] *erat mitissimus atque sapientissimus super*
omnes reges, qui fuerunt ante eum in Francia, moderantissime illud deportavit.

Transactis igitur quibusdam diebus transmisit rex ipsos Thuringos una cum
missis suis aliquos in Italiam et ad sanctum Petrum, quosdam vero in Neustriam
atque in Equitaniam per corpora sanctorum, scilicet ut iurarent fidelitatem regi
liberisque eius, quod et ita actum esse conprobatur. Qui exinde revertentes non-
nulli ex illis detenti sunt in via et evulsi esse noscuntur oculi eorum. Aliqui vero per-
venerunt ad civitatem Uuagionum et ibidem conprehensi sunt et exinde exiliati et
illuc evulsi esse cognoscentur oculi eorum. Possessiones vero vel agros eorum omnes
infiscati esse noscuntur. Rex ergo inlesus atque incolomis permanens optime regens
regnum Francorum atque Langobardorum Romanorumque eo, quod celorum rex
protector eius esse conprobatur. Etiam prefatus rex ad Romam perrexit.[73]

The story, with its peculiar sequence of events and bald account of the pun-
ishments meted out *after* the oathtaking, resembles that of the Hardrad revolt

only in so far as the rebels met a very similar fate. It is only in the account of the rebellion in the Lorsch annals and the *Annales nazariani* that the judgement was given at Worms and the King went to Rome thereafter. From other sources we know that there was indeed an assembly at Worms in 786, after which the King journeyed to Rome. There is a great deal more circumstantial detail in the account of the Thuringians, which alters the emphasis considerably, not least the extra story concerning the Thuringian's daughter and her betrothal to a Frank and the Thuringians' seeking of refuge at the tomb of Boniface in Fulda. It is important to note that the narrative appears to include the betrothal story as an instance of Charlemagne adding fuel to flames already ignited. Indeed, noting the account in the *Annales nazariani* of Thuringian rebels who were tried at the Assembly, or Synod, of Worms in 786, Eberhard Katz *in*flated the Hardrad rebellion to one of a large group comprising east Franks *and* Thuringians.[74] Brunner, on the other hand, was inclined to *con*flate the two and identify the east Franks *as* the Thuringians, though his discussion leaves room for association between two connected groups of nobles.[75] Stuart Airlie also conflates the Hardrad and Thuringian revolts, save for the important observations on the relations between king and aristocratic families implied by the incident (or both incidents).[76] I think we should take the reference to Thuringians seriously, and thus assume that it is more likely that there are indeed two different revolts east of the Rhine, one in 785, recorded in the original "D" version and revised, or "E," version of the *Annales regni francorum*, Einhard's *Vita Karoli*, and the *Annales fuldenses*, and another in 786, recorded in the Lorsch annals and the *Annales nazariani*. This is the more likely given the prominence of the dukes of Thuringia in late Merovingian political life.[77] In the *Annales nazariani* the king appears to have promised clemency after the rebels themselves had sought the intercession of both the saints and Abbot Baugulf of Fulda. The conclusion seems to me deliberately circumspect. The king is not presented in this passage as behaving in a noble manner, despite the occasional words of praise and the fact that he "remains unharmed and safe" in contrast to the unfortunate rebels.

I should also like to draw attention to the phrase "it is reported that one of them said to the king" (*Fertur namque unum ex illis dixisse ad regem*) before the portion recording the defiance of the Thuringian, for this is a precious indication of annals reflecting methods of communication and possibly oral as well as written processes of gathering information. The long story for 786, moreover, is the climax of the annal entries in the manuscript, with every indication that it is a contemporary account. Further, the unusually long entry for 786 in Vat., pal. lat. 966, is marked out for special attention in the manuscript. It comes on the last leaf of a quire; half the preceding page was left blank; and the new section of text beginning on fol. 57r has an enlarged *T* to draw attention to it. A bifolium was then added to the codex to contain the end of the 786 story and the account of Tassilo's hopeless attempt to stand up to his cousin Charlemagne. Again, these leaves contain detail found nowhere else, especially under 788. The last entry in the book is 790 and reads only *Franci quieverunt.* The single scribe wrote the date 791 but never wrote anything else.

This scribe, wherever he was, presented a text whose omissions are as important as his additions for a reflection of his historical perspective. He certainly preserved the memory of the Thuringian revolt, just as the scribes or compilers of the "D" and revised versions of the *Annales regni francorum* preserved the memory of the Hardrad *coniuratio*. Certainly, similarities between the various annal collections might spring from current understandings of history and the circulation of news and perceptions of events that reverberated at the local level.

Individual perceptions of the past, and individual local voices, therefore, can be heard through the medium of the great variety of annals produced in the Carolingian period. The annal accounts witness, in their undoubted echoing of information to be found in the "major" annals, such as the *Annales regni francorum*, to the efficient circulation and dissemination of the latter's narrative. Nevertheless the triumphalist tone to which the *Annales regni francorum* have accustomed us is tempered in these local annals by at least a local memory of disaffection, as well as observations on other topics. Above all, what the manuscripts of the *Annales nazariani* and Lorsch annals, and of the Murbach group, suggest is that the process of annal composition was probably not piecemeal at all but a retrospective presentation of a century of Frankish history. This has profound implications for our understanding not only of these authors' perceptions of the Frankish past, but also of the means by which their perceptions were communicated to their audiences.

Conclusion

In the first chapter of this book, I discussed universal histories of the Carolingian period which brought the history of the world either from the Creation or the Incarnation up to the Franks in the ninth century. By emphasizing Frankish annals and presentations of the immediate Frankish past in my final chapter I may have given the impression that these are two separate developments. I want to end this book, however, by suggesting that the long and the local views are in fact part of a complex of perceptions of the past in the Carolingian period.

First of all, the charting in so many local histories of the slow rise of the Carolingian family to conquest and dominance throughout the Frankish realms is in itself a strong statement of confidence and certainty, set in the context of the history of Rome and of the Franks in the Merovingian period. One can think of the conclusion to the *Annales nazariani*'s entry for 786:

The king remains unharmed and safe therefore, ruling the kingdom of the Franks and the Lombards and Romans most excellently inasmuch as the king

of heaven is proved to be his protector. And the aforementioned king journeyed to Rome.

*Rex ergo inlesus atque incolomis permanens optime regens regnum Francorum
atque Langobardorum Romanorumque eo, quod celorum rex protector eius esse
conprobatur. Etiam prefatus rex ad Romam perrexit.*[1]

Secondly, these Frankish histories cannot be regarded as isolated. The chronicles
of 741, Ado of Vienne, and Regino, quite apart from the older *Liber historiae francorum* or Fredegar's chronicle, showed us a perception of both a new age and of
the continuity of human history. Even the annal texts themselves do this: the
manuscripts from which past modern editors extracted the annals turn out in
many cases to be compilations of sequential historical texts, of which the annals
form an essential portion, designed to be read as history books, with a chronology
extending back to beginnings, whether to the creation of the world or to the origin of the Franks. Alternatively, the annals form part of a continuous history.
Frankish history books, by the simple means of codicological context, create a different chronological perspective for the compilation as a whole. One example
is the Paris manuscript, BnF, lat. 10911, which prefaces the *Annales regni francorum*
with the *Liber historiae francorum* and its account of the Trojan origin of the
Franks, and uses Fredegar's continuations to fill the gap between 727 (the end of
the *Liber historiae Francorum*) and 741 (the beginning of the *Annales regni francorum*).[2] Another is Saint Omer, Bibliothèque Municipale, MS 697 + 706, which
concludes with the *Annales regni francorum* in the "C" redaction and its continuation as the annals of Saint Bertin. The first part of the collection, however, com-
prises abridged versions of Eutropius's *Breviarium* (Breviary of Roman history),
the chronicle of Count Marcellinus, which was itself a continuation of the chronicle of Eusebius-Jerome, Gregory of Tours's *Historiae*, and the fourth book of the
chronicle of Fredegar and its continuations, as well as a list of the provinces of
the Roman empire. It thus contrives to place the Franks firmly in the succession of
Roman history.[3]

Similarly, the *Annales nazariani* in Vat., pal. lat. 966, are preceded by the
Liber historiae francorum's account of the origin of the Franks. This is connected
with the *Annales nazariani* in the way the manuscript is laid out. The 708 entry
recording Drogo's death comes at the bottom of the page, after a new heading
Anni ab incarnatione d[omi]ni inserted between the end of the *Liber historiae francorum* and the first annal entry, as if to indicate a new branch of the narrative.

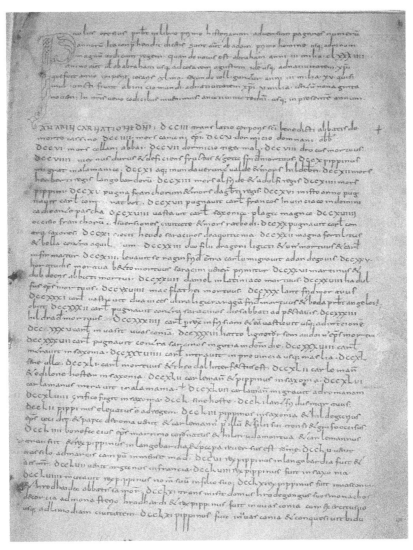

Fig. 8. "Lorsch Annals," Sankt Paul in Lavanttal, Stiftsarchiv, Cod. 8/1, fol. 1r

Even more striking is the complete text of the Lorsch annals in Sankt Paul in La-vanttal, Stiftsarchiv, Cod. 8/1. At the beginning of the text is a preface referring to Orosius's chronological perspective which contrives to bring the chronology from Adam to Abraham, and from Abraham to Caesar and the birth of Christ, and thereafter to the present day (fig. 8).[4] The annals' first year entry is for 703 and the *translatio* of the relics of Saint Benedict. The annalist thus creates a long view similar to that presented by the universal historians. He specifically connects Frankish annals and universal history, leaping from the Creation to the Frankish world in seven lines.

Christianity is essentially an historical religion. The Bible, saints' lives, sermons, and liturgy all taught history.[5] So, more obviously, did the histories of the early church, especially the chronicle of Eusebius-Jerome. As we saw in my second chapter, Christian history in the western middle ages was one in which Rome—the city of the emperors and of Saints Peter and Paul, of the martyrs and saints—loomed large and was communicated in a great range of texts and material objects. The final chapter of this book focussed on the Franks and local perceptions of the more immediate past in order to demonstrate above all how, in the Frankish cultural affiliations and identities I have charted, time, chronology, and geography play crucial roles. In the rich, complex, and sometimes contradictory early medieval perceptions of a past stretching back to the creation of the world, the Franks claimed their own special place.

Notes

Introduction

1. Rosamond McKitterick, *History and Memory in the Carolingian World* (Cambridge, 2004).

2. For a wider context see Anthony Grafton, *Joseph Scaliger: A Study in the History of Classical Scholarship.* vol. 2, *Historical Chronology* (Oxford, 1993).

3. See Franz-Josef Schmale, *Funktion und Formen mittelalterlicher Geschichtsschreibung: Eine Einführung* (Darmstadt, 1985) and Hans-Werner Goetz, *Geschichtßchreibung und Geschichtsbewußtsein im hohen Mittelalter*, Orbis medievalis: Vorstellungswelten des Mittelalters 1 (Berlin, 1999); Hans-Werner Goetz, "Historical Consciousness and Institutional Concern in European Medieval Historiography," in Sølvi Sogner, ed., *Making Sense of Global History: The Nineteenth International Congress of the Historical Sciences, Oslo, 2000, Commemorative Volume* (Oslo, 2002), pp. 350–65; and Paul Magdalino, "Introduction," in Paul Magdalino, ed., *The Perception of the Past in Twelfth-Century Europe* (London, 1992), p. xi. See also Bernard Guenée, *Histoire et culture historique dans l'Occident médiéval* (Paris, 1980) and Jean-Philippe Genet, *L'Historiographie médiévale en Europe* (Paris, 1991).

4. M. R. P. McGuire, "Annals and Chronicles," *New Catholic Encyclopedia*, 2nd ed. (New York, 2003), vol. 1, pp. 459–65 (p. 465).

5. Rosamond McKitterick, "History, Law and Communication with the Past in the Early Middle Ages," in *Comunicare e significare nell'alto Medioevo*, Settimane di Studio del Centro Italiano di studi sull'alto medioevo 52 (Spoleto, 2005), pp. 941–79, and Joyce Hill, "Authority and Intertextuality in the Works of Aelfric," *Proceedings of the British Academy* 131 (2004), pp. 157–81.

6. See Hayden White, *The Content of the Form: Narrative Discourse and Historical Representation* (Baltimore, 1987) and Sarah Foot, "Finding the Meaning of Form: Narratives in

Annals and Chronicles," in Nancy Partner, ed., *Writing Medieval History* (London and New York, 2005), pp. 88–108, and earlier discussions of historical narrative there cited.

7. See Gabriele Spiegel, *The Past as Text: The Theory and Practice of Medieval Historiography* (Baltimore, 1997) and Erik Kooper, ed., *The Medieval Chronicle*, 2 (Amsterdam and New York, 2002).

One.   Chronology and Empire

1. Athanasius, *De Incarnatione* [original in Greek], ed. Charles Kannengiesser, Sources chrétiennes 199 (Paris, 1973), p. 263.

2. See Andrew Louth and Marco Conti, *Genesis 1–11*, Ancient Christian Commentaries on Scripture: Old Testament 1 (Chicago and London, 2001).

3. Origen, *Homiliae in Genesim*, 1.1, in Willem A. Baehrens, ed., *Origenes Werke*, vol. 6, Die griechischen christlichen Schriftsteller 29 (Leipzig, 1929), p. 1.

4. On Jerome's own contributions to the assembly of Latin texts comprising the Vulgate see J. N. D. Kelly, *Jerome* (London, 1975), pp. 153–67.

5. Jerome, *Liber Hebraicarum Quaestionum in Genesim*, in D. Vallarsi, ed., *Patrologia Latina*, vol. 23 (Paris, 1845), col. 938; English trans. Robert Hayward, *Saint Jerome's Hebrew Questions on Genesis* (Oxford, 1995) p. 30; and compare Adam Kamesar, *Jerome, Greek Scholarship, and the Hebrew Bible: A Study of the "Quaestiones Hebraicae in Genesim"* (Oxford, 1993).

6. See Cyrille Vogel, *Medieval Liturgy: An Introduction to the Sources*, revised trans. William Storey and Niels Rasmussen (Washington, D.C., 1986), pp. 301–3, and Walter H. Frere, *Studies in Early Roman liturgy*, vol. 3, *The Roman Epistle-Lectionary* (Oxford, 1935), pp. 9 and 12.

7. See Frank E. Robbins, "The Hexaemeral Literature: A Study of the Greek and Latin Commentaries on Genesis" (Ph.D. dissertation, University of Chicago, 1912), consulted in the 1966 Ann Arbor micrograph reproduction, and Thomas O'Loughlin, *Teachers and Code Breakers: The Latin Genesis tradition, 430–800*, Instrumenta patristica 35 (Turnhout, 1998). See also John J. Contreni, "Carolingian Biblical Culture," in Gerd van Riel, Carlos Steel, and James McEvoy, *Johannes Scottus Eriugena: The Bible and Hermeneutics*, Ancient and Medieval Philosophy Series 1 (Leuven, 1996), pp. 1–23, and for Hraban Maur's commentaries on some of the historical books see Mayke de Jong, "The Empire as *ecclesia*: Hrabanus Maurus and Biblical *historia* for Rulers," in Yitzhak Hen and Matthew Innes, eds., *The Uses of the Past in the Early Middle Ages* (Cambridge, 2000), pp. 191–226.

8. Inglis P. Sheldon-Williams, ed., *Johannis Scottis Eriugenae Periphyseon (De divisione naturae), Liber II*, Scriptores Latinae Hiberniae 9 (Dublin, 1972), p. 1.

9. Michael Gorman, *Biblical Commentaries from the Early Middle Ages*, Millennio Medievale 32, reprints 4 (Florence, 2002). See also Claudio Leonardi on the period s. VII-X in Magne Sæbø, ed., *Hebrew Bible/Old Testament: The History of Its Interpretation*, vol 1.1 (Göttingen, 1996), pp. 180–95, and Burton van Name Edwards, "Introduction: The

Study of the Bible and Carolingian Culture" and Michael Fox, "Alcuin the Exegete: The Evidence of the *Quaestiones in Genesim*," in Celia Chazelle and Burton van Name Edwards, eds., *The Study of the Bible in the Carolingian Era*, Medieval Church Studies 3 (Turnhout, 2003), pp. 1–16 and 39–60.

10. Dorothea von den Brincken, *Studien zur lateinischen Weltchronistik bis in das Zeitalter Ottos von Freising* (Düsseldorf, 1957), table 3, p. 252, reproduced in Karl H. Krüger, *Die Universalchroniken*, Typologie des sources du moyen âge occidental 16 (Turnhout, 1976), p. 39 (table 3). See also Dorothea von den Brincken, "Die lateinische Weltchronistik," in Alexander Randa, ed., *Mensch und Weltgeschichte: Zur Geschichte der Universalgeschichtsschreibung* (Salzburg and Munich, 1969), especially pp. 43–58, discussion, pp. 59–76 and tables, 77–86, and Michael I. Allen, "Universal History, 300–1000: Origins and Western Developments," in Deborah Mauskopf Deliyannis, ed., *Historiography in the Middle Ages* (Leiden, 2003), pp. 117–42.

11. Frutolf of Michelsberg actually depicted all medieval peoples as descending from the languages dispersed from the tower of Babel: Frutolf, *Chronicon*, in Franz-Josef Schmale and Irene Schmale-Ott, eds. and trans., *Frutolfs und Ekkehards Chroniken und die anonyme Kaiserchronik* (Darmstadt, 1972). See also Arno Borst, *Der Turmbau zu Babel: Geschichte der Meinungen über Ursprung und Vielfalt der Sprachen und Völker*, 4 vols. (Stuttgart, 1957–63).

12. Orosius, *Historiarum adversus paganos libri septem*, I, i–v, in Marie-Pierre Arnaud-Lindet, ed., *Orose, Histoires (contre les païens)* (Paris, 1990), vol. 1 (books 1–3), p. 10; trans. Irving W. Raymond, *Orosius, The Seven Books of History against the Pagans* (New York, 1936), p. 32.

13. See Andrew H. Merrills, *History and Geography in Late Antiquity* (Cambridge, 2005), pp. 35–99. See also Jocelyn Hillgarth, "The *Historiae* of Orosius in the Early Middle Ages," in Jean-Claude Fredouille, Louis Holtz, and Marie-Hélène Jullien, eds., *De Tertullien aux Mozarabes: Mélanges offerts à Jacques Fontaine*, vol. 2, *Antiquité tardive et christianisme ancien, VIe–IXe siècles*, Études Augustiniennes: Série Moyen-Âge et temps modernes 26 (Paris, 1992), pp. 157–70.

14. See Janet M. Bately, *The Old English Orosius*, Early English Texts Society S.S. 6 (Oxford, 1980), from British Library, Add. 47967, and compare Michael Hunter, "Germanic and Roman Antiquity and the Sense of the Past in Anglo-Saxon England," *Anglo-Saxon England* 3 (1974), pp. 29–50, and Janet Bately, "World History in the Anglo-Saxon Chronicle: Its Sources and Its Separateness from the Old English Orosius," *Anglo-Saxon England* 8 (1979), pp. 177–94.

15. See Timothy D. Barnes, *Constantine and Eusebius* (Cambridge, MA, 1981), David Wallace-Hadrill, "The Eusebian Chronicle: The Extent and Date of Composition of Its Early Editions," *Journal of Theological Studies*, new series, 6 (1955), pp. 248–53, Robert M. Grant, *Eusebius as Church Historian* (Oxford, 1980), and Alden A. Mosshammer, *The Chronicle of Eusebius and Greek Chronographic Tradition* (Lewisburg, PA, 1979).

16. Postscript to Eusebius-Jerome, *Chronicon*, in Rudolf Helm, ed., *Eusebius Werke*, vol. 7, Die griechischen christlichen Schriftsteller der ersten Jahrhundert 70, 2nd ed.

(Berlin, 1956), p. 250, and compare John Knight Fotheringham, ed., *Eusebii Pamphili Chronici canones latini vertiti adauxit ad sua tempora produxit S. Eusebius Hieronymus* (London and Oxford, 1923), p. 332; trans. Malcolm D. Donaldson, *A Translation of Jerome's "Chronicon" with Historical Commentary* (Lewiston, Queenston, and Lampeter, 1996), p. 57.

17. Jerome, preface to his portion of Eusebius-Jerome, *Chronicon*, in Fotheringham, ed., p. 4, and compare Eusebius-Jerome, *Chronicon*, in Helm, ed., p. 6; trans William H. Fremantle, *The Principal Works of St Jerome*, A Select Library of Nicene and Post-Nicene Fathers of the Christian Church, 2nd series, 6 (Oxford and New York, 1893), p. 484. See also Malcolm D. Donaldson, *A Translation of Jerome's "Chronicon" with Historical Commentary*, p. 54, and for Helm's Latin text with French translation, Benoît Jeanjean and Bertrand Lançon, *Saint Jérôme, Chronique: Continuation de la Chronique d'Eusèbe, années 326–378, suivie de quatre études sur les Chroniques et chronographies dans l'Antiquité tardive (IVe–VIe siècles)* (Rennes, 2004), p. 60. See also Giorgio Brugnoli, *Curiosissimus excerptor: Gli "Additamenti" di Girolamo ai "Chronica" di Eusebio* (Pisa, 1995), Rudolf Helm, *Hieronymus Zusätze in Eusebius Chronik und ihr Wert für die Literaturgeschichte*, Philologus, Supplementband 21.2 (Leipzig, 1929), and the online translation, coordinated by Roger Pearse, (2005). The preface to this edition can be accessed at http://www.tertullian.org/fathers/jerome_chronicle_00_eintro.htm; the edition uses in particular the digital facsimile of Oxford, Merton College Library, F.3.2 (Coxe 315), dated s. IX 2/4, from Alemannia, to which the website provides a link. The facsimile can also be consulted directly on http://image.ox.ac.uk.

18. Bede, *De temporum ratione*, in Charles W. Jones, ed., *Bedae opera didascalica*, Corpus Christianorum: Series Latina 123B, *De temporum ratione liber. Chronica maiora includens (id est capita LXVI–LXXXI) transcripta ex editione a Th. Mommsen divulgata una cum commentariis et glossis scriptis a.d. dcclxxiii e codice Mettensi (Berlin MS Phillipps 1832) cura et studio C. W. Jones* (Turnhout, 1977), p. 463; trans. Faith Wallis, *Bede: The Reckoning of Time* (Liverpool, 1999), pp. 157–58.

19. Brian Croke, *Count Marcellinus and His Chronicle* (Oxford, 2001) and Brian Croke, ed. and trans., *The Chronicle of Marcellinus* (Sydney, 1995). See also Bertrand Lançon, "La Contribution à l'histoire de l'église de la Chronique de Marcellin d'Illyricum," in Bernard Pouderon and Yves-Marie Duval, eds., *L'Historiographie de l'église des premiers siècles*, Théologie Historique 114 (Paris, 2001), pp. 469–80, Hervé Inglebert, *Interpretatio Christiana: Les Mutations des savoirs (cosmographie, géographie, ethnographie, histoire) dans l'Antiquité chrétienne (30–630 après J.-C.)* (Paris, 2001), and Hervé Inglebert, "Les Chrétiens et l'histoire universelle dans l'Antiquité tardive," in Jeanjean and Lançon, eds., *Saint Jérôme, Chronique*, pp. 123–36.

20. Arnaldo Momigliano, "Pagan and Christian Historiography in the Fourth Century A.D.," in Arnaldo Momigliano, ed., *The Conflict between Paganism and Christianity in the Fourth Century* (Oxford, 1963), pp. 79–99. See also William Adler, "Eusebius' Chronicle and Its Legacy," in Harold W. Attridge and Gohei Hata, eds., *Eusebius, Christianity, and Judaism* (Detroit, 1992), pp. 467–91, and Richard W. Burgess with the assistance of Witold

Witakowski, *Studies in Eusebian and Post-Eusebian Chronography*, Historia: Zeitschrift für alte Geschichte, Einzelschriften 135 (Stuttgart, 1999), and Brian Croke and Alanna M. Emmett, eds., *History and Historians in Late Antiquity* (Sydney and Oxford, 1983).

    21. Eusebius-Jerome, *Chronicon*, in Helm, ed., pp. 39a–45a, 72a, 87b, 88b, 91b, 94b.

    22. See Christopher Kelly, "Past Imperfect: The Conversion of the Classical Past in Late Antiquity," (forthcoming). I am very grateful to Christopher Kelly for permitting me to read his work in advance of publication.

    23. Eusebius-Jerome, *Chronicon*, in Helm, ed., p. 113, and the opening reproduced in Franz Steffens, *Lateinische Paläographie*, 2nd ed. (Trier, 1909) and French version trans. Rémi Coulon, *Paléographie Latine* (Paris, 1910); plate 17 from Oxford, Bodleian Library, Auct.T.II.26, published in facsimile by John Knight Fotheringham, *The Bodleian Manuscript of Jerome's Version of the Chronicle of Eusebius* (Oxford, 1905); and compare Elias Avery Lowe, *Codices Latini Antiquiores* (Oxford, 1972), vol. 2, 2nd ed., no. 233a. For Oxford, Merton College, Coxe 315, see http://image.ox.ac.uk.

    24. Jeanjean and Lançon, eds., *Saint Jérôme, Chronique*, pp. 19–26.

    25. Ibid., *Saint Jérôme, Chronique*, pp. 30–41, and see also Aline Canellis, "Saint Jérôme et les ariens," in *Les Chrétiens face à leurs adversaires dans l'Occident latin au IVe siècle* (Rouen, 2001), pp. 155–94.

    26. See Yves-Marie Duval, "Jérôme et l'histoire de l'Église du IVe siècle," Benoît Jeanjean, "De la *Chronique* à la Consolation à Heliodore (Epist. 60): Les Mutations de la matière historique chez Jérôme," and Stéphane Ratti, "Les sources de la *Chronique* de Jérôme pour les années 357–364: nouveaux éléments," in Bernard Pouderon and Yves-Marie Duval, eds., *L'Historiographie de l'église des premiers siècles*, Théologie historique 114 (Paris, 2001), pp. 381–408, 409–23 and 425–50.

    27. Eusebius-Jerome, *Chronicon*, in Helm, ed., p. 241; trans. Donaldson, *Jerome's "Chronicon,"* p. 50.

    28. Eusebius-Jerome, *Chronicon*, in Helm, ed., p. 242.

    29. Ibid. p. 245; trans. Donaldson, *Jerome's "Chronicon,"* p. 53.

    30. Eusebius-Jerome, *Chronicon*, in Helm, ed., pp. 246–47; trans. Donaldson, *Jerome's "Chronicon,"* p. 54.

    31. Eusebius-Jerome, *Chronicon*, in Helm, ed., p. 245; trans. Donaldson, *Jerome's "Chronicon,"* p. 55.

    32. For useful comments on concepts of time see Wesley Stevens, "A Present Sense of Things Past: *Quid est enim tempus?*" in Gerhard Jaritz and Gerson Moreno-Riaño, eds., *Time and Eternity: The Medieval Discourse*, International Medieval Research 9 (Turnhout, 2003), pp. 9–28. See also Robert A. Markus, Saeculum: *History and Society in the Theology of St. Augustine* (Cambridge, 1970) and Bianca Kühnel, *The End of Time in the Order of Things: Science and Eschatology in Early Medieval Art* (Regensburg, 2003). For geographical conceptualization see Natalia Lozovsky, *"The Earth Is Our Book": Geographical Knowledge in the Latin West, ca. 400–1000* (Madison, 2000) and "Carolingian Geographical Tradition: Was It Geography?" *Early Medieval Europe* 5 (1996), pp. 25–44.

33. Eusebius-Rufinus, *Historia ecclesiastica*, V (preface), in Theodor Mommsen and Eduard Schwartz, eds., *Eusebius Werke*, vol. 2, *Die Kirchengeschichte: Die lateinische Übersetzung des Rufinus*, pt. 1, *Die Bücher I bis V*, Die griechischen christlichen Schriftsteller der ersten drei Jahrhunderte, Eusebius, 2.1 and 2.2 (Leipzig, 1903 and 1908), and Momigliano, "Pagan and Christian Historiography."

34. See, for example, Theodor Mommsen, *Chronica minora saec. IV–VII*, 2 vols., MGH Auctores Antiquissimi 9 (Berlin, 1892) and 11 (Berlin, 1894), which includes Prosper of Aquitaine's *Chronica gallica ab Adamo ad a. 511*. See also Richard W. Burgess, "The Gallic Chronicle of 452: A New Critical Edition with a Brief Introduction" and "The Gallic Chronicle of 511: A New Critical Edition with a Brief Introduction," in Ralph Mathisen and Danuta Schanzer, eds., *Society and Culture in Late Antique Gaul: Revisiting the Sources* (Aldershot, 2001), pp. 52–84 and 85–100, Brian Croke, *Christian Chronicles and Byzantine History: Fifth–Sixth Centuries* (Aldershot, 1992), Croke and Emmett, eds., *History and Historians in Late Antiquity*, and Benoît Jeanjean, "Saint Jérôme, patron des chroniqueurs en langue latine," in Jeanjean and Lançon, eds., *Saint Jérôme, Chronique*, pp. 137–78. For later emulators see, for example, Paul Basset, "The Use of History in the *Chronicon* of Isidore of Seville," *History and Theory* 15 (1976), pp. 278–92; Isidore, *Chronica*, ed. José Carlos Martin, Corpus Christianorum: Series Latina 112 (Turnhout, 2003).

35. Bede, *De temporum ratione*, in Jones, ed., *Bedae opera didascalica;* trans. Wallis, *Bede.*

36. See also Paul Hilliard, "Bede's World Chronicle and the *De temporum ratione* in Its Chronographical and Exegetical Context" (M.Phil. dissertation, Faculty of History, University of Cambridge, 2004) and Roger D. Ray, "Bede, the Exegete, as Historian," in Gerald Bonner, ed., Famulus Christi: *Essays in Commemoration of the Thirteenth Centenary of the Birth of the Venerable Bede* (London, 1976), pp. 125–40.

37. Bede, *De temporum ratione*, in Jones, ed., *Bedae opera didascalica*, pp. 468–69; trans. Wallis, *Bede*, pp. 163–64.

38. Bede, *De temporum ratione*, in Jones, ed., *Bedae opera didascalica*, p. 475; trans. Wallis, *Bede*, p. 167.

39. Bede, *De temporum ratione*, in Jones, ed., *Bedae opera didascalica*, p. 503; trans. Wallis, *Bede*, p. 205.

40. Bede, *De temporum ratione*, in Jones, ed., *Bedae opera didascalica*, pp. 519–20; trans. Wallis, *Bede*, p. 223.

41. Bede, *De temporum ratione*, Jones, ed., *Bedae opera didascalica*, p. 521; trans Wallis, *Bede*, pp. 224–25.

42. In addition to Oxford, Bodleian Library, Auct.T.II.26 (see above, note 23), see Paris, BnF, lat. 6400B + Leiden, Universiteitsbibliotheek, Voss. lat. Q.110A + Vat., reg. lat. 1709; Lowe, *Codices Latini Antiquiores*, vol. 5 (Oxford, 1950), no. 563; Valenciennes, Bibliothèque Municipale, 495; Lowe, *Codices Latini Antiquiores*, vol. 6 (Oxford, 1953), no. 841; and Bern, Burgerbibliothek, 219 (written in uncial 627–99); Lowe, *Codices Latini Antiquiores*, vol. 7 (Oxford, 1956), no. 860.

43. See above, note 34. The Oxford copy, Bodleian Library, Auct. T. II.26, for example, has Count Marcellinus's chronicle added to it (fols. 146–78) in a later sixth- or early seventh-century hand. See Lowe, *Codices Latini Antiquiores*, vol. 2, no. 233b.

Ages," in *Comunicare e significare nell'alto Medioevo*, Settimane di Studio del Centro Italiano di Studi sull'alto medioevo 52 (Spoleto, 2005), pp. 941–79 (pp. 949–58). Please note that on pp. 952–53 of this paper a sentence has been omitted by mistake so that the Dagulf Psalter (Vienna, ÖNB, Lat. 1861) is wrongly described. It is the so-called Godescale Evangelistary (Paris, BnF, n.a. lat. 1203), dated 781, which, according to an inscription in the manuscript, was commissioned by Charlemagne and Queen Hildegard.

    67. Ado, *Chronicon*, in *Patrologia Latina*, vol. 123, cols. 135–38.

    68. Regino, *Chronicon*, in Friedrich Kurze, ed., *Reginonis abbatis prumiensis Chronicon cum continuatione treverensi*, MGH Scriptores rerum germanicarum (Hannover, 1890). Paul Schulz, *Die Chronik des Regino vom Jahre 813 an* (Halle, 1888). Simon MacLean has a study of Regino of Prüm in hand. For preliminary comments about Regino's account of late ninth-century politics see Simon MacLean, *Kingship and Politics in the Late Ninth Century: Charles the Fat and the End of the Carolingian Empire* (Cambridge, 2003), pp. 169–71 and 191–98. See also Hans-Henning Körtum, "Weltgeschichte am Ausgang der Karolingerzeit: Regino von Prüm," in Anton Scharer and Georg Schreibelreiter, eds., *Historiographie im frühen Mittelalter*, Veröffentlichungen des Instituts für Österreichische Geschichtsforschung 32 (Vienna and Munich, 1994), pp. 499–513.

    69. Joseph Werra, *Über den Continuator Reginonis* (Leipzig, 1883) and Bernhard Zeller, "Liudolfinger als fränkische Könige? Überlegungen zur sogenannten Continuatio Reginonis," in Richard Corradini, Christina Pössel, Rob Meens, and Philip Shaw, eds., *Texts and Identities in the Early Middle Ages* (Vienna, 2006), pp. 205–24.

    70. Wolf-Rüdiger Schleidgen, *Die Überlieferungsgeschichte der Chronik des Regino von Prüm*, Quellen und Abhandlungen zur mittelrheinischen Kirchengeschichte 31 (Mainz 1977). Compare the criticism by Otto Prinz, "Die Überarbeitung der Chronik Reginos aus sprachlicher Sicht," in Alf Önnerfors, Johannes Rathofer, and Fritz Wagner, eds., *Literatur und Sprache im europäischen Mittelalter: Festschrift für Karl Langosch zum 70. Geburtstag* (Darmstadt, 1973), pp. 122–41. See also Hubert Herkommer, *Überlieferungsgeschichte der Sächsischen Weltchronik: Ein Beitrag zur deutschen Geschichtsschreibung des Mittelalters* (Munich, 1972).

    71. Von den Brincken explains how Regino went astray in this respect in *Studien zur lateinischen Weltchronistik*, pp. 128–33.

    72. Heinz Löwe, "Geschichtsschreibung der ausgehenden Karolingerzeit," *Deutsches Archiv für Erforschung des Mittelalters* 23 (1967), pp. 1–30, reprinted in Heinz Löwe, *Von Cassiodor zu Dante: Ausgewählte Aufsätze zur Geschichtsschreibung und politischen Ideenwelt des Mittelalters* (Berlin and New York, 1973), pp. 180–205.

    73. For studies see Hubert Ermisch, *Die Chronik des Regino bis 813* (Göttingen, 1871), summarized in *Neues Archiv* 15 (1891), pp. 312–24.

    74. Regino, *Chronicon*, in Kurze, ed., pp. 131–33.

    75. On historical collections of canon law see McKitterick, *History and Memory*, pp. 249–56.

    76. Lothar Boschen, *Die Annales Prumienses: Ihre nähere und ihre weitere Verwandtschaft* (Düsseldorf, 1972), pp. 186–94 and 210–26.

77. Karl-Ferdinand Werner, "Zur Arbeitsweise des Regino von Prüm," *Die Welt als Geschichte* 2 (1959), pp. 96–116, reprinted in Karl-Ferdinand Werner, *Einheit der Geschichte: Studien zur Historiographie* (Sigmaringen, 1999), pp. 136–56. See also below, pp. 38–41.

Two.   The Franks and Rome

1. Eusebius-Jerome, *Chronicon*, in Rudolf Helm, ed., *Eusebius Werke*, vol. 7, Die griechischen christlichen Schriftsteller der ersten Jahrhundert 70, 2nd ed. (Berlin, 1956), pp. 232, 237, 240, 244–45. Compare Theodor Mommsen, ed., *Chronica minora, saec. IV–VII*, vol. 1, MGH Auctores Antiquissimi 9 (Berlin, 1892) and John Knight Fothering-ham, ed., *Eusebii Pamphili Chronici canones latini vertiti adauxit ad sua tempora produxit S. Eusebius Hieronymus* (London and Oxford, 1923).

2. Eusebius-Jerome, *Chronicon*, in Helm, ed., pp. 236, 238, 246.

3. Ibid., p. 239

4. Ibid., pp. 240–41 and 242–43 and above, p. 15.

5. Bede, *De temporum ratione, s.a.* 4021 and 4258, in Charles W. Jones, ed., *Bedae opera didascalica*, Corpus Christianorum: Series Latina 123B, *De temporum ratione liber. Chronica maiora includens (id est capita LXVI–LXXXI) transcripta ex editione a Th. Momm-sen divulgata una cum commentariis et glossis scriptis a.d. dcclxxiii e codice Mettensi (Berlin MS Phillipps 1832) cura et studio C. W. Jones* (Turnhout, 1977), pp. 497 and 508; trans. Faith Wallis, *Bede: The Reckoning of Time* (Liverpool, 1999), pp. 198 and 210–11.

6. Bede, *De temporum ratione, s.a.* 4290, Jones, ed., *Bedae opera didascalica*, pp. 509–10; trans. Wallis, *Bede*, p. 212–23.

7. Above, p. 23 and Freculf, *Chronicon*, in Michael I. Allen, ed., *Freculfi Lexoviensis episcopi opera omnia*, Corpus Christianorum: Continuatio Mediaevalis 169 (Turnhout, 2002), p. 202*.

8. See above, pp. 23–26, and Jones, ed., *Bedae opera didascalica*, p. 246, and Wallis, *Bede*, pp. lxxxv–xcii.

9. Milan, Biblioteca Ambrosiana, M12 sup. (pp. 1–238), and Bernhard Bischoff, *Katalog der festländischen Handschriften des neunten Jahrhunderts (mit Ausnahme der wisi-gotischen)*, vol. 2, *Laon-Paderborn* (Wiesbaden, 2004), no. 2645, pp. 162–63. Compare Bernhard Bischoff, "Das karolingische Kalendar der Palimpsesthandschrift Ambros. M.12 sup.," in Bonifatius Fischer and Virgil Fiala eds., *Colligere fragmenta: Festschrift Alban Dold* (Beuron, 1952), pp. 247–60. Jones, ed., *Bedae opera didascalica*, p. 248, lists it as from Corvey, second half of the ninth century. This manuscript can also be consulted in its microfilm copy in the library of the Medieval Institute, University of Notre Dame. The calendar is illustrated in Christoph Stiegemann and Matthias Wemhoff, eds., *799, Kunst und Kultur der Karolingerzeit: Karl der Große und Papst Leo III. in Paderborn* (Mainz, 1999), vol. 2, p. 523, and for discussion see Joseph Prinz, "Der karolingische Kalender der HS. Ambros. M12 sup," in *Festschrift für Hermann Heimpel*, Veröffentlichungen des Max-Planck-Instituts für Geschichte 36.3 (Göttingen, 1972), pp. 290–327.

10. See, for example, Martin Hellmann, *Tironische Noten in der Karolingerzeit, am Beispiel eines Persius-Kommentars aus der Schule von Tours*, MGH Studien und Texte 27 (Hannover, 2000), especially pp. 6–21.

11. Ado of Vienne, *Chronicon* [reprint of Paris 1561 edition], in *Patrologia Latina*, vol. 123, col. 79.

12. Paul the Deacon, *Liber de episcopis mettensibus*, ed. Georg Pertz, MGH Scriptores 2 (Hannover, 1829), p. 26, and see Walter Goffart, "Paul the Deacon's *Gesta episcoporum mettensium* and the Early Design of Charlemagne's Succession," *Traditio* 42 (1986), pp. 59–94; see also Michel Sot, "Local and Institutional History (300–1000)," in Deborah Mauskopf Deliyannis, ed., *Historiography in the Middle Ages* (Leiden, 2003), pp. 89–114 (p. 102), and Michel Sot, "La Rome antique dans l'historiographie épiscopale de Gaule," in Settimane di Studio del Centro Italiano di studi sull'alto medioevo, La Mendola, 1998, Milan (Spoleto, 2001), pp. 163–88.

13. *Actus pontificum Cenomannis in urbe degentium*, ed. Gustave Busson and Ambroise Ledru (Le Mans, 1901), pp. 11–13

14. Flodoard, *Historia remensis ecclesiae*, I, i–iii, in Martina Stratmann, ed., *Flodoard von Reims: Die Geschichte der reimser Kirche*, MGH Scriptores 36 (Hannover, 1998), pp. 61–67. See also Michel Sot, "Autorité du passé lointain, autorité du passé proche dans l'historiographie épiscopale (VIII–XI siècles): Les Cas de Metz, Auxerre et Reims," in Jean-Marie Sansterre, ed., *L'Autorité du passé dans les sociétés médiévales*, Collection de l'école française de Rome 333 (Rome, 2004), pp. 139–62.

15. Flodoard, *Historia remensis ecclesiae*, in Stratmann, ed., pp. 61–62.

16. See Michel Sot, *Un Historien et son église au Xe siècle: Flodoard de Reims* (Paris, 1993), pp. 357–66.

17. Regino, *Chronicon*, s.a. 842, in Friedrich Kurze, ed., *Reginonis abbatis prumiensis Chronicon cum continuatione treverensi*, MGH Scriptores rerum germanicarum 50 (Hannover, 1890), p. 75; trans. Lucy McKitterick.

18. Ado of Vienne, *Chronicon*, in *Patrologia Latina*, vol. 123, cols. 104–7.

19. Regino, *Chronicon*, in Kurze, ed., pp. 1–2 and 3.

20. Ibid., p. 8.

21. Ibid., p. 6.

22. Ibid., p. 11. On the importance of chronology and place in the history of Christian writers and martyrs see also Rosamond McKitterick, *History and Memory in the Carolingian World* (Cambridge, 2004), pp. 218–44.

23. Regino, *Chronicon*, in Kurze, ed., p. 5.

24. Ibid., pp. 15 and 30.

25. Ibid., pp. 1 and 40; trans. Lucy McKitterick. The preface addressed to Bishop Adalbero is also printed in Reinhold Rau, ed., *Quellen zur karolingischen Reichsgeschichte* (Darmstadt, 1975), vol. 3, p. 180.

26. Thomas F. X. Noble, *The Republic of St. Peter: The Birth of the Papal State, 680–825* (Philadelphia, 1984) and Thomas F. X. Noble, "The Papacy in the Eighth and Ninth Centuries," in Rosamond McKitterick, ed., *The New Cambridge Medieval History*, vol. 2, *c.700–c.900* (Cambridge, 1995), pp. 563–86.

27. See the essays assembled in Julia M. H. Smith, ed., *Early Medieval Rome and the Christian West: Essays in Honour of Donald A. Bullough* (Leiden, 2000), especially those by Paolo Delogu, Rudolf Schieffer, and Julia Smith.

28. Jean Gaudemet, "Survivances romaines dans le droit de la monarchie franque, du Ve au Xe siècle," *Tijdschrift voor Rechtsgeschiedenis* 23 (1955), pp. 149–206, and Janet L. Nelson, "Translating Images of Authority: The Christian Roman Emperors in the Carolingian World," in Mary M. Mackenzie and Charlotte Roueché, eds., *Images of Authority: Papers Presented to Joyce Reynolds on the Occasion of Her Seventieth Birthday* (Cambridge, 1992), pp. 194–205, reprinted in Janet L. Nelson, *The Frankish World* (London, 1996), pp. 89–98. See also Hans Hubert Anton, *Fürstenspiegel und Herrscherethos in der Karolingerzeit* (Bonn, 1968) and the discussion by Patrick Wormald, *The Making of English Law: King Alfred to the Twelfth Century*, vol.1, *Legislation and Its Limits* (Oxford, 2000), pp. 28–92.

29. Peter Classen, *Karl der Große, das Papsttum und Byzanz: Die Begründung des karolingischen Kaisertums*, Beiträge zur Geschichte und Quellenkunde des Mittelalters 9 (Sigmaringen, 1985). For the older literature see Elisabeth Pfeil, *Die fränkische und deutsche Romidee des frühen Mittelalters*, Forschungen zur mittelalterlichen und neueren Geschichte 3 (Munich, 1929).

30. Augustine, *De civitate dei* 18.22.612, in Bernard Dombart and Alphonse Kalb, eds., *Sancti Aurelii Augustini De Civitate Dei*, Corpus Christianorum: Series Latina 48, pts. 14.1 and 14.2 (Turnhout, 1955), p. 628, and see the discussion of Augustine's two cities and the critique of the Roman tradition in Lawrence Nees, *A Tainted Mantle: Hercules and the Classical Tradition at the Carolingian Court* (Philadelphia, 1991), pp. 77–109. For an introduction to early medieval Apocalypse commentaries see E. Ann Matter, "The Apocalypse in Early Medieval Exegesis," in Richard K. Emmerson and Bernard McGinn, eds., *The Apocalypse in the Middle Ages* (Ithaca and London, 1992), pp. 38–50.

31. Richard Krautheimer, "The Carolingian Revival of Early Christian Architecture," *Art Bulletin* 24 (1942), pp. 1–38, reprinted with postscript in Richard Krautheimer, *Studies in Early Christian, Medieval, and Renaissance Art* (New York, 1971), pp. 203–56. See also Richard Krautheimer, *Corpus basilicarum Christianarum Romae*, 5 vols. (Rome and New York, 1937–77), Richard Krautheimer, *Rome: Profile of a City, 312–1308* (Princeton, 1980), E. Baldwin Smith, *Architectural Symbolism of Imperial Rome and the Middle Ages* (Princeton, 1956), and John Crook, *The Architectural Setting of the Cult of Saints in the Early Christian West, c.300–c.1200* (Oxford, 2000). For studies which address the Krautheimer thesis about early Christian revival in the Carolingian period see Charles McLendon, "Louis the Pious, Rome, and Constantinople," in Cecil L. Striker, ed., *Architectural Studies in Memory of Richard Krautheimer* (Mainz am Rhein, 1996), pp. 103–6; Judson J. Emerick, "Focusing on the Celebrant: The Column Display inside Santa Prassede," in *Mededelingen van het Nederlands Instituut te Rome*, vol. 59 (Rome, 2000), pp. 129–59, and Franz Alto Bauer, "The Liturgical Arrangement of Early Medieval Roman Church Buildings," in ibid., pp. 101–28; Federico Guidobaldi and Alessandra Guiglia Guidobaldi, eds., *Ecclesiae Urbis: Atti del congresso internazionale di studi sulle chiese di Roma (IV–X secolo)*, 3 vols., Studi di antichità cristiana 59 (Vatican City, 2002). I am grateful to Doctor Claudia Bolgia

of Pembroke College, Cambridge, for discussion of the Krautheimer thesis. On the significance of *spolia* see Arnold Esch, *Wiederverwendung von Antike im Mittelalter* (Berlin and New York, 2005), and especially his "Ausgewählte Bibliographie zur Spolien-Forschung," pp. 61–70.

32. Eric Palazzo, *Liturgie et société au moyen âge* (Paris, 2000), pp. 199–202, and Yitzhak Hen, *The Royal Patronage of Liturgy in Frankish Gaul to the Death of Charles the Bald (877)*, Henry Bradshaw Society Subsidia 3 (London, 2001).

33. Jacques Viret, "La Réforme liturgique carolingienne et les deux traditions du chant romain," in Pierre Riché, Carol Heitz, and François Héber-Suffrin, eds., *Autour de la reine Hildegarde*, Paris Nanterre Études, 5 (Paris 1987), pp. 117–27; Philippe Bernard, *Du chant romain au chant grégorien (IVe–XIIIe siècle)* (Paris, 1996), Kenneth Levy, *Gregorian Chant and the Carolingians* (Princeton, 1998), and the review article by Rosamond McKitterick, *Early Music History* 19 (2000), pp. 279–90.

34. Janneke Raaijmakers, *Sacred Time, Sacred Space: History and Identity at the Monastery of Fulda (744–856)* (academisch proefschrift, Ph. D., University of Amsterdam, 2003), pp. 104–10.

35. Leighton D. Reynolds, *Texts and Transmission: A Survey of the Latin Classics* (Oxford, 1983).

36. McKitterick, *History and Memory*, pp. 205–10.

37. Compare, for example, Rudolf Schieffer, "Karolingische Herrscher in Rom," in *Roma fra oriente e occidente*, Settimane di Studio del Centro Italiano di studi sull'alto medioevo 49 (Spoleto, 2002), vol. 1, pp. 101–28, and Heinz Hoffmann, "Roma caput mundi: Rom und 'imperium romanum' zwischen Spätantike und dem 9 Jht," in ibid., pp. 492–556 (though the latter examines primarily literary texts before the eighth century).

38. Facsimile ed., Franz Unterkircher, ed., *Alkuin-Briefe und andere Traktate*, Codices selecti 20 (Graz, 1969).

39. *Notitia ecclesiarum urbis Romae* and *De locis sanctis martyrum quae sunt foris civitatis Romae*, in RobertoValentini and Giusseppi Zucchetti, eds., *Codice topografico della Città di Roma* vol. 2, in Fonti per la storia d'Italia (Rome, 1942), pp. 72–99 and 106–31, drawing on Giovanni B. de Rossi, *Roma sotteranea Christiana*, vol. 1 (Rome, 1864), pp. 128–57, and P. Geyer and O. Cuntz et al., eds., *Itineraria et alia geographica*, Corpus Christianorum: Series Latina 175 (Turnhout, 1965), pp. 304–11 and 314–22. See Donatella Bellardini and Paolo Delogu, "Liber Pontificalis e altre fonti: La topografia di Roma nell'VIII secolo," in Herman Geertman, ed., *Il Liber Pontificalis e la storia materiale*, Atti del colloquio internazionale Roma, 21–22 Febbraio 2002, Mededelingen van het Nederlands Instituut te Rome 60/61 (Rome, 2003), pp. 205–23. On the manuscript and text transmission see Maximilian Diesenberger, "Rom als virtueller Raum der Märtyrer: Zur gedanklichen Aneignung der Roma suburbana in bayerischen Handschriften um 800," in Elisabeth Vavra, ed., *Imaginäre Räume*, Internationaler Kongress Krems, 2003, Veröffentlichungen des Instituts für Realienkunde (Krems, forthcoming), pp. 43–68. I am very grateful to Max Diesenberger for letting me read his paper in advance of publication.

40. Compare Pope Julius I (337–52) in the *Liber Pontificalis*, in Louis Duchesne, ed., *Le Liber pontificalis*, 2 vols. (Paris, 1886–92), vol. 1, pp. 83–84.

41. Geyer and Cuntz, eds., *Itineraria*, p. 306.

42. See also the maps in Franz Alto Bauer, "Das Bild der Stadt Rom in der Karolingerzeit: Der Anonymus Einsiedlensis," *Römische Quartalschrift* 92 (1997), pp. 190–228.

43. Geyer and Cuntz, eds., *Itineraria*, p. 315.

44. For a useful survey of pilgrimage to Rome see Debra J. Birch, *Pilgrimage to Rome in the Middle Ages* (Woodbridge, 1998). See also Maribel Dietz, *Wandering Monks, Virgins, and Pilgrims: Ascetic Travel in the Mediterranean World, A.D. 300–800* (University Park, PA, 2005).

45. *Itinerarium Egeriae*, ed. A. Franceschini and R. Weber, in Geyer and Cuntz, eds., *Itineraria*, pp. 35–90, and Hugeburc of Heidenheim, *Hodoeporicon*, ed. Oswald Holder-Egger, MGH Scriptores 15.1 (Hannover, 1887), pp. 80–117.

46. For the original manuscript (Einsiedeln, Stiftsbibliothek, codex 326, fols. 67–79 and 79–85) see the description by Franz Alto Bauer in Stiegemann and Wemhoff, eds., *799, Kunst und Kultur der Karolingerzeit*, vol. 2, pp. 607–9, and Klaus Herbers, "Die Stadt Rom und die Päpste von der Spätantike bis zum 9. Jahrhundert," in ibid., pp. 594–606, and his bibliography. For a full edition and commentary with facsimile see Gerold Walser, ed., *Die Einsiedler Inschriftensammlung und der Pilgerführer durch Rom (Codex Einsidlensis 326)* (Stuttgart, 1987).

47. *Itinerarium Einsidlense*, in Roberto Valentini and Giuseppe Zucchetti, eds., *Codice topografico della Città di Roma* vol. 2, Fonti per la storia d'Italia 88 (Rome, 1942), pp. 169–207, and in Geyer and Cuntz, eds., *Itineraria*, pp. 329–43.

48. See Joanna Story, *Charlemagne and Rome: The Epitaph of Pope Hadrian I*, Medieval History and Archaeology (Oxford, forthcoming).

49. Giovanni B. de Rossi, ed., *Inscriptiones Christianae Urbis Romae septimo saeculo antiquiores*, 2 vols. (Rome, 1857–88), vol. 2 (1888), pp. 95–118.

50. Veronica Ortenberg, "Archbishop Sigeric's Journey to Rome in 990," *Anglo-Saxon England* 19 (1990), pp. 197–246.

51. On Alcuin see L .A. J. R. Houwen and Alastair A. MacDonald, eds., *Alcuin of York*, Germania latina 3 (Groningen, 1998) and Philippe Depreux and Bruno Judic, eds., *Alcuin de York à Tours: Écriture, pouvoir et réseau dans l'Europe du haut moyen âge*, Annales de Bretagne et des pays de l'Ouest 111 (2004).

52. Donald A. Bullough, *Alcuin: Achievement and Reputation. Being Part of the Ford Lectures delivered in Oxford in the Hilary Term 1980* (Leiden and Boston, 2004), pp. 44–51, concentrated on the letters.

53. Herwig Wolfram and Maximilian Diesenberger, "Arn und Alkuin bis 804: Zwei Freunde und ihre Schriften," in Meta Niederkorn-Bruck and Anton Scharer, eds., *Erzbischof Arn von Salzburg*, Veröffentlichungen des Instituts für Österreichische Geschichtsforschung (Vienna and Munich, 2004), pp. 81–106.

54. Conrad Leyser. "The Temptations of Cult: Roman Martyr Piety in the Age of Gregory the Great," *Early Medieval Europe* 9 (2000), pp. 289–307 (p. 298).

55. Alcuin, *Epistolae*, epp. 140 and 156, ed. Ernst Dümmler, MGH Epistolae karolini aevi (Berlin, 1895), pp. 222, 253–55; and *Carmen* 44, ed. Ernst Dümmler, MGH Poetae latini aevi karolini 1 (Berlin, 1888), pp. 255–57.

56. *Annales regni francorum, s.a.* 787, ed. Friedrich Kurze, MGH Scriptores rerum germanicarum 6 (Hannover, 1895), p. 74.

57. See Alcuin, *Epistolae*, ep.146, ed. Dümmler, vol. 2, pp. 235–36, and Heinrich Schmidinger, "Das Papsttum und die Salzburger Kirche im 8. Jahrhundert," in Eberhard Zwink, ed., *Frühes Mönchtum in Salzburg*, Salzburg Diskussionen (Salzburg, 1983), pp. 145–55, and Herwig Wolfram, *Salzburg, Bayern, Österreich: Die Conversio Bagoariorum et Carantanorum und die Quellen ihrer Zeit*, Mitteilungen des Instituts für Österreichische Geschichtsforschung Ergänzungsband 31 (Vienna and Munich, 1995), pp. 290–94, and Heinz Dopsch, "Die Zeit der Karolinger und Ottonen," in Heinz Dopsch, ed., *Geschichte Salzburgs*, vol. 1.1 (Salzburg, 1981), pp. 157–228.

58. Compare Wolfram and Diesenberger, "Arn und Alkuin," p. 89, with Bullough, *Alcuin*, p. 51–52.

59. Bernhard Bischoff, *Die südostdeutschen Schreibschulen und Bibliotheken in der Karolingerzeit*, vol. 2, *Die vorwiegend Österreichischen Diözesen* (Wiesbaden, 1980), pp. 115–19.

60. Leyser, "The Temptations of Cult," p. 298, and compare the discussion of the seventh-century dates in Herman Geertman, *More veterum: Il Liber pontificalis e gli edifici ecclesiastici di Roma nella tarda antichità e nell'alto medioevo*, Archaeologia Traiectina 10 (Groningen, 1975), pp. 198–202. See also Diesenberger, "Rom als virtueller Raum," especially pp. 47–52.

61. I owe this suggestion about the elegiac tone of the itineraries in Vienna, ÖNB, lat. 795, to Tom Noble, made during the discussion after my second Conway lecture in Notre Dame. On sacred topography see also Raaijmakers, *Sacred Time, Sacred Space*, pp. 167–99.

62. See Marios Costambeys, "The Culture and Practice of Burial in and around Rome in the Sixth Century," in Guidobaldi and Guiglia Guidobaldi, eds., *Ecclesiae urbis*, pp. 721–32, and compare Alan Thacker, "In Search of Saints: The English Church and the Cult of Roman Apostles and Martyrs in the Seventh and Eighth centuries," in Smith, ed., *Early Medieval Rome*, pp. 247–78.

63. *Liber Pontificalis*, ed. Duchesne, vol. 1, pp. xxxiii–xlviii. On the problems raised by the notion of different recensions in the light of the early manuscripts see Patrizia Carmassi, "La prima redazione del *Liber Pontificalis* nel quadro delle fonti contemporanee: Osservazioni in margine alla *vita* di Simmaco," and Herman Geertman, "Documenti, redattori e la formazione del testo dei Liber Pontificalis," in Herman Geertman, ed., *Il Liber Pontificalis e la storia materiale*, Atti del colloquio internazionale, Roma, 21–22 Febbraio 2002, Mededelingen van het Nederlands Instituut te Rome 60/61 (Rome, 2003), pp. 235–66 and 267–355.

64. *Liber Pontificalis*, ed. Duchesne, vol. 2, life 98, pp. 17–25, and see Raymond Davis, *The Lives of the Eighth-Century Popes (Liber Pontificalis)* (Liverpool, 1992), pp. 175–78 and 209–18, Geertman, *More veterum*, pp. 82–129, L. Edward Phillips, "A Note on the Gifts

of Leo III to the Church of Rome: *Vestes cum storiis," Ephemerides liturgicae* 102 (1988), pp. 72–78, and Guy Ferrari, *Early Roman Monasteries: Notes for the History of the Monasteries and Convents at Rome from the Fifth through the Tenth Century*, Studi di antichità cristiana 23 (Vatican, 1957).

65. *Liber Pontificalis*, ed. Duchesne, vol. 1, p. cxciii. The other manuscripts with life 98 are Italian, dating from the ss. X/XI, XIV, and XV respectively. It has also been suggested that the list was originally a *libellus* and inserted into the life as a self-contained addition. On Leo III in the *Liber Pontificalis* see Klaus Herbers, "Das Bild Papst Leo III in der Perspektive des *Liber Pontificalis*," in Niederkorn-Bruck and Scharer, eds., *Erzbischof Arn von Salzburg*, pp. 137–54.

66. *Liber Pontificalis*, ed. Duchesne, vol. 2, life 98, p. 20.

67. For discussion of some of the implications of these descriptions see Thomas F. X. Noble, "Paradoxes and Possibilities in the Sources for Roman Society in the Early Middle Ages," in Smith, ed., *Early Medieval Rome*, pp. 55–83.

68. *Liber Pontificalis*, ed. Duchesne, vol. 1, life 34, p. 179.

69. Ibid., lives 24, 25, 27–31, pp. 69, 71–77, and 154–64.

70. Ibid., life 30, pp. 72 and 162.

71. Ibid., lives 55 and 60, pp. 275 and 290–93.

72. Ibid., life 25, p. 155.

73. Ibid., life 18, pp. 63 and 143.

74. Ibid., life 11, p. 132. This is an addition to the life of Pius I referring to "Praxedes and her sister Pudentiana and the church dedicated to Pudentiana at the baths of Novata," found only in the late eleventh-century Vatican manuscript, Vat., lat. 3764, from Cava and its later derivatives. Compare Davis, *The Lives of the Eighth-Century Popes*, p. 81, note 6. On the church see Matilda Webb, *The Churches and Catacombs of Early Christian Rome* (Brighton, 2001), pp. 65–71.

75. See Charles Pietri, *Roma Christiana: Recherches sur l'église de Rome (311–440)*, Bibliothèque des Écoles françaises d'Athène et de Rome 224 (Rome, 1976), pp. 468–70.

76. *Liber Pontificalis*, ed. Duchesne, vol. 1, life 92:13, p. 420; life 94:52, p. 455; life 95:3, pp. 464 and 466.

77. Ibid., life 17, pp. 62 and 141.

78. Ibid., life 55, p. 276. Compare Henri Leclercq, "Domitille (Cimitière de)," in Fernand Cabrol and Henri Leclercq, eds., *Dictionnaire d'archéologie chrétienne et de liturgie*, vol. 4.2 (Paris, 1921), cols. 1409–39.

79. *Liber Pontificalis*, ed. Duchesne, vol. 1, life 20, pp. 64, 65, and 147; trans. Raymond Davis, *The Book of the Pontiffs ("Liber Pontificalis"): The Ancient Biographies of the First Ninety Roman Bishops to AD 715*, rev. ed. (Liverpool, 2000), p. 8.

80. *Liber Pontificalis*, ed. Duchesne, vol. 1, life 21, pp. 64 and 148, and see the Manchester University project led by Kate Cooper and Clare Pilsworth on the *Gesta martyrum* of the fifth and sixth centuries at http://www.art.man.ac.uk/cla/Romanmartyrs.htm.

81. Marianne Sághy, "*Scinditur in partes populus*: Pope Damasus and the Martyrs of Rome," in Kate Cooper, ed., *The Roman Martyrs and the Politics of Memory*, special issue of

Early Medieval Europe 9 (2000), pp. 273–87. See also Kate Blair-Dixon, "Damasus and the Fiction of Unity: The Urban Shrines of Saint Laurence," in Guidobaldi and Guiglia Guidobaldi, eds., *Ecclesiae urbis*, vol. 1, pp. 331–52.

82. *Liber Pontificalis*, ed. Duchesne, vol. 1, life 22, pp. 66 and 150.

83. Ibid., life 22, p. 150 (the earlier version, ibid. p. 66 has *in templo, in monte Aurea, in vaticano palacii*); trans. Davis, *The Book of the Pontiffs*, p. 9. See Kate Cooper, "The Martyr, the *matrona* and the Bishop: The Matron Lucina and the Politics of Martyr Cult in Fifth- and Sixth-Century Rome," *Early Medieval Europe* 8 (1999), pp. 297–318.

84. Krautheimer, *Rome*, pp. 33, 53–55.

85. Isa Belli Barsali, "Sulla topografia di Roma in periodo carolingio: La 'civitas leoniana' e la Giovannipoli," in *Roma e l'età carolingia* (Rome, 1976), pp. 201–14, Letizia Pani Ermini, ed., *Christiana loca: Lo spazio cristiana nella Roma del primo millennio*, 2 vols. (Rome, 2000), *Roma fra oriente e occidente*, and Maria Andaloro and Serena Romano, eds., *Römisches Mittelalter: Kunst und Kultur in Rom von der Spätantike bis Giotto* (Darmstadt, 2002).

86. On the stational liturgy see John F. Baldovin, "The Urban Character of Christian Worship: The Origins, Development and Meaning of Stational Liturgy," *Orientalia Christiana analecta* 228 (Rome, 1987), pp. 105–66.

87. See, for example, Sághy, "*Scinditur in partes populus*," Leyser, "The Temptation of Cult," and Clare Pilsworth, "Dating the *Gesta martyrum*: A Manuscript-Based Approach," in Cooper, ed., *The Roman Martyrs*, pp. 309–24.

88. Daniel Caner, *Wandering, Begging Monks: Spiritual Authority and the Promotion of Monasticism in Late Antiquity* (Berkeley, CA, 2002), pp. 228–34.

89. *Liber Pontificalis*, ed. Duchesne, vol. 1, pp. clxiv–ccvi, summarized by Davis, *Eighth-Century Popes*, pp. xv–xviii.

90. Bede, *Historia ecclesiastica gentis anglorum*, in Bertram Colgrave and Roger A. B. Mynors, eds. and trans., *Bede's Ecclesiastical History of the English People*, Oxford Medieval Texts (Oxford, 1969), p. 592.

91. *Liber Pontificalis*, ed. Duchesne, vol. 1, life 97, pp. 499–514.

92. Geyer and Cuntz, eds., *Itineraria*, p. 332.

93. Diana Wood, ed., *Martyrs and Martyrologies*, Studies in Church History 30 (Oxford, 1993) and Jacques Dubois, *Les Martyrologes du moyen âge latin*, Typologie des sources du moyen âge occidental 26 (Turnhout,1978).

94. *Hieronymian Martyrology*, ed. Giovanni B. de Rossi, Louis Duchesne, "Martyrologium Hieronymianum," *Acta Sanctorum* November 2/1 (1894), pp. xlii–xliii, Henri Quentin, *Acta Sanctorum* November 2/2 (1931), and see Dubois, *Martyrologes*, pp. 29–37. See also Felice Lifshitz, *The Name of the Saint: The Martyrology of Jerome and Access to the Sacred in Francia, 627–827*, Publications in Medieval Studies (Notre Dame, IN, 2006).

95. For Bede, see Henri Quentin, *Les Martyrologes historiques du moyen âge: Étude sur la formation du martyrologe romain* (Paris, 1908), pp. 2–119, Jacques Dubois and Geneviève Renant, eds., *Édition pratique des martyrologes de Bède, de l'anonyme Lyonnais et de Florus*

(Paris, 1976), and Meta Niederkorn-Bruck, "Das Salzburger historische Martyrolog aus der Arn-Zeit und seine Bedeutung für die Textgeschichte des 'Martyrologium Bedae,'" in Niederkorn-Bruck and Scharer, eds., *Erzbischof Arn von Salzburg*, pp. 155–71; Jacques Dubois, *Le Martyrologe d'Usuard: Texte et commentaire*, Subsidia Hagiographica 40 (Brussels, 1965) (based on the possibly autograph manuscript in Paris, BnF, lat. 13745) and Hraban Maur, *Martyrology*, in John McCulloh, ed., *Rabani Mauri martyrologium*, Corpus Christianorum Continuatio Medievalis 44 (Turnhout, 1979). For an English translation and attempted reconstruction of Bede's martyrology see Felice Lifshitz, in Thomas Head, ed., *Medieval Hagiography: An Anthology* (New York and London, 2000), pp. 169–97. See also Jacques Dubois, *Martyrologes: D'Usuard au Martyrologe Romain* (Abbeville, 1990).

    96. Above, p. 44.

    97. Lupus of Ferrières, *Epistolae*, ep. 110 (dated 859–60), in Léon Levillain, ed., *Loup de Ferrières: Correspondance*, Les Classiques de l'histoire de France au moyen âge 10 (Paris, 1964), vol. 2, pp. 150–52; trans. Graydon W. Regenos, *The Letters of Lupus of Ferrières* (The Hague, 1966), p. 128.

    98. See Dominique Iogna-Prat, Colette Jeudy, and Guy Lobrichon, eds., *L'École carolingienne d'Auxerre de Murethach à Rémi, 830–908* (Auxerre, 1991).

    99. Ado, *Martyrologium*, in Jacques Dubois and Geneviève Renaud, eds., *Le Martyrologe d'Adon* (Paris, 1984).

    100. *Concilium Aquisgranense* (817), ed. Kassius Hallinger, Corpus consuetudinum monasticarum 1 (Siegburg, 1963), p. 480.

    101. Wandalbert of Prüm, *Martyrologium*, in Hans-Walter Stork, ed., *Das Martyrologium für Kaiser Lothar: Faksimile Cod. Reg. lat. 438*, Codices e Vaticanis selecti 83 (Zurich, 1997), Jacques Dubois, "Le Martyrologe métrique de Wandelbert, ses sources, son originalité, son influence sur le martyrologe d'Usuard," *Analecta Bollandiana* 79 (1961), pp. 257–93, and Wolfgang Haubrichs, *Die Kultur der Abtei Prüm zur Karolingerzeit: Studien zur Heimat des althochdeutschen Georgsliedes*, Rheinisches Archiv 105 (Bonn, 1979).

    102. For the saints, but without the place in historical time see Peter Brown, *The Cult of the Saints* (Chicago and London, 1981), especially pp. 1–22. See also Alan Thacker, "*Loca sanctorum*: The Significance of Place in the Study of the Saints," in Alan Thacker and Richard Sharpe, eds., *Local Saints and Local Churches in the Medieval West* (Oxford, 2002), pp. 1–43, emphasizing primary shrine and secondary relics.

    103. See Einhard, *Translatio sanctorum Marcellini et Petri*, ed. Georg Waitz, MGH Scriptores 15.1 (Hannover, 1887), pp. 238–64; trans. Paul E. Dutton, *Charlemagne's Courtier: The Complete Einhard* (Peterborough, ON, 1998), pp. 69–130. See Hans Reinhard Seeliger, "Einhards römische Reliquien: Zur Übertragung der heiligen Marzellinus und Petrus ins Frankenreich," *Römische Quartalschrift* 83 (1988), pp. 58–75, and Julia M. H. Smith, "'Emending Evil Ways and Praising God's Omnipotence': Einhard and the Uses of Roman Martyrs," in Kenneth Mills and Anthony Grafton, eds., *Conversion in Late Antiquity and the Early Middle Ages: Seeing and Believing* (Rochester, 2003), pp. 189–223.

    104. *Lex Salica*, D and E, ed. Karl August Eckhardt, MGH Leges nationum germanicarum 4.2 (Hannover, 1969), pp. 6 and 8 (variant wording is to be found on pp. 7 and

9); trans. Katherine Fischer Drew, *The Laws of the Salian Franks* (Philadelphia, 1991), p. 171. See also Smith, "Old Saints, New Cults," in Smith, ed., *Early Medieval Rome*, pp. 317–40.

105.   The best study of these is Martin Heinzelmann, *Translationsberichte und andere Quellen der Reliquienkulte*, Typologie des sources du moyen âge occidental 33 (Turnhout, 1979). See also Klaus Herbers, "Mobilität und Kommunikation in der Karolingerzeit: Die Reliquienreisen der heiligen Chrysanthus und Daria," in Nine Miedema and Rudolf Suntrup, eds., *Literatur— Geschichte—Literaturgeschichte: Beiträge zur mediävistischen Literaturwissenschaft. Festschrift für Volker Honemann zum 60. Geburtstag* (Frankfurt am Main, 2003), pp. 647–60.

106.   For Einhard see the references cited in note 103. On Hilduin of Saint Denis see Giles Brown, "Politics and Patronage at the Abbey of Saint-Denis (814–98): The Rise of a Royal Patron Saint," (D.Phil. thesis, University of Oxford, 1989).

107.   Erconrad, *Translatio S. Liborii episcopi*, in A. Cohausz and Robert Latouche, eds. and French trans., *La Translation de S. Liboire du diacre Erconrad* (Le Mans, 1967); and see Hans-Jürgen Brandt and Karl Hengst, eds., *Felix Paderae civitas: Der heilige Liborius, 836–1985*, Studien und Quellen zur westfälischen Geschichte 24 (Paderborn, 1986) and Volker de Vry, *Liborius. Brückenbauer Europas: Die mittelalterlichen Viten und Translationsberichte* (Paderborn, 1997). See also Klaus Herbers, "Rom im Frankenreich: Rombeziehung durch Heilige in der Mitte des 9. Jhts," in Dieter R. Bauer, Rudolf Hiestand, Brigitte Kasten and Sonke Lorenz, eds., *Mönchtum—Kirche—Herrschaft, 750–1050: Josef Semmler zum 65. Geburtstag* (Sigmaringen, 1998), pp. 133–69, and John M. McCulloh, "From Antiquity to the Middle Ages: Continuity and Change in Papal Relic Policy from the Sixth to the Eighth Century," *Jahrbuch für Antike und Christentum* 22 (1980), pp. 313–24.

108.   See Bernhard Bischoff, *Mittelalterliche Schatzverzeichnisse* (Munich, 1967). The Chelles relic labels were discovered by Jean-Pierre Laporte and edited by Hartmut Atsma and Jean Vezin, *Authentiques de reliques provenant de l'ancien monastère Notre-Dame de Chelles (VIIe–VIIIe siècles)*, Chartae Latinae Antiquiores 18 (Zurich, 1985), no. 669, pp. 84–108. See also Jean-Pierre Laporte, *Le Trésor des saints de Chelles*, Société archéologique et historique de Chelles (Chelles, 1988), pp. 115–60, who includes a discussion of the ninth-century collection.

109.   See André Wilmart, "Reliques réunies à Jouarre," in *Analecta reginensia*, Studi e testi 59 (Vatican City, 1933), pp. 9–17. For the eighth century see Rosamond McKitterick, "Nuns' Scriptoria in England and Francia in the Eighth Century," *Francia* 19.1 (1992), pp. 1–35 (p. 11), reprinted in Rosamond McKitterick, *Books, Scribes and Learning in the Frankish Kingdoms, Sixth–Ninth Centuries* (Aldershot, 1994), chapter 7. Michael McCormick, *Origins of the European Economy: Communications and Commerce, A.D. 300–900* (Cambridge, 2001), p. 286, note 11, in challenging the possibility of a group of relics possibly to be associated with Jouarre, has missed my limiting of the Chelles relic labels that might be attributed to Jouarre hands to the small group of thirty labels in b-minuscule.

110.   Hariulf, *Chronicon Centulense*, in Ferdinand Lot, ed., *Hariulf, Chronique de l'abbaye de Saint-Riquier, Ve siècle–1004* (Paris, 1894), pp. 57–67, and Susan Rabe, *Faith, Art, and Politics at Saint-Riquier: The Symbolic Vision of Angilbert* (Philadelphia, 1995).

111. Maurice Prou and Eugène Chartraire, "Authentiques de reliques conservées au trésor de la cathédrale de Sens,"*Mémoires de la Société Nationale des Antiquaires de France,* 6th series, 9 (1900), pp. 129–72, and facsimiles, plates 7–9, and see McCormick, *Origins of the European Economy,* pp. 283–318.

112. The definitive work is Hedwig Röckelein, *Reliquientranslationen nach Sachsen im 9. Jahrhundert: Über Kommunikationen, Mobilität und Öffentlichkeit im Frühmittelalter* (Stuttgart, 2002). See also Rudolf Schieffer, "Reliquientranslationen nach Sachsen," in Stiegemann and Wemhoff, eds., *799, Kunst und Kultur,* vol. 3, pp. 484–93, and the earlier important contribution by Klemens Honselmann, "Reliquientranslationen nach Sachsen," in Viktor H. Elbern, ed., *Das erste Jahrtausend: Kultur und Kunst im werdenden Abendland an Rhein und Ruhr* (Düsseldorf, 1962), pp. 159–93.

113. Röckelein, *Reliquientranslationen,* pp. 27, 29, and 374.

114. Hedwig Röckelein, "Über Hagio-Geo-Graphien: Mirakel in Translationsberichten des 8. und 9. Jahrhunderts," in Martin Heinzelmann, Klaus Herbers, and Dieter R. Bauer, eds., *Mirakel im Mittelalter: Konzeptionen, Erscheinungsformen, Deutungen,* Beiträge zur Hagiographie 3 (Stuttgart, 2002), pp. 166–79.

115. McKitterick, *History and Memory,* pp. 249–56. See also Rosamond McKitterick, "History, Law and Communication with the Past in the Carolingian period," in *Comunicare e significare nell'alto medioevo,* Settimane di Studio del Centro Italiano di studi sull'alto medioevo 52 (Spoleto, 2005), pp. 941–79.

116. Livy, *Ab urbe condita* V.52.2, in B.O. Foster, ed. and trans., *Livy in Fourteen Volumes,* vol. 3, *Books V, VI, VII* (Cambridge, MA, 1967), pp. 174 and 175. See Catherine Conybeare, "*Terrarum Orbi Documentum*: Augustine, Camillus, and Learning from History," in Mark Vessey, Karla Pollmann, and Allan D. Fitzgerald, eds., *History, Apocalypse, and the Secular Imagination: New Essays on Augustine's "City of God"* (Bowling Green, OH, 1999), pp. 45–58.

117. Nicholas Purcell, "The City of Rome," in Richard Jenkyns, ed., *The Legacy of Rome* (Oxford, 1992), pp. 421–55, Diane Farro, *The Urban Image of Augustan Rome* (Cambridge, 1996), and Catharine Edwards, *Writing Rome: Textual Approaches to the City* (Cambridge, 1996).

118. On the building programmes of the fifth to ninth centuries see Robert Coates Stevens, "Dark Age Architecture in Rome," *Papers of the British School at Rome* 65 (1997), pp. 177–232. See also Crook, *The Architectural Setting of the Cults of Saints,* especially pp. 80–134.

119. See Herbers, "Die Stadt Rom und die Päpste," in Stiegemann and Wemhoff, eds., *799, Kunst und Kultur,* vol. 2, pp. 595–606; catalogue entries, "Rom zur Zeit der Karolinger," in ibid., vol. 2, pp. 607–65; and Riccardo Santangeli Valenzani, "Profanes Bauwesen in Rom um das Jahr 800," in ibid., vol. 3, pp. 550–57.

120. For example, *Annales q.d. Einhardi,* ed. Friedrich Kurze, MGH Scriptores rerum germanicarum 6 (Hannover, 1895), p. 55, and Reynolds, *Texts and Transmission,* pp. 205–14.

121. See McKitterick, *History and Memory,* especially pp. 186–217.

122. See Robert A. Markus, Saeculum: *History and Society in the Theology of St. Augustine* (Cambridge, 1970), Johannes van Oort, *Jerusalem and Babylon: A Study into Augustine's "City of God" and the Sources of His Doctrine of the Two Cities* (Leiden, 1991), Nees, *A Tainted Mantle*, pp. 77–109, Vessey, Pollmann, and Fitzgerald, eds., *History, Apocalypse, and the Secular Imagination*; and on Augustine and Orosius and their sense of place see Andrew H. Merrills, *History and Geography in Late Antiquity* (Cambridge, 2005), pp. 35–99.

123. Ben Witherington III, ed., *History, Society and Literature in the Book of Acts* (Cambridge, 1996).

124. Alastair P. MacKinlay, "Studies in Arator I: The Manuscript Tradition of the *capitula* and *tituli*," *Harvard Studies in Classical Philology* 43 (1932), pp. 123–66, and *Arator: The Codices* (Cambridge, MA, 1942).

125. Regino, *Chronicon, s.a.* 459–97, in Kurze, ed., p. 20.

126. Arator, *De actibus apostolorum*, in Alastair P. MacKinlay, ed., *Aratoris subdiaconi de actibus apostolorum*, Corpus Scriptorum Ecclesiasticorum Latinorum (Vienna, 1951); trans. Richard J. Schrader, Joseph L. Roberts, and John F. Makowski, *Arator's On the Acts of the Apostles* (Atlanta, 1992). See also Michael Roberts, *Biblical Epic and rhetorical Paraphrase in Late Antiquity* (Liverpool, 1985) and Alastair P. MacKinlay, "Latin Commentaries: Arator," *Scriptorium* 6 (1952), pp. 151–56.

127. See Claudia Rapp, "Literary Culture under Justinian," in Michael Maas, ed., *The Cambridge Companion to Justinian* (Cambridge, 2005), pp. 376–97 (p. 379).

128. For an analysis of Arator's language see Schrader, Roberts, and Makowski, trans., *Arator*, pp. 9–15.

129. Schrader, Roberts, and Makowski, trans., *Arator*, p. 93, ed. MacKinlay, p. 147.

130. See Dominique Iogna-Prat, "Lieu de culte et exégèse liturgique à l'époque carolingienne," in Celia Chazelle and Burton van Name Edwards, eds., *The Study of the Bible in the Carolingian Era*, Medieval Church Studies 3 (Turnhout, 2003), pp. 215–44.

131. See Jan M. Ziolkowski and Michael C. J. Putnam, eds., *The Virgilian Tradition: The First Fifteen Hundred Years* (New Haven, CT, and London, 2006). I am very grateful to Jan Ziolkowski for kindly telling me about this collection in advance of publication.

132. Suetonius, *De vita caesarum*, ed. Otto Wittstock (Berlin, 1993).

133. See McKitterick, *History and Memory*, pp. 41–42.

134. Bern, Burgerbibliothek, MS 366. See Bernhard Bischoff, *Katalog der festländischen Handschriften des neunten Jahrhunderts (mit Ausnahme der wisigotischen)*, pt. 1, *Aachen-Lambach* (Wiesbaden, 1998), no. 586, p. 125, and Reynolds, *Texts and Transmission*, pp. 428–29.

135. Lupus of Ferrières, *Epistolae*, ep. 37, ed. Léon Levillain, vol. 1, p. 165; trans. Regenos, *The Letters of Lupus of Ferrières*, p. 55.

136. Valerius Maximus, *Factorum et dictorum memorabilium libri*, in David R. Shackleton Bailey, ed. and trans., *Valerius Maximus, Memorable Doings and Sayings* (Cambridge, MA, 2000) and G. Maslakov, "Valerius Maximus and Roman Historiography: A Study of the Exempla Tradition," in Hildegard Temporini and Wolfgang Haase, eds., *Aufstieg und Niedergang der römischen Welt: Geschichte und Kultur Roms im Spiegel der neueren Forschung,*

vol. 2, *Principat* (Berlin, 1984), pp. 437–96. See also the essays by Anthony J. Woodman, "Velleius Paterculus" and C. J. Carter, "Valerius Maximus," in Thomas A. Dorey, ed., *Empire and Aftermath* (London, 1975), pp. 1–25 and 26–56 respectively.

137. See E. David Hunt, *Holy Land Pilgrimage in the Later Roman Empire, AD 312–460* (Oxford, 1982) and Bianca Kühnel, *From the Earthly to the Heavenly Jerusalem: Representations of the Holy City in Christian Art of the First Millennium*, Römische Quartalschrift für christliche Altertumskunde und Kirchengeschichte, Supplementband 42 (Rome, Freiburg im Breisgau, and Vienna, 1987).

138. See Chris Wickham, "Ninth-Century Byzantium through Western Eyes," in Leslie Brubaker, ed., *Byzantium in the Ninth Century: Dead or Alive?* (Birmingham, 1998), pp. 246–56. For the claims apparently about Aachen but possibly Paderborn, see, for example, the Paderborn epic, in Helmut Beumann, Franz Brunhölzl, and Wilhelm Winkelmann, eds., *Karolus Magnus et Leo Papa: Ein Paderborner Epos vom Jahr 799* (Paderborn, 1966), lines 91–135, pp. 66–68, and see Wilhelm Heintz, ed., *De Karolo rege et Leone papa*, Studien und Quellen zur westfälischen Geschichte 36 (Paderborn, 1999). See also Deborah Mauskopf Deliyannis, "Charlemagne's Silver Tables: The Ideology of an Imperial Capital," *Early Medieval Europe* 12 (2003), pp. 159–78.

139. See McKitterick, *History and Memory*, pp. 218–45.

Three.   The Franks and Their History

1. Chris Wickham, "Gossip and Resistance among the Medieval Peasantry," *Past and Present* 160 (1998), pp. 3–24. For a discussion of the importance of oral communication see Michael Richter, *The Formation of the Medieval West: Studies in the Oral Culture of the Barbarians* (Dublin, 1994).

2. *Annales regni francorum*, ed. Friedrich Kurze, MGH Scriptores rerum germanicarum 6 (Hannover, 1895), pp. 68–70.

3. Aspects are covered by Heinrich Büttner, "Mission und Kirchenorganisation des Frankenreiches bis zum Tode Karls des Großen, in Wolfgang Braunfels, ed., *Karl der Große: Lebenswerk und Nachleben*, vol. 1, *Persönlichkeit und Geschichte* (Düsseldorf, 1965), pp. 454–87, Rudolf Schieffer, *Die Entstehung von Domkapiteln in Deutschland* (Bonn, 1976), Henry Mayr-Harting, "Charlemagne, the Saxons and the Imperial Coronation of 800," *English Historical Review* 111 (1996), pp. 1113–33, and Christopher Carroll, "The Bishoprics of Saxony in the First Century after Christianization," *Early Medieval Europe* 9 (1999), pp. 219–46. See also Timothy Reuter, "Charlemagne and the World beyond the Rhine," in Joanna Story, ed., *Charlemagne: Empire and Society* (Manchester, 2005), pp. 183–94.

4. See Eric J. Goldberg, "Popular Revolt, Dynastic Politics, and Aristocratic Factionalism in the Early Middle Ages: The Saxon *stellinga* Reconsidered," *Speculum* 70 (1995), pp. 467–501; but compare Carroll, "The Bishoprics of Saxony," p. 221, note 9, and Angelika Lampen, "Die Sachsenkriege," in Christoph Stiegemann and Matthias Wemhoff, eds., *799, Kunst und Kultur der Karolingerzeit: Karl der Große und Papst Leo III. in Paderborn* (Mainz, 1999), vol. 1, pp. 264–72.

5. I make the case for this in Rosamond McKitterick, *History and Memory in the Carolingian World* (Cambridge, 2004), pp. 84–119.

6. See Matthew Innes and Rosamond McKitterick, "The Writing of History," in Rosamond McKitterick, ed., *Carolingian Culture: Emulation and Innovation* (Cambridge, 1994), pp. 193–222. For details of modern editions of the texts see also Wilhelm Wattenbach, Wilhelm Levison, and Heinz Löwe, *Deutschlands Geschichtsquellen des Mittelalters: Vorzeit und Karolinger*, bk. 2 (Weimar, 1953) and bk. 3 (Weimar, 1957) and above pp. 51–54.

7. Sarah Foot, "Finding the Meaning of Form: Narrative in Annals and Chronicles," in Nancy Partner, ed., *Writing Medieval History* (London and New York, 2005), pp. 88–108. See also Sarah Foot, "The Making of Angelcynn: English Identity before the Norman Conquest," *Transactions of the Royal Historical Society*, 6th series, 6 (1996), pp. 25–50, and Sarah Foot, "Remembering, Forgetting and Inventing: Attitudes to the Past in England after the First Viking Age," *Transactions of the Royal Historical Society*, 6th series, 9 (1999), pp. 185–200.

8. See Friedrich Kurze, "Ueber die karolingischen Reichsannalen von 741–829 und ihre Ueberarbeitung: 1. Die handschriftliche Ueberlieferung," *Neues Archiv* 19 (1894), pp. 295–339, and "Zur Ueberlieferung der karolingischen Reichsannalen und ihrer Ueberarbeitung," *Neues Archiv* 29 (1903), pp. 619–69, Gabriel Monod, *Études critiques sur les sources de l'histoire carolingienne* (Paris, 1898), and Louis Halphen, *Études critiques sur l'histoire de Charlemagne* (Paris, 1921).

9. For constructive suggestions about the potential value of thirty-eight of these "minor" annals see Jennifer Davis, "Conceptions of Kingship under Charlemagne," (M.Litt. thesis, University of Cambridge, 1999).

10. Hincmar of Rheims, *De villa Novilliaco*, ed. Georg Waitz, MGH Scriptores 15.2 (Hannover, 1888), p. 1167, and see also *Annales fuldenses, s.a.* 863, ed. Georg Pertz and Friedrich Kurze, MGH Scriptores rerum germanicarum 7 (Hannover, 1891), p. 58. Walahfrid Strabo refers to Thegan's life of Louis the Pious (*Gesta Hludowici imperatoris*) as *annales*. See his prologue to the *Gesta Hludowici* in Ernst Tremp, ed., *Thegan, Die Taten Kaiser Ludwigs; Astronomus, Das Leben Kaiser Ludwigs*, MGH Scriptores rerum germanicarum 64 (Hannover, 1995), p. 168. I am very grateful to Helmut Reimitz and Richard Corradini for discussion of this point and of these instances of ninth-century usage of *annales* to refer to history writing.

11. McKitterick, *History and Memory*, pp. 19–22.

12. Davis, "Conceptions of Kingship," p. 176.

13. See ibid., p. 177. See also Matthew Innes, *State and Society in the Early Middle Ages: The Middle Rhine Valley, 400–1000* (Cambridge, 2000), pp. 118–24 and 143–53, and Christina Pössel, "Symbolic Communication and the Negotiation of Power at Carolingian Regnal Assemblies, 814–840," (Ph.D. thesis, University of Cambridge, 2003).

14. Davis, "Conceptions of Kingship," p. 175.

15. *Annales regni francorum*, ed. Kurze, p. 3, prints only the revised version for 741. For the text of the "original" *Annales regni francorum* for 741 see Reinhold Rau, ed., *Quellen zur karolingischen Geschichte*, vol. 1 (Darmstadt, 1974), p. 10. On the significance of the beginning in 741 and the variety of information under that date in different annal ac-

counts see Matthias Becher, "Eine verschleierte Krise: Die Nachfolge Karl Martells 741 und die Anfänge der karolingischen Hofgeschichtsschreibung," in Johannes Laudage, ed., *Von Fakten und Fiktionen: Mittelalterliche Geschichtsdarstellungen und ihre kritische Aufarbeitung* (Cologne, Weimar, and Vienna, 2003), pp. 95–133.

16. *Annales fuldenses*, ed. Pertz and Kurze, p. 1.

17. *Annales mettenses priores*, ed. Bernhard von Simson, MGH Scriptores rerum germanicarum 10 (Hannover, 1905), p. 1. See Yitzhak Hen, "The Annals of Metz and the Merovingian Past," in Yitzhak Hen and Matthew Innes, eds., *The Uses of the Past in the Early Middle Ages* (Cambridge, 2000), pp. 175–90, and Paul Fouracre, "The Long Shadow of the Merovingians," in Story, ed., *Charlemagne*, pp. 5–21.

18. See Norbert Schröer, *Die Annales S. Amandi und ihre Verwandten: Untersuchungen zu einer Gruppe karolingischer Annalen des 8. und frühen 9. Jahrhunderts*, Göppinger Akademische Beiträge 85 (Göppingen, 1975) and on the *Annales Tiliani*, Wattenbach, Levison, and Löwe, *Deutschlands Geschichtsquellen*, bk. 2, p. 183–84.

19. See Walter Lendi, *Untersuchungen zur frühalemannischen Annalistik: Die Murbacher Annalen, mit Edition*, Scrinium Friburgense 1 (Freiburg in der Schweiz, 1971).

20. Recently reiterated, for example, by Joaquín Martínez Pizarro, "Ethnic and National History, ca. 500–1000," in Deborah Mauskopf Deliyannis, ed., *Historiography in the Middle Ages* (Leiden, 2003), pp. 43–88 (p. 73), and more cautiously by Michael Lapidge, "Annals," in Michael Lapidge, John Blair, Simon Keynes, and Donald Scragg, eds., *The Blackwell Encyclopaedia of Anglo-Saxon England* (Oxford, 1999), p. 39, though without reference to recent discussion of the issue elsewhere.

21. I am grateful to Joanna Story for discussion of this. See Joanna Story, "The Frankish Annals of Lindisfarne and Kent," *Anglo-Saxon England* 34 (2005), pp. 59–109, which she kindly let me read in advance of publication. See also Foot, "Finding the Meaning of Form," pp. 92–94. On the Christian era, see Georges Declercq, *Anno domini: Les Origines de l'ère chrétienne* (Turnhout, 2000).

22. *Annales floriacenses*, ed. Georg Pertz, MGH Scriptores 2 (Hannover, 1829), pp. 254–55. I am indebted to the anonymous reader for the University of Notre Dame Press for supplying this example. See also Alexandre Vidier, *L'Historiographie à Saint-Benoît-sur-Loire et les miracles de saint Benoît* (Paris, 1965), pp. 51–52, 83–84, and "Appendice III Annales floriacenses (ou Chronicon floriacensis) MS Paris lat. 5543, fols 9v–23r.," in ibid., pp. 217–20.

23. Thomas Scharff, *Die Kämpfe der Herrscher und der Heiligen: Krieg und historische Erinnerung in der Karolingerzeit* (Darmstadt, 2002), pp. 189–214.

24. Revised text of the *Annales regni francorum* under the title *Annales q.d. Einhardi*, ed. Friedrich Kurze, MGH Scriptores rerum germanicarum 6 (Hannover, 1895), p. 69; trans. P. David King, *Charlemagne: Translated Sources* (Kendal, 1987), pp. 118–19; and see again Lampen, "Die Sachsenkriege."

25. *Annales q.d. Einhardi*, ed. Kurze, p. 71.

26. *Annales mosellani* (703–797/98), ed. Johann M. Lappenberg, MGH Scriptores 16 (Hannover, 1859), pp. 494–99 (p. 497), from Saint Petersburg, Saltykov-Schedrin Library,

O.v.IV.1, fols. 65v–72v; for discussion see Wattenbach, Levison, and Löwe, *Deutschlands Geschichtsquellen*, bk. 2, pp. 185–89. The *Annales mosellani* omit an entry for 786.

27. *Annales q.d. Einhardi*, ed. Kurze, p. 71, trans. King, *Charlemagne*, p. 119.

28. *Annales regni francorum*, ed. Kurze, p. 148; compare the English translation offered by Bernhard W. Scholz, *Carolingian Chronicles* (Ann Arbor, 1970), pp. 103–4.

29. *Annales regni francorum*, ed. Kurze, p. 70.

30. For a useful survey with an emphasis on *coniurationes* as social groupings, see Otto-Gerhard Oexle, "*Coniuratio* und Gilde im frühen Mittelalter," in Berent Schwineköper, ed., *Gilden und Zünfte: Kaufmännische und gewerbliche Genossenschaften im frühen und hohen Mittelalter*, Vorträge und Forschungen 29 (Sigmaringen, 1985), pp. 151–213, and Otto-Gerhard Oexle, "Coniuratio et gilde dans l'Antiquité et dans le haut moyen âge: Remarques sur la continuité des formes de la vie sociale," *Francia* 10 (1982), pp. 1–19. I am grateful to Mayke de Jong for bringing these articles to my attention. See also Hans-Werner Goetz, "Social and Military Institutions," in Rosamond McKitterick, ed., *The New Cambridge Medieval History*, vol. 2, *c.700–c.900* (Cambridge, 1995), pp. 451–80 (pp. 477–78).

31. *Capitulare Haristallense* (779), in Alfred Boretius, ed., *Capitularia*, MGH Capitularia regum francorum 1 (Hannover, 1883), no. 20, c. 14, pp. 50 and 51; trans. King, *Charlemagne*, p. 204.

32. *Concilium Francofurtense* (794), in Albert Werminghoff, ed., *Concilia*, MGH Concilia aevi karolini 2.1 (Hannover and Leipzig, 1906), no. 19, c. 31, p. 169; trans. King, *Charlemagne*, p. 228.

33. *Capitulare missorum in Theodonis villa datum secundum, generale*, in Boretius, ed., *Capitularia*, no. 44, c. 10, p. 124; trans. King, *Charlemagne*, p. 249.

34. *Duplex legationis edictum*, in Boretius, ed., *Capitularia*, no. 23, c. 18, p. 63; trans. King, *Charlemagne*, p. 221. On the oaths see Thomas F. X. Noble, "From Brigandage to Justice: Charlemagne, 785–794," in Celia M. Chazelle, ed., *Literacy, Politics, and Artistic Innovation in the Early Medieval West: Papers Delivered at "A Symposium on Early Medieval Culture," Bryn Mawr College, Bryn Mawr, PA* (Lanham, New York, and London), pp. 49–75 (pp. 53–54), Matthias Becher, *Eid und Herrschaft: Untersuchungen zum Herrscherethos Karls des Großen*, Vorträge und Forschungen, Sonderband 39 (Sigmaringen, 1993), and Matthew Innes, "Charlemagne's government," in Story, ed., *Charlemagne*, pp. 71–89 (p. 80).

35. Boretius gave this the title *Capitulare missorum* and dated it "792 vel 786," *Capitularia*, no. 25, c. 1, p. 66; trans. King, *Charlemagne*, p. 223. According to Hubert Mordek, *Bibliotheca capitularium regum Francorum manuscripta: Überlieferung und Traditionszusammenhang der fränkischen Herrschererlasse*, MGH Hilfsmittel 15 (Munich, 1995), p. 472, this capitulary should be dated 789 vel 792/93. It survives only in the tenth-century manuscript, Paris, BnF, lat. 4613, from Italy, fols. 67v–69r.

36. *Capitulare missorum in Theodonis villa datum secundum, generale*, in Boretius, ed., *Capitularia*, no. 44, c. 9, p. 124; trans. King, *Charlemagne*, p. 249, and compare *Capitularia missorum specialia*, in Boretius, ed., *Capitularia*, no. 34, after c. 19, pp. 101–2; trans. King, *Charlemagne*, p. 244.

37. For some discussion see Jürgen Hannig, *Consensus fidelium: Frühfeudale Interpretationen des Verhältnisses von Königtum und Adel am Beispiel des Frankenreiches* (Stuttgart, 1982); see also Becher, *Eid und Herrschaft*.

38. See the map of the Saxon wars in Stiegemann and Wemhoff, eds., *799, Kunst und Kultur*, vol. 1, p. 265.

39. *Annales nazariani*, ed. Georg Pertz, MGH Scriptores 1 (Hannover, 1826), pp. 41–42, and Karl Brunner, *Oppositionelle Gruppen im Karolingerreich*, Veröffentlichungen des Instituts für Österreichische Geschichtsforschung 25 (Vienna, 1979), pp. 47–52, and, more briefly, in the Lorsch annals. See the discussion of the Lorsch annals and *Annales nazariani* below, pp. 75–76 and 84–89.

40. Brunner, *Oppositionelle Gruppen*, pp. 48–52, and see further below, pp. 87–88.

41. See Matthias Becher, "Die Sachsen im 7. und 8. Jahrhundert," in Stiegemann and Wemhoff, eds., *799. Kunst und Kultur*, vol. 1, pp. 188–94 (pp. 190–92), and "VI.4 Canones apostolorum und Mainzer Geiselverzeichnis," in ibid., pp. 327–28, illustrating Sankt Paul in Lavanttal, Benediktinerstift, Cod. 6/1, fols. 191v–192r.

42. Goldberg, "Popular Revolt," citing the older German scholarship.

43. Helmut Reimitz, "Ein fränkisches Geschichtsbuch aus Saint-Amand und der Codex Vindobonensis palat. 473," in Christoph Egger and Herwig Wiegl, eds., *Text—Schrift—Codex. Quellenkundliche Arbeiten aus dem Institut für Österreichische Geschichtsforschung* (Vienna, 1999), pp. 34–90.

44. Bernhard Bischoff, *Katalog der festländischen Handschriften des neunten Jahrhunderts (mit Ausnahme der wisigotischen)*, vol. 2, *Laon-Paderborn* (Wiesbaden, 2004), no. 2166, p. 46. I am grateful to David Ganz and Helmut Reimitz for comments on this manuscript.

45. *Annales laureshamenses*, s.a. 786, ed. Georg Pertz, MGH Scriptores 1 (Hannover, 1926), pp. 32–33; trans. King, *Charlemagne*, pp. 37–38.

46. *Annales q.d. Einhardi*, ed. Kurze, p. 73.

47. Cambridge University Library, Kk.5.16, and see Bernhard Bischoff, "Die Hofbibliothek Karls des Großen," *Mittelalterliche Studien*, vol. 3 (Stuttgart, 1981), pp. 149–70 (pp. 160–61); trans. Michael Gorman, "The Court Library of Charlemagne," in Bernhard Bischoff, *Manuscripts and Libraries in the Age of Charlemagne* (Cambridge, 1994), pp. 56–75 (p. 67).

48. See Wilfried Hartmann, *Die Synoden der Karolingerzeit im Frankenreich und in Italien: Konziliengeschichte* (Paderborn, Munich, Vienna, and Zurich, 1989), p. 102. On the character and function of Carolingian assemblies see Pössel, "Symbolic Communication," Paul Barnwell and Marco Mostert, eds., *Political Assemblies in the Earlier Middle Ages*, Studies in the Early Middle Ages 7 (Turnhout, 2003) and Timothy Reuter, "Assembly Politics in Western Europe from the Eighth Century to the Twelfth," in Peter Linehan and Janet L. Nelson, eds., *The Medieval World* (London, 2002), pp. 432–50.

49. Franz Unterkircher, ed., *Das Wiener Fragment der Lorscher Annalen, Christus und die Samariterin, Katechese des Niceta von Remesiana, Codex Vindobonensis 515 der Österreichischen Nationalbibliothek, Facsimile Ausgabe*, Codices selecti 15 (Graz, 1967).

50. Elias Avery Lowe, *Codices Latini Antiquiores*, vol. 10 (Oxford, 1963), no. 1482. Compare the discussion in Bernhard Bischoff, *Die sudostdeutchen Schreibschulen und Bib-*

liotheken, vol. 1, *Die bayrischen Diözesen*, 3rd ed. (Wiesbaden, 1974), pp. 145–46, which identifies Hand "A" of the Vienna fragment with the first hand of Munich, Bayerische Staatsbibliothek, Clm 6330, a miscellany of ecclesiastical texts, and was inclined to see two, rather than four, scribes.

51. Unterkircher, ed., *Das Wiener Fragment*, pp. 18–20. See McKitterick, *History and Memory*, pp. 104–11. Since *History and Memory* was published and the lectures on which this book is based were first delivered, Roger Collins's essay, "Charlemagne's Imperial Coronation and the Annals of Lorsch," in Story, ed., *Charlemagne*, pp. 52–70, has appeared. Collins covers some of the same ground I do here, though his focus is on the events of 799–800.

52. *Annales laureshamenses*, in Eberhard Katz, ed., *Annalium laureshamensium editio emendata secundum codicem St Paulensem*, Separatabdruck vom Jahresbericht des Öffentlichen Stiftsuntergymnasium der Benediktiner zu St Paul (Sankt Paul, 1889). This has a number of different readings form those offered by Pertz in the MGH Scriptores 1 edition cited above. On the manuscript see also Peter Hans Pascher, "9.7 *Annales Laureshamenses*," in Hartwig Pucker, ed., *Schatzhaus Kärntens: Landesausstellung St. Paul, 1991: 900 Jahre Benediktinerstift*, vol. 1, *Katalog* (Klagenfurt, 1991), p. 156, Kurt Holter, "Die Bibliothek: Handschriften und Inkunabeln," in Karl Ginhart, ed., *Die Kunstdenkmäler des Benediktinerstiftes St. Paul im Lavanttal und seiner Filialkirchen*, Österreichische Kunsttopographie 37 (Vienna, 1969), pp. 360–61 and plate 495 on p. 362, and Sascha Käuper, "II.3. Annales Laureshamenses (Lorscher Annalen)," in Stiegemann and Wemhoff, eds., *799, Kunst und Kultur*, vol. 1, pp. 38–40.

53. Heinrich Fichtenau, "Abt Richbod und die Annales laureshamenses," in *Beiträge zur Geschichte des Klosters Lorsch*, 2nd ed., Geschichtsblätter für den Kreis Bergstraße, Sonderband 4 (Lorsch, 1980), pp. 277–304.

54. Collins, "Charlemagne's Imperial Coronation," p. 57.

55. Lendi, *Untersuchungen zur frühalemannischen Annalistik*, pp. 94–131.

56. McKitterick, *History and Memory*, p. 108.

57. Heinrich Canisius, *Antiquae Lectiones*, vol. 3 (Ingolstadt, 1603), pp. 187–217; his text is based on a transcript in the Bavarian ducal library of an "old manuscript from Lorsch."

58. Einhard, *Vita Karoli* (c. 20) ed. Oswald Holder-Egger, reprinted in Rau, *Quellen zur karolingischen Reichsgeschichte*, vol. 1, p. 192; trans. Paul E. Dutton, *Charlemagne's Courtier* (Peterborough, ON, 1998), p. 29. On Fastrada see Janet L. Nelson, "Women at the Court of Charlemagne: A Case of Monstrous Regiment?" in John C. Parsons, ed., *Medieval Queenship* (Stroud, 1993), pp. 43–61, reprinted in Janet L. Nelson, *The Frankish World, 750–900* (London, 1996), pp. 223–42 (pp. 235–36); Janet L. Nelson, "The Siting of the Council at Frankfort: Some Reflections on Family and Politics" and Franz Staab, "Die Königin Fastrada," in Rainer Berndt, ed., *Das Frankfurter Konzil von 794: Kristallisationspunkt karolingischer Kultur*, Quellen und Abhandlungen zur mittelrheinischen Kirchengeschichte 80 (Mainz, 1997), pp. 149–66 and 183–218.

59. Innes and McKitterick, "The Writing of History," pp. 203–8, and compare McKitterick, *History and Memory*, pp. 29–30.

60. On the Frankish court in the reign of Charlemagne see Janet. L. Nelson, "Aachen as a Place of Power," in Mayke de Jong, Frans Theuws with Carine van Rhijn, eds., *Topographies of Power in the Early Middle Ages*, Transformation of the Roman World 6 (Leiden, 2001), pp. 217–42, and Donald Bullough, "*Aula renovata:* The Carolingian Court before the Aachen Palace," in Donald Bullough, *Carolingian Renewal* (Manchester, 1991), pp. 123–160.

61. *Annales fuldenses*, ed. Pertz and Kurze, p. 11; trans. Jan Ziolkowski, to whom I am grateful for discussion of the Fulda Annals.

62. See McKitterick, *History and Memory*, pp. 9–22, and Richard Corradini, *Die Wiener Handschrift Cvp 430 *: Ein Beitrag zur Historiographie in Fulda im frühen 9. Jahrhundert* (Frankfurt am Main, 2000) and Richard Corradini, "Zeiträume—Schrifträume: Überlegungen zur Komputistik und Marginalchronographie am Beispiel der Annales Fuldenses antiquissimi," in Walter Pohl and Paul Herolds, eds., *Von Nutzen des Schreibens: Soziales Gedächtnis, Herrschaft und Besitz*, Forschungen zur Geschichte des Mittelalters 5, Österreichische Akademie der Wissenschaften, phil.-hist. Klasse Denkschriften 306 (Vienna, 2003), pp. 113–66.

63. *Annales fuldenses*, ed. Pertz and Kurze, p. vi, and see above, p. 3. But for the portion to 838 see Richard Corradini, "Überlegungen zur sächsischen Ethnogenese anhand der Annales Fuldenses und deren sächsisch-ottonischer Rezeption," in Walter Pohl, ed., *Die Suche nach den Ursprüngen: Von der Bedeutung des frühen Mittelalters*, Forschungen zur Geschichte des Mittelalters 8, Österreichische Akademie der Wissenschaften, phil.-hist. Klasse Denkschriften 322 (Vienna, 2004), pp. 211–32.

64. Rau, *Quellen zur karolingischen Reichsgeschichte*, vol. 3, pp. 21–23.

65. Timothy Reuter, trans., *The Annals of Fulda* (Manchester, 1992), p. 8.

66. "Astronomer," *Vita Hludowici Imperatori*, I.7, in Tremp, *Thegan: Die Taten Kaiser Ludwigs; Astronomus, Das Leben Kaiser Ludwigs*, p. 306; compare English trans. Allen Cabaniss, *Son of Charlemagne: A Contemporary Life of Louis the Pious* (Syracuse, 1961), p. 39. On the possible date of composition see Hugh Doherty, "The Maintenance of Royal Power and Prestige in the Carolingian *regnum* of Aquitaine under Louis the Pious," (M.Phil. dissertation, Faculty of History, University of Cambridge, 1998).

67. Astronomer, *Vita Hludowici Imperatori*, II. 29, p. 382, and compare *Annales regni francorum, s.a.* 817, ed. Kurze, p. 148.

68. *Annales petaviani*, ed. Georg Pertz, MGH Scriptores 1 (Hannover, 1826), pp. 7–18, noted by Friedrich Kurze, in *Annales regni francorum*, p. 14, note 6, and p. 16, note 1.

69. Bischoff, *Die Sudostdeutsche Schreibschulen und Bibliotheken in der Karolingerzeit*, vol. 1, p. 21. The hand of fol. 2v, lines 106, resembles that of the Wessobrunner Gebet (Munich, Bayerische Staatsbibliothek, Clm 22053) written ca 814 in Augsburg. The last entry for 814 is by a different scribe.

70. See Lendi, *Untersuchungen zur frühalemannischen Annalistik*, pp. 82–93. I am very grateful to the Stiftsarchiv in Sankt Gallen and especially to Doctor Peter Erhart for his kindness in letting me see this manuscript and for supplying me with photographs of it subsequently.

71. Lowe, *Codices latini antiquiores*, vol. 1, no. 98, where the first text is wrongly described as Gregory of Tours's *Historiae*, following the heading in the manuscript itself,

fol. 1v (*Incipit liber Gregorii Toronis ep[iscop]i gesta regu[m] Francorum*) and Bernhard Bischoff, *Die Abtei Lorsch im Spiegel ihrer Handschriften* (Lorsch, 1989), p. 128. See also Helmut Reimitz, "Social Networks and Identities in Frankish Historiography: New Aspects of the Textual History of Gregory of Tours' *Historiae*," in Richard Corradini, Maximilian Diesenberger, and Helmut Reimitz, eds., *The Construction of Communities in the Early Middle Ages: Texts, Resources and Artefacts*, The Transformation of the Roman World 12 (Leiden, 2003), pp. 229–68 (p. 240, note 63).

72. This is Lendi's suggested expansion for the abbreviation *qn*.

73. Transcribed from Vat., pal. lat. 966, fols. 57r–58r, and also checked against another transcription kindly supplied by Helmut Reimitz, to whom I am also very grateful for discussion of this manuscript as well as supplying the photograph for reproduction here. The manuscript's text has a number of erasures, additions, and ambiguous abbreviations that we have solved as best we could in the text offered here. See also Lendi, *Untersuchungen zur frühalemannischen Annalistik*, pp. 159–63 for a modern edition and compare *Annales nazariani*, ed. Pertz, pp. 40–44 (pp. 41–42); trans. (from the MGH edition) King, *Charlemagne*, pp. 154–55. Note at the start of the entry (*Thuringi autem consilium fecerunt*) the word used is *consilium*, not the technical term *coniuratio* or even *conspiratio*.

74. *Annales laureshamenses*, ed. Katz, p. 17.

75. Brunner, *Oppositionelle Gruppen*, pp. 47–53.

76. Stuart Airlie, "Charlemagne and the Aristocracy: Captains and Kings," in Story, ed., *Charlemagne*, pp. 90–102 (p. 98). See also Timothy Reuter, "Charlemagne and the world beyond the Rhine," in ibid., pp. 183–94 (pp. 187–88).

77. See the interesting suggestions in Hubert Mordek, "Die Hedenen als politische Kraft im austrasischen Frankenreich," in Jörg Jarnut, Ulrich Nonn, and Michael Richter, eds., Karl Martell in seiner Zeit (Sigmaringen, 1994), pp. 345–66.

Conclusion

1. *Annales nazariani*, in Walter Lendi, *Untersuchungen zur frühalemannischen Annalistik: Die Murbacher Annalen*, Scrinium Friburgense 1 (Freiburg in der Schweiz, 1971), p. 161, and in Georg Pertz, ed., MGH Scriptores 1 (Hannover, 1826), p. 42 (Vat., pal. lat. 966, fol. 58r); trans. P. David King, *Charlemagne: Translated Sources* (Kendal, 1987), p. 155.

2. Rosamond McKitterick, *History and Memory in the Carolingian World* (Cambridge, 2004), pp. 13–19.

3. Ibid., pp. 50–51.

4. *Annales laureshamenses*, in Eberhard Katz, ed., *Annalium laureshamensium editio emendata secundum codicem St Paulensem*, Separatabdruck vom Jahresbericht des Öffentlichen Stiftsuntergymnasium der Benediktiner zu St Paul (Sankt Paul, 1889), p. 27.

5. Compare above p. 8 and remarks in Brian Croke, *Count Marcellinus and His Chronicle* (Oxford, 2003), pp. 257–65.

Bibliography

Primary Sources

Actus pontificum Cenomannis in urbe degentium. Ed. Gustave Busson and Ambroise Ledru (Le Mans, 1901)

Ado of Vienne. *Chronicon* [reprint of Paris 1561 edition], in *Patrologia Latina*, vol. 123, cols. 23–138.

———— *Martyrologium*, in Jacques Dubois and Geneviève Renaud, eds., *Le Martyrologe d'Adon* (Paris, 1984).

Alcuin. *Carmina*, ed. Ernst Dümmler, MGH Poetae latini aevi karolini 1 (Berlin, 1888).

———— *Epistolae*, ed. Ernst Dümmler, MGH Epistolae karolini aevi (Berlin, 1895); facsimile ed. Franz Unterkircher, ed., *Alkuin-Briefe und andere Traktate*, Codices selecti 20 (Graz, 1969).

Annales floriacenses. Ed. Georg Pertz, MGH Scriptores 2 (Hannover, 1829).

Annales fuldenses. Ed. Georg Pertz and Friedrich Kurze, MGH Scriptores rerum germanicarum 7 (Hannover, 1891); trans. Timothy Reuter, *The Annals of Fulda* (Manchester, 1992).

Annales laureshamenses. In Eberhard Katz, ed., *Annalium laureshamensium editio emendata secundum codicem St Paulensem*, Separatabdruck vom Jahresbericht des Öffentlichen Stiftsuntergymnasium der Benediktiner zu St Paul (Sankt Paul, 1889); ed. Georg Pertz, MGH Scriptores 1 (Hannover, 1926); facsimile Franz Unterkircher, ed., *Das Wiener Fragment der Lorscher Annalen, Christus und die Samariterin, Katechese des Niceta von Remesiana, Codex Vindobonensis 515 des Österreichischen Nationalbibliothek, Faksimile Ausgabe*, Codices Selecti 15 (Graz, 1967).

Annales maximiani. Ed. Georg Waitz, MGH Scriptores 13 (Hannover, 1881), pp. 19–25.

Annales mettenses priores. Ed. Bernhard von Simson, MGH Scriptores rerum germanicarum 10 (Hannover, 1905).

Annales mosellani (703–97/98). Ed. Johann M. Lappenberg, MGH Scriptores 16 (Hannover, 1859), pp. 494–99.

Annales murbacenses. In Walter Lendi, ed., *Untersuchungen zur frühalemannischen Annalistik: Die Murbacher Annalen mit Edition,* Scrinium Friburgense 1 (Freiburg in der Schweiz, 1971), pp. 146–93.

Annales nazariani. Ed. Georg Pertz, MGH Scriptores 1 (Hannover, 1826), pp. 40–44, and Walter Lendi, *Untersuchungen zur frühalemannischen Annalistik: Die Murbacher Annalen,* Scrinium Friburgense 1 (Freiburg in der Schweiz, 1971), pp. 159–63; trans. of extracts, P. David King, *Charlemagne: Translated Sources* (Kendal, 1987), pp. 154–55.

Annales petaviani. Ed. Georg Pertz, MGH Scriptores 1 (Hannover, 1826), pp. 7–18.

Annales q.d. Einhardi [= "revised" version of *Annales regni francorum*]. Ed. Friedrich Kurze, MGH Scriptores rerum germanicarum 6 (Hannover, 1895); trans. of extracts, P. David King, *Charlemagne: Translated Sources* (Kendal, 1987), pp. 108–31.

Annales regni francorum. Ed. Friedrich Kurze, MGH Scriptores rerum germanicarum 6 (Hannover, 1895); trans. Bernard W. Scholz, in *Carolingian Chronicles* (Ann Arbor, MI, 1970).

Anonymous of Lyon. *Martyrology,* ed. Jacques Dubois and Geneviève Renant, *Édition pratique des martyrologes de Bède, de l'Anonyme Lyonnais et de Florus* (Paris, 1976).

Arator. *De actibus apostolorum,* in Alastair P. MacKinlay, ed., *Aratoris subdiaconi de actibus apostolorum,* Corpus scriptorum ecclesiasticarum latinorum (Vienna, 1951); trans. Richard J. Schrader, Joseph L. Roberts, and John F. Makowski, *Arator's On the Acts of the Apostles* (Atlanta, 1992).

Astronomer. *Vita Hludowici Imperatori,* in Ernst Tremp, ed., *Thegan, Die Taten Kaiser Ludwigs; Astronomus, Das Leben Kaiser Ludwigs,* MGH Scriptores rerum germanicarum 64 (Hannover, 1995); trans. Allen Cabaniss, *Son of Charlemagne: A Contemporary Life of Louis the Pious* (Syracuse, 1961).

Athanasius. *De Incarnatione,* ed. Charles Kannengiesser, Sources chrétiennes 199 (Paris, 1973).

Augustine. *Sancti Aurelii Augustini De Civitate Dei,* ed. Bernard Dombart and Alphonse Kalb, Corpus Christianorum: Series Latina 48 (Turnhout, 1955).

Bede. *De temporum ratione,* in Charles W. Jones, ed., *Bedae opera didascalica,* Corpus Christianorum: Series Latina 123B, *De temporum ratione liber. Chronica maiora includens (id est capita LXVI–LXXXI) transcripta ex editione a Th. Mommsen divulgata una cum commentariis et glossis scriptis a.d. dcclxxiii e codice Mettensi (Berlin MS Phillipps 1832) cura et studio C. W. Jones* (Turnhout, 1977); trans. Faith Wallis, *Bede: The Reckoning of Time* (Liverpool, 1999).

———. *Historia ecclesiastica gentis anglorum,* in Roger A. B. Mynors and Bertram Colgrave, eds. and trans., *Bede's Ecclesiastical History of the English People,* Oxford Medieval Texts (Oxford, 1969).

———. *Martryology,* in Henry Quentin, ed., *Les Martyrologes historiques du moyen âge: Étude sur la formation du martyrologe romain* (Paris, 1908), pp. 2–119, and in Jacques Dubois and Geneviève Renant, eds., *Édition pratique des Martyrologes de Bède, de l'Anonyme Lyonnais et de Florus* (Paris, 1976); an attempted reconstruction in English trans., Felice Lifshitz, in Thomas Head, ed., *Medieval Hagiography: An Anthology* (New York and London, 2000), pp. 179–97.

Canisius, Heinrich, ed. *Antiquae Lectiones*, vol. 3 (Ingolstadt, 1603).

Capitularia. Ed. Alfred Boretius, MGH Capitularia regum francorum 1 (Hannover, 1883).

Chelles, relic labels. Ed. Hartmut Atsma and Jean Vezin, *Authentiques de reliques provenant de l'ancien monastère Notre-Dame de Chelles (VIIe–VIIIe siècles)*, Chartae Latinae Antiquiores 18 (Zurich, 1985), no. 669, pp. 84–108.

Chronica minora, saec. IV–VII. Ed. Theodor Mommsen, 2 vols., MGH Auctores Antiquissimi 9 (Berlin, 1892) and 11 (Berlin, 1894).

Chronicon universale—741 [incomplete]. Ed. Georg Waitz, MGH Scriptores 13 (Hannover, 1881).

Concilia. Ed. Albert Werminghoff, MGH Concilia aevi karolini 2.1 (Hannover and Leipzig, 1906).

Concilium Aquisgranense (817). Ed. Kassius Hallinger, Corpus consuetudinum monasticarum 1 (Siegburg, 1963).

Decretum Aquisgranensi de processione spiritus sancti a patre et filio (809). In Harald Willjung, ed., *Das Konzil von Aachen 809*, MGH Concilia 2, Supplementum 2 (Hannover, 1998).

Einhard. *Translatio sanctorum Marcellini et Petri*, ed. Georg Waitz, MGH Scriptores 15.1 (Hannover, 1887), pp. 238–64; trans. Paul E. Dutton, *Charlemagne's Courtier: The Complete Einhard* (Peterborough, ON, 1998) pp. 69–130.

———. *Vita Karoli*, ed. Oswald Holder-Egger, reprinted in Reinhard Rau, ed., *Quellen zur karolingischen Reichsgeschichte*, vol. 1 (Darmstadt, 1974), pp. 163–212; trans. Paul E. Dutton, *Charlemagne's Courtier: The Complete Einhard* (Peterborough, ON, 1998).

Erconrad. *Translatio S. Liborii episcopi*, in A. Cohausz and Robert Latouche, eds. and French trans., *La Translation du S. Liboire de diacre Erconrad* (Le Mans, 1967).

Eriugena, John Scotus. In Inglis P. Sheldon-Williams, ed., *Johannis Scottis Eriugenae Periphyseon (De divisione naturae), Liber II*, Scriptores Latinae Hiberniae 9 (Dublin, 1972).

Eusebius-Jerome. *Chronicon*, in Rudolf Helm, ed., *Eusebius Werke*, vol. 7, Die griechischen christlichen Schriftsteller der ersten Jahrhundert 70, 2nd ed. (Berlin, 1956); John Knight Fotheringham, ed., *Eusebii Pamphili Chronici canones latini vertiti adauxit ad sua tempora produxit S. Eusebius Hieronymus* (London and Oxford, 1923); trans. Malcolm D. Donaldson, *A Translation of Jerome's "Chronicon" with Historical Commentary* (Lewiston, Queenston, and Lampeter, 1996); French trans. (with Helm's Latin text) Benoît Jeanjean and Bertrand Lançon, *Saint Jérôme, Chronique: Continuation de la Chronique d'Eusèbe, années 326–378, suivie de quatre études sur les Chroniques et chronographies dans l'Antiquité tardive (IVe–VIe siècles)* (Rennes, 2004); facsimile ed. of Oxford, Bodleian Library, Auct. T II, John Knight Fotheringham, ed., *The Bodleian Manuscript of Jerome's Version of the Chronicle of Eusebius* (Oxford, 1905); digital images of Oxford, Merton College Library MS Coxe 315 at http://image.ox.ac.uk.

Eusebius-Rufinus. *Historia ecclesiastica*, in Theodor Mommsen and Eduard Schwartz, eds., *Eusebius Werke*, vol. 2, *Die Kirchengeschichte: Die lateinische Übersetzung des Ru-*

finus, pt. 1, *Die Bücher I bis V,* Die griechischen Schriftsteller der ersten drei Jahrhunderte, Eusebius, 2.1 and 2.2 (Leipzig, 1903 and 1908).

Flodoard. *Historia remensis ecclesiae,* in Martina Stratmann, ed., *Flodoard von Reims: Die Geschichte der reimser Kirche,* MGH Scriptores 36 (Hannover, 1998).

Florus. *Martyrology,* ed. Jacques Dubois and Geneviève Renant, *Édition pratique des martyrologes de Bède, de l'anonyme Lyonnais et de Florus* (Paris, 1976).

Freculf. *Chronicon,* in Michael Allen, ed., *Frecvlfi Lexoviensis episcopi opera omnia,* Corpus Christianorum: Continuatio Mediaevalis 169 (Turnhout, 2003).

Frutolf. *Chronicon,* in Franz-Josef Schmale and Irene Schmale-Ott, eds., with German trans., *Frutolfs und Ekkehards Chroniken und die anonyme Kaiserchronik* (Darmstadt, 1972).

Hariulf. *Chronicon Centulense,* in Ferdinand Lot, ed., *Hariulf, Chronique de l'abbaye de Saint-Riquier, Ve siècle–1004* (Paris, 1894).

Hieronymian Martyrology. Ed. Giovanni B. de Rossi, Louis Duchesne, "Martyrologium Hieronymianum," *Acta Sanctorum* November 2/1 (1894), and Henri Quentin, *Acta Sanctorum* November 2/2 (1931).

Hincmar of Rheims. *De villa Novilliaco,* ed. Georg Waitz, MGH Scriptores 15.2 (Hannover, 1888), pp. 1167–69.

Hraban Maur. *Martyrology,* in John McCulloh, ed., *Rabani Mauri martyrologium,* Corpus Christianorum Continuatio Medievalis 44 (Turnhout, 1979).

Hugeburc of Heidenheim, *Hodoeporicon,* ed. Oswald Holder-Egger, MGH Scriptores 15.1 (Hannover, 1887), pp. 80–117.

Inscriptions of Rome. Ed. Giovanni B. de Rossi, *Inscriptiones Christianae urbis Romae septimo saeculo antiquiores,* 2 vols. (Rome, 1857–88).

Isidore. *Chronica,* ed. José Carlos Martin, Corpus Christianorum: Series Latina 112 (Turnhout, 2003).

Itinerarium Egeriae. Ed. A. Franceschini and R. Weber, in P. Geyer and O. Cuntz, et al., eds., *Itineraria et alia geographica,* Corpus Christianorum: Series Latina 175 (Turnhout,1965), pp. 35–90.

Itinerarium Einsiedlense. In Roberto Valentini and Giuseppe Zucchetti, eds., *Codice topografico della Città di Roma,*vol. 2, Fonti per la storia d'Italia 88 (Rome, 1942), pp. 169–207, and in P. Geyer and O. Cuntz, eds., *Itineraria et alia geographica,* Corpus Christianorum: Series Latina 175 (Turnhout, 1965), pp. 329–43; Gerold Walser, ed., *Die Einsiedler Inschriftensammlung und der Pilgerführer durch Rom (Codex Einsidlensis 326)* (Stuttgart, 1987).

Jerome. *Liber Hebraicarum Quaestionum in Genesim,* in D. Vallarsi, ed., *Patrologia Latina,* vol. 23 (Paris, 1845); trans. Robert Hayward, *Saint Jerome's Hebrew Questions on Genesis* (Oxford, 1995).

Jerome-Gennadius. *De viris inlustribus,* ed. Ernest C. Richardson, Texte und Untersuchungen der altchristlichen Literatur 14 (Leipzig, 1896).

Lex Salica. Ed. Karl August Eckhardt, MGH Leges nationum germanicarum 4.2 (Hannover, 1969); trans. Katherine Fischer Drew, *The Laws of the Salian Franks* (Philadelphia, 1991).

Liber Pontificalis. In Louis Duchesne, ed., *Le Liber pontificalis*, 2 vols. (Paris, 1886–92); trans. Raymond Davis, *The Book of the Pontiffs ("Liber Pontificalis"): The Ancient Biographies of the First Ninety Roman Bishops to AD 715*, rev. ed. (Liverpool, 2000); *The Lives of the Eighth-Century Popes (Liber Pontificalis)* (Liverpool, 1992); *The Lives of the Ninth-Century Popes* (Liverpool, 1995).

Livy. *Ab urbe condita*, in *Livy in Fourteen Volumes*. ed. and trans. B. O. Foster, vol. 3, *Books V, VI, VIII* (Cambridge, MA, 1967).

Lupus of Ferrières. *Epistolae*, in Léon Levillain, ed., *Loup de Ferrières, Correspondance*, Les Classiques de l'histoire de France au moyen âge 10 (Paris, 1964); trans. Graydon W. Regenos, *The Letters of Lupus of Ferrières* (The Hague, 1966).

Marcellinus. *Chronicon*, ed. and trans. Brian Croke, *The Chronicle of Marcellinus* (Sydney, 1995).

Notitia ecclesiarum urbis Romae and *De locis sanctis martyrum quae sunt foris civitatis Romae*. In Roberto Valentini and Giuseppe Zucchetti, eds., *Codice topografico della Città di Roma* vol. 2, Fonti per la storia d'Italia (Rome, 1942), pp. 72–99 and 106–31; in Giovanni B. de Rossi, ed., *Roma sotteranea christiana*, vol. 1 (Rome, 1864), pp. 128–57, and in Giovanni de Rossi ed., *Inscriptiones Christianae Urbis Romae septimo saeculo antiquiores*, 2 vols. (Rome, 1857–88), vol. 2 (1888), pp. 95–118; and in P. Geyer and O. Cuntz, et al., eds., *Itineraria et alia geographica*, Corpus Christianorum: Series Latina 175 (Turnhout, 1965), pp. 304–11 and 314–22.

Origen. *Homiliae in Genesim*, in Willem A. Baehrens, ed., *Origenes Werke*, vol. 6, Die griechischen christlichen Schriftsteller 29 (Leipzig, 1929).

Orosius. *Historiarum adversus paganos libri septem*, in Marie-Pierre Arnaud-Lindet, ed., *Orose: Histoires (contre les païens)* (Paris, 1990); trans. Irving W. Raymond, *Orosius: The Seven Books of History Against the Pagans* (New York, 1936).

Paderborn epic. In Helmut Beumann, Franz Brunhölzl, and Wilhelm Winkelmann, eds., *Karolus Magnus et Leo Papa: Ein Paderborner Epos vom Jahr 799* (Paderborn, 1966) and Wilhelm Heintz, ed., *De Karolo rege et Leone papa*, Studien und Quellen zur westfälischen Geschichte 36 (Paderborn, 1999).

Paul the Deacon. *Liber de episcopis mettensibus*, ed. Georg Pertz, MGH Scriptores 2 (Hannover, 1829).

Regino. *Chronicon*, in Friedrich Kurze, ed., *Reginonis abbatis prumiensis Chronicon cum continuatione treverensi*, MGH Scriptores rerum germanicarum 50 (Hannover, 1890).

Sens, relic labels. Ed. Maurice Prou and Eugène Chartraire, "Authentiques de reliques conservées au trésor de la cathédrale de Sens," *Mémoires de la Société Nationale des Antiquaires de France*, 6th series, 9 (1900), pp. 129–72 and facsimiles, plates 7–12.

Suetonius. *De vita caesarum*, ed. Otto Wittstock (Berlin, 1993).

Thegan. *Gesta Hludowici imperatoris*, in Ernst Tremp, ed., *Thegan, Die Taten Kaiser Ludwigs; Astronomus, Das Leben Kaiser Ludwigs*, MGH Scriptores rerum germanicarum 64 (Hannover, 1995); trans. Paul E. Dutton, *Carolingian Civilisation: A Reader*, 2nd ed. (Peterborough, 2004).

Treasure lists. Ed. Bernhard Bischoff, *Mittelalterliche Schatzverzeichnisse* (Munich, 1967).

Usuard. *Martyrologium*, in Jacques Dubois, ed., *Le Martyrologe d'Usuard: Texte et commentaire*, Subsidia Hagiographica 40 (Brussels, 1965).

Valerius Maximus. *Factorum et dictorum memorabilium libri*, in David R. Shackleton Bailey, ed. and trans., *Valerius Maximus, Memorable Doings and Sayings* (Cambridge, MA, 2000).

Wandalbert of Prüm. *Martyrologium*, in Hans-Walter Stork, ed., *Das Martyrologium für Kaiser Lothar: Faksimile Cod. Reg. lat. 438*, Codices e Vaticanis selecti 83 (Zurich, 1997).

Secondary Literature

Adler, William. "Eusebius' Chronicle and its legacy," in Harold W. Attridge and Gohei Hata, eds., *Eusebius, Christianity, and Judaism* (Detroit, 1992), pp. 467–91.

Airlie, Stuart. "Charlemagne and the Aristocracy: Captains and Kings," in Joanna Story, ed., *Charlemagne: Empire and Society* (Manchester, 2005), pp. 90–102.

Allen, Michael I. "The Chronicle of Claudius of Turin," in Alexander C. Murray, ed., *After Rome's Fall: Narrators and Sources of Early Medieval History. Essays Presented to Walter Goffart* (Toronto, 1998), pp. 288–319.

———. "Universal History, 300–1000: Origins and Western Developments," in Deborah Mauskopf Deliyannis, ed., *Historiography in the Middle Ages* (Leiden, 2003), pp. 17–42.

Andaloro, Maria, and Serena Romano, eds. *Römisches Mittelalter: Kunst und Kultur in Rom von der Spätantike bis Giotto* (Darmstadt, 2002).

Anton, Hans Hubert. *Fürstenspiegel und Herrscherethos in der Karolingerzeit* (Bonn, 1968).

———. "Origo gentis (Franken)," *Reallexikon der Germanischen Altertumskunde*, 2nd ed., vol. 22 (Berlin and New York, 2003), pp. 189–95.

Baldovin, John F. "The Urban Character of Christian Worship: The Origins, Development and Meaning of Stational Liturgy," *Orientalia Christiana analecta* 228 (Rome, 1987), pp. 105–66.

Barnes, Timothy D. *Constantine and Eusebius* (Cambridge, MA, 1981).

Barnwell, Paul, and Marco Mostert, eds. *Political Assemblies in the Earlier Middle Ages*, Studies in the Early Middle Ages 7 (Turnhout, 2003).

Barsali, Isa Belli. "Sulla topografia di Roma in periodo carolingio: La 'civitas leoniana' e la Giovannipoli," in *Roma e l'età carolingia* (Rome, 1976), pp. 201–14.

Basset, Paul. "The Use of History in the *Chronicon* of Isidore of Seville," *History and Theory* 15 (1976), pp. 278–92.

Bately, Janet M. "World History in the Anglo-Saxon Chronicle: Its Sources and Its Separateness from the Old English Orosius," *Anglo-Saxon England* 8 (1979), pp. 177–94.

———. *The Old English Orosius*, Early English Texts Society S.S. 6 (Oxford, 1980).

Bauer, Franz Alto. "Das Bild der Stadt Rom in der Karolingerzeit: Der Anonymus Einsiedlensis," *Römische Quartalschrift* 92 (1997), pp. 190–228.

———. "IX.1 Einsiedler Pilgerführer," in Christoph Stiegemann and Matthias Wemhoff, eds., *799, Kunst und Kultur der Karolingerzeit: Karl der Große und Papst Leo III. in Paderborn* (Mainz, 1999), vol. 2, pp. 607–9.

———. "The Liturgical Arrangement of Early Medieval Roman Church Buildings," in *Mededelingen van het Nederlands Instituut te Rome*, vol. 59 (Rome, 2000), pp. 101–28.

Becher, Matthias. *Eid und Herrschaft: Untersuchungen zum Herrscherethos Karls des Großen*, Vorträge und Forschungen Sonderband 39 (Sigmaringen, 1993).

———. "Die Sachsen im 7. und 8. Jahrhundert," in Christoph Stiegemann and Matthias Wemhoff eds., *799, Kunst und Kultur der Karolingerzeit: Karl der Große und Papst Leo III. in Paderborn* (Mainz, 1999), vol. 1, pp. 188–94.

———. "Eine verschleierte Krise: Die Nachfolge Karl Martells 741 und die Anfänge der karolingischen Hofgeschichtsschreibung," in Johannes Laudage, ed., *Von Fakten und Fiktionen: Mittelalterliche Geschichtsdarstellungen und ihre kritische Aufarbeitung* (Cologne, Weimar, and Vienna, 2003), pp. 95–133.

Bellardini, Donatella, and Paolo Delogu. "Liber Pontificalis e altre fonti: La topografia di Roma nell'VIII secolo," in *Il Liber Pontificalis e la storia materiale*, ed. Herman Geertman, Atti del colloquio internazionale Roma, 21–22 Febbraio 2002, Mededelingen van het Nederlands Instituut te Rome 60/61 (Rome, 2003), pp. 205–23.

Bernard, Philippe. *Du chant romain au chant grégorien (IVe–XIIIe siècle)* (Paris, 1996).

Birch, Debra J. *Pilgrimage to Rome in the Middle Ages* (Woodbridge, 1998).

Bischoff, Bernhard. "Das karolingische Kalendar der Palimpsesthandschrift Ambros. M.12 sup.," in Bonifatius Fischer and Virgil Fiala, eds., *Colligere fragmenta: Festschrift Alban Dold* (Beuron, 1952), pp. 247–60.

———. *Die südostdeutschen Schreibschulen und Bibliotheken*, vol. 1, *Die bayrischen Diözesen*, 3rd ed. (Wiesbaden, 1974).

———. *Die südostdeutschen Schreibschulen und Bibliotheken in der Karolingerzeit*, vol. 2, *Die vorwiegend Österreichischen Diözesen* (Wiesbaden, 1980).

———. "Die Hofbibliothek Karls des Großen," *Mittelalterliche Studien*, vol. 3 (Stuttgart, 1981), pp. 149–70; trans. Michael Gorman, "The Court Library of Charlemagne," in Bernhard Bischoff, *Manuscripts and Libraries in the Age of Charlemagne* (Cambridge, 1994), pp. 56–75.

———. *Die Abtei Lorsch im Spiegel ihrer Handschriften*, 2nd ed. (Lorsch, 1989).

———. *Katalog der festländischen Handschriften des neunten Jahrhunderts (mit Ausnahme der wisigotischen)*, vol. 1, *Aachen-Lambach* (Wiesbaden, 1998).

———. *Katalog der festländischen Handschriften des neunten Jahrhunderts (mit Ausnahme der wisigotischen)*, vol. 2, *Laon-Paderborn* (Wiesbaden, 2004).

Blair-Dixon, Kate. "Damasus and the Fiction of Unity: The Urban Shrines of Saint Laurence," in Federico Guidobaldi and Alessandra Guiglia Guidobaldi, eds., *Ecclesiae Urbis: Atti del congresso internazionale di studi sulle chiese di Roma (IX–X secolo)*, vol. 1, Studi di antichita cristiana 59 (Vatican City, 2002), pp. 331–52.

Borst, Arno. *Der Turmbau zu Babel: Geschichte der Meinungen über Ursprung und Vielfalt der Sprachen und Völker*, 4 vols. (Stuttgart, 1957–63).

Boschen, Lothar. *Die Annales Prumienses: Ihre nähere und ihre weitere Verwandtschaft* (Düsseldorf, 1972).

Brandt, Hans-Jürgen, and Karl Hengst, eds. *Felix Paderae civitas: Der heilige Liborius, 836–1985*, Studien und Quellen zur westfälischen Geschichte 24 (Paderborn, 1986).

Brincken, Dorothea von den. *Studien zur lateinischen Weltchronistik bis in das Zeitalter Ottos von Freising* (Düsseldorf, 1957).

———. "Die lateinische Weltchronistik," in Alexander Randa, ed., *Mensch und Weltgeschichte: Zur Geschichte der Universalgeschichtsschreibung* (Salzburg and Munich, 1969).

Brown, Giles. "Politics and Patronage at the Abbey of Saint-Denis (814–898): The Rise of a Royal Patron Saint," (D.Phil. thesis, University of Oxford, 1989).

Brown, Peter. *The Cult of the Saints* (Chicago and London, 1981).

Brugnoli, Giorgio. *Curiosissimus excerptor" Gli "Additamenti" di Girolamo ai "Chronica" di Eusebio* (Pisa, 1995).

Brunner, Karl. *Oppositionelle Gruppen im Karolingerreich*, Veröffentlichungen des Instituts für Österreichische Geschichtsforschung 25 (Vienna, 1979).

Bullough, Donald A. "*Aula renovata:* The Carolingian Court before the Aachen Palace," in Donald Bullough, *Carolingian Renewal* (Manchester 1991), pp. 123–60.

———. *Alcuin: Achievement and Reputation. Being Part of the Ford Lectures Delivered in Oxford in the Hilary Term 1980* (Leiden and Boston, 2004).

Burgess, Richard W. "The Gallic Chronicle of 452: A New Critical Edition with a Brief Introduction," in Ralph Mathisen and Danuta Schanzer, eds., *Society and Culture in Late Antique Gaul: Revisiting the Sources* (Aldershot, 2001), pp. 52–84.

———. "The Gallic Chronicle of 511: A New Critical Edition with a Brief Introduction," in Ralph Mathisen and Danuta Schanzer, eds., *Society and Culture in Late Antique Gaul: Revisiting the Sources* (Aldershot, 2001), pp. 85–100.

———, with the assistance of Witold Witakowski. *Studies in Eusebian and Post-Eusebian Chronography*, Historia: Zeitschrift für alte Geschichte, Einzelschriften 135 (Stuttgart, 1999).

Büttner, Heinrich. "Mission und Kirchenorganisation des Frankenreiches bis zum Tode Karls des Großen," in Wolfgang Braunfels, ed., *Karl der Große: Lebenswerk und Nachleben*, vol. 1, *Persönlichkeit und Geschichte* (Düsseldorf, 1965), pp. 454–87.

Canellis, Aline. "Saint Jérôme et les ariens," in *Les Chrétiens face à leurs adversaires dans l'Occident latin au IVe siècle* (Rouen, 2001), pp. 155–94.

Caner, Daniel. *Wandering, Begging Monks: Spiritual Authority and the Promotion of Monasticism in Late Antiquity* (Berkeley, CA, 2002).

Carmassi, Patrizia. "La prima redazione del *Liber Pontificalis* nel quadro delle fonti contemporanee: Osservazioni in margine alla *vita* di Simmaco," in *Il Liber Pontificalis e la storia materiale*, ed. Herman Geertman, Atti del colloquio internazionale Roma, 21–22 Febbraio 2002, Mededelingen van het Nederlands Instituut te Rome 60/61 (Rome, 2003), pp. 235–66.

Carroll, Christopher: "The Bishoprics of Saxony in the First Century after Christianization," *Early Medieval Europe* 9 (1999), pp. 219–46.

Carter, C. J. "Valerius Maximus," in Thomas A. Dorey, ed., *Empire and Aftermath* (London, 1975), pp. 26–56.

Chazelle, Celia, and Burton van Name Edwards, eds. *The Study of the Bible in the Carolingian Era*, Medieval Church Studies 3 (Turnhout, 2003).

Classen, Peter. *Karl der Große, das Papsttum und Byzanz: Die Begründung des karolingischen Kaisertums*, Beiträge zur Geschichte und Quellenkunde des Mittelalters 9 (Sigmaringen, 1985).

Coates Stevens, Robert. "Dark Age Architecture in Rome," *Papers of the British School at Rome* 65 (1997), pp. 177–232.

Collins, Roger. "Charlemagne's Imperial Coronation and the Annals of Lorsch," in Joanna Story, ed., *Charlemagne: Empire and Society* (Manchester, 2005), pp. 52–70.

Contreni, John, J. "Carolingian Biblical Culture," in Gerd van Riel, Carlos Steel, and James McEvoy, *Johannes Scottus Eriugena: The Bible and Hermeneutics*, Ancient and Medieval Philosophy Series 1 (Leuven, 1996), pp. 1–23.

Conybeare, Catherine. *"Terrarum Orbi Documentum:* Augustine, Camillus, and Learning from History," in Mark Vessey, Karla Pollmann, and Allan Fitzgerald, eds., *History, Apocalypse, and the Secular Imagination: New Essays on Augustine's "City of God"* (Bowling Green, OH, 1999), pp. 45–58.

Cooper, Kate. "The Martyr, the *matrona* and the Bishop: The Matron Lucina and the Politics of Martyr Cult in Fifth- and Sixth-Century Rome," *Early Medieval Europe* 8 (1999), pp. 297–318.

———, ed. *The Roman Martyrs and the Politics of Memory*, special issue of *Early Medieval Europe* 9 (2000).

Cooper, Kate, and Clare Pilsworth. "The Roman Martyrs Project," at http://www.art.man.ac.uk/cla/Romanmartyrs.htm.

Corradini, Richard. *Die Wiener Handschrift Cvp 430*: Ein Beitrag zur Historiographie in Fulda im frühen 9. Jahrhundert* (Frankfurt am Main, 2000).

———. "Zeiträume—Schrifträume. Überlegungen zur Komputistik und Marginalchronographie am Beispiel der Annales Fuldenses antiquissimi," in Walter Pohl and Paul Herolds, eds., *Von Nutzen des Schreibens. Soziales Gedächtnis, Herrschaft und Besitz*, Forschungen zur Geschichte des Mittelalters 5, Österreichische Akademie der Wissenschaften, phil.-hist. Klasse Denkschriften 306 (Vienna, 2003), pp. 113–66.

———. "Überlegungen zur sächsischen Ethnogenese anhand der Annales Fuldenses und deren sächsisch-ottonischer rezeption," in Walter Pohl, ed., *Die Suche nach den Ursprüngen: Von der Bedeutung des frühen Mittelalters*, Forschungen zur Geschichte des Mittelalters 8, Österreichische Akademie der Wissenschaften, phil.-hist. Klasse Denkschriften 322 (Vienna, 2004), pp. 211–32.

Costambeys, Marios. "The Culture and Practice of Burial in and around Rome in the Sixth Century," in Federico Guidobaldi and Alessandra Guiglia Guidobaldi, eds., *Ecclesiae Urbis: Atti del congresso internazionale di studi sulle chiese di Roma (IV–X secolo)*, 3 vols, Studi di antichità cristiana 59 (Vatican City, 2002), pp. 721–32.

Croke, Brian. *Christian Chronicles and Byzantine History: Fifth–Sixth Centuries* (Aldershot, 1992).

———. *Count Marcellinus and His Chronicle* (Oxford, 2001).

Croke, Brian, and Alanna M. Emmett, eds. *History and Historians in Late Antiquity* (Sydney and Oxford, 1983).

Crook, John. *The Architectural Setting of the Cult of Saints in the Early Christian West, c.300–c.1200* (Oxford, 2000).

Davis, Jennifer. "Conceptions of Kingship under Charlemagne" (M.Litt thesis, University of Cambridge, 1999).

Declercq, Georges. *Anno domini: Les Origines de l'ère chrétienne* (Turnhout, 2000).

Deliyannis, Deborah Mauskopf. "Charlemagne's Silver Tables: The Ideology of an Imperial Capital," *Early Medieval Europe* 12 (2003), pp. 159–78.

———, ed. *Historiography in the Middle Ages* (Leiden, 2003).

Depreux, Philippe, and Bruno Judic, eds. *Alcuin de York à Tours. Écriture, pouvoir et réseau dans l'Europe du haut moyen âge,* Annales de Bretagne et des pays de l'Ouest 111 (2004).

Diesenberger, Maximilian. "Rom als virtueller Raum der Märtyrer: Zur gedanklichen Aneignung der Roma suburbana in bayerischen Handschriften um 800," in Elizabeth Vavra, ed., *Imaginäre Räume,* Internationaler Kongress Krems 2003, Veröffentlichungen des Instituts für Realienkunde (Krems, forthcoming), pp. 43–68.

Dietz, Maribel. *Wandering Monks, Virgins and Pilgrims: Ascetic Travel in the Mediterranean World, A.D. 300–800* (University Park, PA, 2005).

Doherty, Hugh. "The Maintenance of Royal Power and Prestige in the Carolingian *regnum* of Aquitaine under Louis the Pious" (M.Phil. dissertation, Faculty of History, University of Cambridge, 1998).

Dopsch, Heinz. "Die Zeit der Karolinger und Ottonen," in Heinz Dopsch, ed., *Geschichte Salzburgs,* vol. 1.1 (Salzburg, 1981), pp. 157–228.

Dubois, Jacques. "Le Martyrologe métrique de Wandelbert, ses sources, son originalité, son influence sur le martyrologe d'Usuard," *Analecta Bollandiana* 79 (1961), pp. 257–93.

———. *Les Martyrologes du moyen âge latin,* Typologie des sources du moyen âge occidental 26 (Turnhout, 1978).

———. *Martyrologes: D'Usuard au Martyrologe Romain* (Abbeville, 1990).

Dummer, Jürgen. "Freculf von Lisieux und die Historia Ecclesiastica Tripartita," *Philologus* 115 (1971), pp. 58–70.

Dümmler, Ernst. "Über Leben und Lehre des Bischofs Claudius von Turin," *Sitzungsberichte der königlich-preussischen Akademie der Wissenschaften zu Berlin* (1895), pp. 427–43.

Duval, Yves-Marie. "Jerôme et l'histoire de l'Église du IVe siècle," in Bernard Pouderon and Yves-Marie Duval, eds., *L'Historiographie de l'église des premiers siècles,* Théologie Historique 114 (Paris, 2001), pp. 381–408.

Edwards, Burton van Name. "Introduction: The Study of the Bible and Carolingian Culture," in Celia Chazelle and Burton van Name Edwards, eds., *The Study of the Bible in the Carolingian Era,* Medieval Church Studies 3 (Turnhout, 2003), pp. 1–16.

Edwards, Catharine. *Writing Rome: Textual Approaches to the City* (Cambridge, 1996).

Emerick, Judson J. "Focusing on the Celebrant: The Column Display inside Santa Pras-sede," in *Mededelingen van het Nederlands Instituut te Rome*, vol. 59 (Rome, 2000), pp. 129–59.

Ermini, Letizia Pani, ed. *Christiana loca: Lo spazio cristiana nella Roma del primo millennio*, 2 vols. (Rome, 2000).

Ermisch, Hubert. *Die Chronik des Regino bis 813* (Göttingen, 1871), summarized in *Neues Archiv* 15 (1891), pp. 312–24.

Esch, Arnold. *Wiederverwendung von Antike im Mittelalter* (Berlin and New York, 2005).

Ewig, Eugen. "Zum Geschichtsbild der Franken und den Anfangen der Merowinger," in Jürgen Petersohn, ed., *Mediaevalia Augiensia: Forschungen zur Geschichte des Mittelalters*, Vorträge und Forschungen 54 (Stuttgart, 2001), pp. 43–58.

Farro, Diane. *The Urban Image of Augustan Rome* (Cambridge, 1996).

Ferrari, Guy. *Early Roman Monasteries: Notes for the History of the Monasteries and Convents at Rome from the Fifth through the Tenth Century*, Studi di antichità cristiana 23 (Vatican, 1957).

Fichtenau, Heinrich. "Abt Richbod und die Annales laureshamenses," in *Beiträge zur Geschichte des Klosters Lorsch*, 2nd ed., Geschichtsblätter für den Kreis Bergstraße, Sonderband 4 (Lorsch, 1980), pp. 277–304.

Foot, Sarah. "The Making of Angelcynn: English Identity before the Norman Conquest," *Transactions of the Royal Historical Society*, 6th series, 6 (1996), pp. 25–50.

———. "Remembering, Forgetting and Inventing: Attitudes to the Past in England after the First Viking Age," *Transactions of the Royal Historical Society*, 6th series, 9 (1999), pp. 185–200.

———. "Finding the Meaning of Form: Narrative in Annals and Chronicles," in Nancy Partner, ed., *Writing Medieval History* (London and New York, 2005), pp. 88–108.

Fotheringham, John Knight. *The Bodleian Manuscript of Jerome's Version of the Chronicle of Eusebius* (Oxford, 1905).

Fouracre, Paul. "The Long Shadow of the Merovingians," in Joanna Story, ed., *Charlemagne: Empire and Society* (Manchester, 2005), pp. 5–21.

Fox, Michael. "Alcuin the Exegete: The Evidence of the *Quaestiones in Genesim*," in Celia Chazelle and Burton van Name Edwards, eds., *The Study of the Bible in the Carolingian Era*, Medieval Church Studies 3 (Turnhout, 2003), pp. 39–60.

Frere, Walter H. *Studies in Early Roman Liturgy*, vol. 3, *The Roman Epistle-Lectionary* (Oxford, 1935).

Gaudemet, Jean. "Survivances romaines dans le droit de la monarchie franque, du Ve au Xe siècle," *Tijdschrift voor Rechtsgeschiedenis* 23 (1955), pp. 149–206.

Geertman, Herman. *More veterum: Il Liber pontificalis e gli edifici ecclesiastici di Roma nella tarda antichità e nell'alto medioevo*, Archaeologia Traiectini 10 (Groningen, 1975).

———. "Documenti, redattori e la formazione del testo dei Liber Pontificalis," in Herman Geertman, ed., *Il Liber Pontificalis e la storia materiale*, Atti del colloquio internazionale, Roma, 21–22 Febbraio 2002, Mededelingen van het Nederlands Instituut te Rome 60/61 (Rome, 2003), pp. 267–355.

——, ed. *Il Liber Pontificalis e la storia materiale*, Atti del colloquio internazionale, Roma, 21–22 Febbraio 2002, Mededelingen van het Nederlands Instituut te Rome 60/61 (Rome, 2003).

Genet, Jean-Philippe. *L'Historiographie médiévale en Europe* (Paris, 1991).

Goetz, Hans-Werner. "Social and Military Institutions," in Rosamond McKitterick, ed., *The New Cambridge Medieval History*, vol. 2, *c.700–c.900* (Cambridge, 1995), pp. 451–80.

——. *Geschichßchreibung und Geschichtsbewußtsein im hohen Mittelalter*, Orbis medievalis: Vorstellungswelten des Mittelalters 1 (Berlin, 1999).

——. "Historical Consciousness and Institutional Concern in European Medieval Historiography," in Sølvi Sogner, ed., *Making Sense of Global History: The Nineteenth International Congress of the Historical Sciences, Oslo, 2000, Commemorative Volume* (Oslo, 2002), pp. 350–65.

Goffart, Walter. "Paul the Deacon's *Gesta episcoporum mettensium* and the Early Design of Charlemagne's Succession," *Traditio* 42 (1986), pp. 59–94.

Goldberg, Eric J. "Popular Revolt, Dynastic Politics, and Aristocratic Factionalism in the Early Middle Ages: The Saxon *stellinga* Reconsidered," *Speculum* 70 (1995), pp. 467–501.

Gorman, Michael. *Biblical Commentaries from the Early Middle Ages*, Millennio Medievale 32, reprints 4 (Florence, 2002).

Grafton, Anthony. *Joseph Scaliger: A Study in the History of Classical Scholarship*, vol. 2, *Historical Chronology* (Oxford, 1993).

Grant, Robert M. *Eusebius as Church Historian* (Oxford, 1980).

Graus, František. "Troja and trojanische Herkunftssage im Mittelalter," in Willi Erzgräber, ed., *Kontinuität und Transformation der Antike im Mittelalter* (Sigmaringen, 1989), pp. 25–44.

Guenée, Bernard. *Histoire et culture historique dans l'Occident médiéval* (Paris, 1980).

Guidobaldi, Federico, and Alessandra Guiglia Guidobaldi, eds. *Ecclesiae Urbis: Atti del congresso internazionale di studi sulle chiese di Roma (IV–X secolo)*, 3 vols., Studi di antichità cristiana 59 (Vatican City, 2002).

Halphen, Louis. *Études critiques sur l'histoire de Charlemagne* (Paris, 1921).

Hannig, Jürgen. *Consensus fidelium: Frühfeudale Interpretationen des Verhältnisses von Königtum und Adel am Beispiel des Frankenreiches* (Stuttgart, 1982).

Hartmann, Wilfried. *Die Synoden der Karolingerzeit im Frankenreich und in Italien: Konziliengeschichte* (Paderborn, Munich, Vienna, and Zurich, 1989).

Haubrichs, Wolfgang. *Die Kultur der Abtei Prüm zur Karolingerzeit: Studien zur Heimat des althochdeutschen Georgsliedes*, Rheinisches Archiv 105 (Bonn, 1979).

Heinzelmann, Martin. *Translationsberichte und andere Quellen der Reliquienkulte*, Typologie des sources du moyen âge occidental 33 (Turnhout, 1979).

Hellmann, Martin. *Tironische Noten in der Karolingerzeit, am Beispiel eines Persius-Kommentars aus der Schule von Tours*, MGH Studien und Texte 27 (Hannover, 2000).

Helm, Rudolf. *Hieronymus Zusätze in Eusebius Chronik und ihr Wert für die Literatur-geschichte*, Philologus, Supplementband 21.2 (Leipzig, 1929).

Hen, Yitzhak. "The Annals of Metz and the Merovingian Past," in Yitzhak Hen and Matthew Innes, eds., *The Uses of the Past in the Early Middle Ages* (Cambridge, 2000), pp. 175–190.

———. *The Royal Patronage of Liturgy in Frankish Gaul to the Death of Charles the Bald (877)*, Henry Bradshaw Society Subsidia 3 (London, 2001).

Hen, Yitzhak and Matthew Innes, eds. *The Uses of the Past in the Early Middle Ages* (Cambridge, 2000).

Herbers, Klaus. "Rom im Frankenreich: Rombeziehung durch Heilige in der Mitte des 9. Jhts," in Dieter R. Bauer, Rudolf Hiestand, Brigitte Kasten and Sonke Lorenz, eds., *Mönchtum—Kirche—Herrschaft, 750–1050: Festschrift Josef Semmler* (Sigmaringen, 1998), pp. 133–69.

———. "Die Stadt Rom und die Päpste von der Spätantike bis zum 9. Jahrhundert," in Christoph Stiegemann and Matthias Wemhoff, eds., *799, Kunst und Kultur der Karolingerzeit: Karl der Große und Papst Leo III. in Paderborn* (Mainz, 1999), vol. 2, pp. 594–606.

———. "Mobilität und Kommunikation in der Karolingerzeit: Die Reliquienreisen der heilige Chrysanthus und Daria," in Nine Miedema and Rudolf Suntrup, eds., *Literatur—Geschichte—Literaturgeschichte: Beiträge zur mediävistischen Literaturwissenschaft: Festschrift für Volker Honemann zum 60. Geburtstag* (Frankfurt am Main, 2003), pp. 647–60.

———. "Das Bild Papst Leo III in der Perspektive des *Liber Pontificalis*," in Meta Niederkorn-Bruck and Anton Scharer, eds., *Erzbischof Arn von Salzburg*, Veröffentlichungen des Instituts für Österreichische Geschichtsforschung 40 (Vienna and Munich, 2004), pp. 137–54.

Herkommer, Hubert. *Überlieferungsgeschichte der Sächsischen Weltchronik: Ein Beitrag zur deutschen Geschichtsschreibung des Mittelalters* (Munich, 1972).

Hill, Joyce. "Authority and Intertextuality in the Works of Aelfric," *Proceedings of the British Academy* 131 (2004), pp. 157–81.

Hillgarth, Jocelyn. "The *Historiae* of Orosius in the Early Middle Ages," in Jean-Claude Fredouille, Louis Holtz, and Marie-Hélène Jullien, eds., *De Tertullien aux Mozarabes: Mélanges offerts à Jacques Fontaine*, vol. 2, *Antiquité tardive et christianisme ancien, VIe–IXe siècles*, Études Augustiniennes: Série Moyen-Âge et temps modernes 26 (Paris, 1992), pp. 157–70.

Hilliard, Paul. "Bede's World Chronicle and the *De temporum ratione* in Its Chronographical and Exegetical Context" (M.Phil. dissertation, Faculty of History, University of Cambridge, 2004).

Hoffmann, Heinz. "Roma caput mundi: Rom und "imperium romanum" zwischen Spätantike und dem 9. Jht," *Roma fra oriente e occidente*, Settimane di Studio del Centro Italiano di studi sull'alto medioevo 49 (Spoleto, 2002), vol. 1, pp. 492–556.

Holter, Kurt. "Die Bibliothek: Handschriften und Inkunabeln," in Karl Ginhart, ed., *Die Kunstdenkmäler des Benediktinerstiftes St. Paul in Lavanttal und seiner Filialkirchen*, Österreichische Kunsttopographie 37 (Vienna, 1969), pp. 360–62.

Honselmann, Klemens. "Reliquientranslationen nach Sachsen," in Viktor H. Elbern, ed., *Das erste Jahrtausend: Kultur und Kunst im werdenden Abendland an Rhein und Ruhr* (Düsseldorf, 1962), pp. 159–93.

Houwen, L. A. J. R., and Alastair A. MacDonald, eds. *Alcuin of York*, Germania latina 3 (Groningen, 1998).

Hunt, E. David. *Holy Land Pilgrimage in the Later Roman Empire, AD 312–460* (Oxford, 1982).

Hunter, Michael. "Germanic and Roman Antiquity and the Sense of the Past in Anglo-Saxon England," *Anglo-Saxon England* 3 (1974), pp. 29–50.

Inglebert, Hervé. *Interpretatio Christiana: Les Mutations des savoirs (cosmographie, géographie, ethnographie, histoire) dans l'Antiquité chrétienne (30–630 après J.-C.)* (Paris, 2001).

———. "Les Chrétiens et l'histoire universelle dans l'Antiquité tardive," in Benoît Jeanjean and Bertrand Lançon, eds., *Saint Jérôme, Chronique: Continuation de la Chronique d'Eusèbe, années 326–378, suivie de quatre études sur les Chroniques et chronographies dans l'Antiqité tardive (IVe–VIe siècles)* (Rennes, 2004), pp. 123–36.

Innes, Matthew. *State and Society in the Early Middle Ages: The Middle Rhine Valley, 400–1000* (Cambridge, 2000).

———. "Teutons or Trojans? The Carolingians and the Germanic Past," in Yitzhak Hen and Matthew Innes, eds., *The Uses of the Past in the Early Middle Ages* (Cambridge, 2000), pp. 227–49.

———. "Charlemagne's government," in Joanna Story ed., *Charlemagne: Empire and society* (Manchester, 2005), pp. 71–89.

Innes, Matthew, and Rosamond McKitterick. "The Writing of History," in Rosamond McKitterick, ed., *Carolingian Culture: Emulation and Innovation* (Cambridge, 1994), pp. 193–222.

Iogna-Prat, Dominique. "Lieu de culte et exégèse liturgique à l'époque carolingienne," in Celia Chazelle and Burton van Name Edwards, eds., *The Study of the Bible in the Carolingian Era*, Medieval Church Studies 3 (Turnhout, 2003), pp. 215–44.

Iogna-Prat, Dominique, Colette Jeudy, and Guy Lobrichon, eds. *L'École carolingienne d'Auxerre de Murethach à Remi, 830–908* (Auxerre, 1991).

Jeanjean, Benoît. "De la *Chronique* à la Consolation à Heliodore (Epist. 60): Les Mutations de la matière historique chez Jérôme," in Bernard Pouderon and Yves-Marie Duval, eds., *L'Historiographie de l'église des premiers siècles*, Théologie Historique 114 (Paris, 2001), pp. 409–23.

Jeanjean, Benoît. "Saint Jérôme, patron des chroniqueurs en langue latine," in Benoît Jeanjean and Bertrand Lançon, eds., *Saint Jérôme, Chronique: Continuation de la Chronique d'Eusèbe, années 326–378, suivie de quatre études sur les Chroniques et chronographies dans l'Antiqité tardive (IVe–VIe siècles)* (Rennes, 2004), pp. 137–78.

Jeanjean, Benoît, and Bertrand Lançon, eds. *Saint Jérôme, Chronique: Continuation de la Chronique d'Eusèbe, années 326–378, suivie de quatre études sur les Chroniques et chronographies dans l'Antiqité tardive (IVe–VIe siècles)* (Rennes, 2004).

Jong, Mayke de. "The Empire as *ecclesia*: Hrabanus Maurus and Biblical *historia* for Rulers," in Yitzhak Hen and Matthew Innes, eds., *The Uses of the Past in the Early Middle Ages* (Cambridge, 2000), pp. 191–226.

Jung, Marc-René. "L'Histoire grecque: Darès et les suites," in Emmanuele Baumgartner and Laurence Harf-Lancner, eds., *Entre fiction et histoire: Troie et Rome au moyen âge* (Paris, 1997), pp. 185–206.

Kamesar, Adam. *Jerome, Greek Scholarship, and the Hebrew Bible: A Study of the "Quaestiones Hebraicae in Genesim"* (Oxford, 1993).

Käuper, Sascha. "II.3. Annales Laureshamenses (Lorscher Annalen)," in Christoph Stiegemann and Matthias Wemhoff, eds., *799, Kunst und Kultur der Karolingerzeit: Karl der Große und Papst Leo III. in Paderborn* (Mainz, 1999), vol. 1, pp. 38–40.

Kelly, Christopher. "Past Imperfect: The Conversion of the Classical Past in Late Antiquity," forthcoming.

Kelly, J. N. D. *Jerome* (London, 1975).

Kooper, Erik, ed. *The Medieval Chronicle*, vol. 2 (Amsterdam and New York, 2002).

Körtum, Hans-Henning. "Weltgeschichte am Ausgang der Karolingerzeit: Regino von Prüm," in Anton Scharer and Georg Scheibelreiter, eds., *Historiographie im frühen Mittelalter*, Veröffentlichungen des Instituts für Österreichische Geschichtsforschung 32 (Vienna and Munich, 1994), pp. 499–513.

Krautheimer, Richard. *Corpus basilicarum Christianarum Romae*, 5 vols. (Rome and New York, 1937–77).

———. "The Carolingian Revival of Early Christian Architecture," *Art Bulletin* 24 (1942), pp. 1–38, reprinted with postscript in Richard Krautheimer, *Studies in Early Christian, Medieval, and Renaissance Art* (New York, 1971), pp. 203–56.

Krautheimer, Richard. *Rome: Profile of a City, 312–1308* (Princeton, 1980).

Kremers, Wilhelm. *Ado von Vienne: Sein Leben und seine Schriften* (Steyl, 1911).

Krüger, Karl. *Die Universalchroniken*, Typologie des sources du moyen âge occidental 16 (Turnhout, 1976).

———. "Neue Beobachtungen zur Datierung von Einhards Karlsvita," *Frühmittelalterliche Studien* 32 (1998), pp. 124–45.

Kühnel, Bianca. *From the Earthly to the Heavenly Jerusalem: Representations of the Holy City in Christian Art of the First Millennium*, Römische Quartalschrift für christliche Altertumskunde und Kirchengeschichte, Supplementband 42 (Rome, Freiburg im Breisgau, and Vienna, 1987).

———. *The End of Time in the Order of Things: Science and Eschatology in Early Medieval Art* (Regensburg, 2003).

Kurze, Friedrich. "Ueber die karolingischen Reichsannalen von 741–829 und ihre Ueberarbeitung: 1. Die handschriftliche Ueberlieferung," *Neues Archiv* 19 (1894), pp. 295–339.

————. "Zur Ueberlieferung der karolingischen Reichsannalen und ihrer Ueberarbeitung," *Neues Archiv* 29 (1903), pp. 619–69.

Lambert, Bernard. *Bibliotheca Hieronymiana Manuscripta: La Tradition manuscrite des oeuvres de saint Jérôme*, Instrumenta patristica 4.3 (Steenbrugge, 1969–72).

Lampen, Angelika. "Die Sachsenkriege," in Christoph Stiegemann and Matthias Wemhoff, eds., *799 Kunst und Kultur der Karolingerzeit: Karl der Große und Papst Leo III. in Paderborn* (Mainz, 1999), vol. 1, pp. 264–72.

Lançon, Bertrand. "La Contribution à l'histoire de l'église de la Chronique de Marcellin d'Illyricum," in Bernard Pouderon and Yves-Marie Duval, eds., *L'Historiographie de l'église des premiers siècles*, Théologie Historique 114 (Paris, 2001), pp. 469–80.

Lapidge, Michael, John Blair, Simon Keynes, and Donald Scragg, eds. *The Blackwell Encyclopaedia of Anglo-Saxon England* (Oxford, 1999).

Laporte, Jean-Pierre. *Le Trésor des saints de Chelles*, Société archéologique et historique de Chelles (Chelles, 1988), pp. 115–60.

Leclercq, Henri. "Domitille (Cimitière de)," in Fernand Cabrol and Henri Leclercq, eds., *Dictionnaire d'archéologie chrétienne et de liturgie*, vol. 4.2 (Paris, 1921), cols. 1409–39.

Lendi, Walter. *Untersuchungen zur frühalemannischen Annalistik: Die Murbacher Annalen, mit Edition*, Scrinium Friburgense 1 (Freiburg in der Schweiz, 1971).

Levy, Kenneth. *Gregorian Chant and the Carolingians* (Princeton, 1998).

Leyser, Conrad. "The Temptations of Cult: Roman Martyr Piety in the Age of Gregory the Great," *Early Medieval Europe* 9 (2000), pp. 289–307.

Lifshitz, Felice. *The Name of the Saint: The Martyrology of Jerome and Access to the Sacred in Francia, 627–827*, Publications in Medieval Studies (Notre Dame, IN, 2006).

Louth, Andrew, and Marco Conti. *Genesis 1–11*, Ancient Christian commentaries on Scripture: Old Testament 1 (Chicago and London, 2001).

Lowe, Elias Avery. *Codices Latini Antiquiores*, 11 vols. plus Supplement (Oxford, 1935–72).

Löwe, Heinz. "Geschichtsschreibung der ausgehenden Karolingerzeit," *Deutsches Archiv für Erforschung des Mittelalters* 23 (1967), pp. 1–30, reprinted in Heinz Löwe, *Von Cassiodor zu Dante: Ausgewählte Aufsätze zur Geschichtsschreibung und politischen Ideenwelt des Mittelalters* (Berlin and New York, 1973), pp. 180–205.

Lozovsky, Natalia. "Carolingian Geographical Tradition: Was It Geography?" *Early Medieval Europe* 5 (1996), pp. 25–44.

————. *"The Earth is Our Book": Geographical Knowledge in the Latin West, ca. 400–1000* (Madison, 2000).

MacKinlay, Alastair P. "Studies in Arator I: The Manuscript Tradition of the *capitula* and *tituli*," *Harvard Studies in Classical Philology* 43 (1932), pp. 123–66.

————. *Arator. The Codices* (Cambridge, MA, 1942).

————. "Latin Commentaries: Arator," *Scriptorium* 6 (1952), pp. 151–56.

MacLean, Simon. *Kingship and Politics in the Late Ninth Century: Charles the Fat and the End of the Carolingian Empire* (Cambridge, 2003).

Magdalino, Paul, ed. *The Perception of the Past in Twelfth-Century Europe* (London, 1992).

Markus, Robert A. Saeculum: *History and Society in the Theology of St. Augustine* (Cambridge, 1970).

Maslakov, G. "Valerius Maximus and Roman Historiography: A Study of the Exempla Tradition," in Hildegard Temporini and Wolfgang Haase, eds., *Aufstieg und Niedergang der römischen Welt: Geschichte und Kultur Roms im Spiegel der neueren Forschung,* vol. 2, *Principat* (Berlin, 1984), pp. 437–96.

Matter, E. Ann. "The Apocalypse in Early Medieval Exegesis," in Richard K. Emmerson and Bernard McGinn, eds., *The Apocalypse in the Middle Ages* (Ithaca and London, 1992), pp. 38–50.

Mayr-Harting, Henry. "Charlemagne, the Saxons and the Imperial Coronation of 800," *English Historical Review* 111 (1996), pp. 1113–33.

McCormick, Michael. *Origins of the European Economy: Communications and Commerce, A.D. 300–900* (Cambridge, 2001).

McCulloh, John M. "From Antiquity to the Middle Ages: Continuity and Change in Papal Relic Policy from the Sixth to the Eighth Century," *Jahrbuch für Antike und Christentum* 22 (1980), pp. 313–24.

McGuire, M. R. P. "Annals and Chronicles," *New Catholic Encyclopedia*, 2nd ed. (New York, 2003), vol. 1, pp. 459–65.

McKitterick, Rosamond, ed. *Carolingian Culture: Emulation and Innovation* (Cambridge, 1994).

———. "Nuns' Scriptoria in England and Francia in the Eighth Century," *Francia* 19.1 (1992), pp. 1–35, reprinted in Rosamond McKitterick, *Books, Scribes and Learning in the Frankish Kingdoms, Sixth–Ninth Centuries* (Aldershot, 1994), chapter 7.

———. Review of Kenneth Levy, *Gregorian Chant and the Carolingians, Early Music History* 19 (2000), pp. 279–90.

———. "Kulturelle Verbindungen zwischen England und den fränkischen Reichen in der Zeit der Karolinger: Kontexte und Implikationen," in Joachim Ehlers, ed., *Deutschland und der Westen Europas im Mittelalter*, Vorträge und Forschungen 56 (Stuttgart, 2002), pp. 121–48.

———. *History and Memory in the Carolingian World* (Cambridge, 2004).

———. "History, Law and Communication with the Past in the Carolingian Period," in *Comunicare e significare nell'alto medioevo*, Settimane di Studio del Centro Italiano di studi sull'alto medioevo 52 (Spoleto, 2005), pp. 941–79.

McLendon, Charles. "Louis the Pious, Rome, and Constantinople," in Cecil L. Striker, ed., *Architectural Studies in Memory of Richard Krautheimer* (Mainz am Rhein, 1996), pp. 103–6.

Merrills, Andrew H. *History and Geography in Late Antiquity* (Cambridge, 2005).

Momigliano, Arnaldo. "Pagan and Christian Historiography in the Fourth Century A.D.," in Arnaldo Momigliano, ed., *The Conflict between Paganism and Christianity in the Fourth Century* (Oxford, 1963), pp. 79–99.

Mommsen, Theodor. "Zur Weltchronik vom J. 741," *Neues Archiv* 22 (1896) pp. 548–53, reprinted in Theodor Mommsen, *Gesammelte Schriften*, vol. 6 (Berlin, 1910), pp. 643–48.

Monod, Gabriel. *Études critiques sur les sources de l'histoire carolingienne* (Paris, 1898).

Mordek, Hubert. "Die Hedenen als politische Kraft im austrasischen Frankenreich," in Jörg Jarnut, Ulrich Nonn, and Michael Richter, eds., *Karl Martell in seiner Zeit* (Sigmaringen, 1994), pp. 345–66.

———. *Bibliotheca capitularium regum Francorum manuscripta: Überlieferung und Traditionszusammenhang der fränkischen Herrschererlasse*, MGH Hilfsmittel 15 (Munich, 1995).

Morton, Catherine. "Boethius in Pavia: The Tradition and the Scholars," in Luca Obertello, ed., *Atti del Congresso internazionale di studi boeziani, Pavia, 1980* (Rome, 1981), pp. 49–58.

Mosshammer, Alden A. *The Chronicle of Eusebius and Greek Chronographic Tradition* (Lewisburg, PA, 1979).

Naturewicz, Chester F. "Freculphus of Lisieux, His Chronicle and a Mont St Michel Manuscript," *Sacris Erudiri* 17 (1966), pp. 90–134.

Nees, Lawrence. *A Tainted Mantle: Hercules and the Classical Tradition at the Carolingian Court* (Philadelphia, 1991).

Nelson, Janet L. "Translating Images of Authority: The Christian Roman Emperors in the Carolingian World," in Mary M. Mackenzie and Charlotte Roueché, eds., *Images of Authority: Papers Presented to Joyce Reynolds on the Occasion of her Seventieth Birthday* (Cambridge, 1992), pp. 194–205, reprinted in Janet L. Nelson, *The Frankish World* (London, 1996), pp. 89–98.

———. "Women at the court of Charlemagne: A Case of Monstrous Regiment?" in John C. Parsons, ed., *Medieval Queenship* (Stroud, 1993), pp. 43–61, reprinted in Janet L. Nelson, *The Frankish World, 750–900* (London, 1996), pp. 223–42.

———. *The Frankish World, 750–900* (London, 1996).

———. "The Siting of the Council at Frankfort: Some Reflections on Family and Politics," in Rainer Berndt, ed., *Das Frankfurter Konzil von 794: Kristallisationspunkt karolingischer Kultur*, Quellen und Abhandlungen zur mittelrheinischen Kirchengeschichte 80 (Mainz, 1997), pp. 149–66.

———. "Aachen as a Place of Power," in Mayke de Jong, Frans Theuws with Carine van Rhijn, eds., *Topographies of Power in the Early Middle Ages*, Transformation of the Roman World 6 (Leiden, 2001), pp. 217–42.

Niederkorn-Bruck, Meta. "Das Salzburger historische Martyrolog aus der Arn-Zeit und seine Bedeutung für die Textgeschichte des 'Martyrologium Bedae,'" in Meta Niederkorn-Bruck and Anton Scharer, eds., *Erzbischof Arn von Salzburg*, Veröffentlichungen des Instituts für Österreichische Geschichtsforschung 40 (Vienna and Munich, 2004), pp. 155–71.

Niederkorn-Bruck, Meta, and Anton Scharer, eds. *Erzbischof Arn von Salzburg*, Veröffentlichungen des Instituts für Österreichische Geschichtsforschung 40 (Vienna and Munich, 2004).

Noble, Thomas F. X. *The Republic of St. Peter: The Birth of the Papal State, 680–825* (Philadelphia, 1984).

————. "From Brigandage to Justice: Charlemagne, 785–794," in Celia M. Chazelle, ed., *Literacy, Politics, and Artistic Innovation in the Early Medieval West: Papers Delivered at "A Symposium on Early Medieval Culture," Bryn Mawr College, Bryn Mawr, PA* (Lanham, New York, and London, 1992), pp. 49–75.

————. "The Papacy in the Eighth and Ninth Centuries," in Rosamond McKitterick, ed., *The New Cambridge Medieval History*, vol. 2, c.*700–c.900* (Cambridge, 1995), pp. 563–86.

————. "Paradoxes and Possibilities in the Sources for Roman Society in the Early Middle Ages," in Julia M. H. Smith, ed., *Early Medieval Rome and the Christian West: Essays in Honour of Donald A. Bullough* (Leiden, 2000), pp. 55–83.

Oexle, Otto-Gerhard. "Coniuratio et gilde dans l'Antiquité et dans le haut moyen age: Remarques sur la continuité des formes de la vie sociale," *Francia* 10 (1982), pp. 1–19.

————. "*Coniuratio* und Gilde im frühen Mittelalter," in Berent Schwineköper, ed., *Gilden und Zünfte: Kaufmännische und gewerbliche Genossenschaften im frühen und hohen Mittelalter*, Vorträge und Forschungen 29 (Sigmaringen, 1985), pp. 151–213.

O'Loughlin, Thomas. *Teachers and Code Breakers: The Latin Genesis Tradition, 430–800*, Instrumenta patristica 35 (Turnhout, 1998).

Oort, Johannes van. *Jurusalem and Babylon: A Study into Augustine's "City of God" and the Sources of His Doctrine of the Two Cities* (Leiden, 1991).

Ortenberg, Veronica. "Archbishop Sigeric's Journey to Rome in 990," *Anglo-Saxon England* 19 (1990), pp. 197–246.

Palazzo, Eric. *Liturgie et société au moyen âge* (Paris, 2000), pp. 199–202.

Pani Ermini, Letizia, ed. *Christiana loca: Lo spazio cristiana nella Roma del primo millennio*, 2 vols (Rome, 2000)

Pascher, Hans Peter. "*9.7 Annales Lauveshamenses*," in Hartwig Pucker, ed., *Schatzhaus Kärntens: Landesausstellung St. Paul, 1991: 900 Jahre Benediktinerstift*, vol. 1, *Katalog* (Klagenfurt, 1991), p. 156.

Pearse, Roger, ed. Preface to the online edition of Jerome, *Chronicle* (2005) at http://www.tertullian.org/fathers/jerome_chronicle_00_eintro.htm.

Pfeil, Elisabeth. *Die fränkische und deutsche Romidee des frühen Mittelalters*, Forschungen zur mittelalterlichen und neueren Geschichte 3 (Munich, 1929).

Phillips, L. Edward. "A Note on the Gifts of Leo III to the Church of Rome: *Vestes cum storiis*," *Ephemerides liturgicae* 102 (1988), pp. 72–78.

Pietri, Charles. *Roma Christiana: Recherches sur l'église de Rome (311–440)*, Bibliothèque des Écoles françaises d'Athène et de Rome 224 (Rome, 1976).

Pilsworth, Clare. "Dating the *Gesta martyrum*: A Manuscript-Based Approach," in Kate Cooper, ed., *The Roman Martyrs and the Politics of Memory*, special issue of *Early Medieval Europe* 9 (2000), pp. 309–24.

Pizarro, Joaquín Martínez. "Ethnic and National History, ca. 500–1000," in Deborah Mauskopf Deliyannis, ed., *Historiography in the Middle Ages* (Leiden, 2003), pp. 43–88.

Pössel, Christina. "Symbolic Communication and the Negotiation of Power at Carolingian Regnal Assemblies, 814–840" (Ph.D. thesis, University of Cambridge, 2003).

Pouderon, Bernard, and Yves-Marie Duval, eds. *L'Historiographie de l'église des premiers siècles*, Théologie historique 114 (Paris, 2001).

Prinz, Joseph. "Der Karolingische Kalender der HS.Ambros.M12 sup," in *Festschrift für Hermann Heimpel*, Veröffentlichungen des Max-Planck-Instituts für Geschichte 36.3 (Göttingen, 1972), pp. 290–327.

Prinz, Otto. "Die Überarbeitung der Chronik Reginos aus sprachlicher Sicht," in Alf Önnerfors, Johnanes Rathofer, and Fritz Wagner, eds., *Literatur und Sprache im europäischen Mittelalter: Festschrift für Karl Langosch zum 70. Geburtstag* (Darmstadt, 1973), pp. 122–41.

Prou, Maurice, and Eugène Chartraire. "Authentiques de reliques conservée au trésor de la cathédrale de Sens," *Mémoires de la Société Nationale des Antiquaires de France*, 6th series, 9 (1900), pp. 129–72.

Purcell, Nicholas. "The City of Rome," in Richard Jenkyns, ed., *The Legacy of Rome* (Oxford, 1992), pp. 421–55.

Quentin, Henri. *Les Martyrologes historiques du moyen âge: Étude sur la formation du martyrologe romain* (Paris, 1908).

Raaijmakers, Janneke. *Sacred Time, Sacred Space: History and Identity at the Monastery of Fulda (744–856)* (academisch proefschrift, Ph.D., University of Amsterdam, 2003).

Rabe, Susan. *Faith, Art, and Politics at Saint-Riquier: The Symbolic Vision of Angilbert* (Philadelphia, 1995).

Rapp, Claudia. "Literary Culture under Justinian," in Michael Maas, ed., *The Cambridge Companion to Justinian* (Cambridge, 2005), pp. 376–97.

Ratti, Stéphane. "Les Sources de la *Chronique* de Jérôme pour les annés 357–364: Nouveaux éléments," in Bernard Pouderon and Yves-Marie Duval, eds., *L'Historiographie de l'église des premiers siècles*, Théologie Historique 114 (Paris, 2001), pp. 425–50.

Ray, Roger D. "Bede, the Exegete, as Historian," in Gerald Bonner, Famulus Christi: *Essays in Commemoration of the Thirteenth Centenary of the Birth of the Venerable Bede* (London, 1976), pp. 125–40.

Reiffenberg, Baron de. "Notices des manuscrits," *Compte-rendu des séances de la commission royale d'histoire* 7 (Brussels, 1844), pp. 167–92, and 8 (Brussels, 1844), pp. 241–60.

Reimitz, Helmut. "Ein fränkisches Geschichtsbuch aus Saint-Amand und der Codex Vindobonensis palat. 473," in Christoph Egger and Herwig Wiegl, eds., *Text–Schrift–Codex: Quellenkundliche Arbeiten aus dem Institut für Österreichische Geschichtsforschung* (Vienna, 1999), pp. 34–90.

———. "Social Networks and Identities in Frankish Historiography: New Aspects of the Textual History of Gregory of Tours' *Historiae*," in Richard Corradini, Maximilian Diesenberger, and Helmut Reimitz, eds., *The Construction of Communities in the Early Middle Ages: Texts, Resources and Artefacts*, The Transformation of the Roman World 12 (Leiden, 2003), pp. 229–68.

———. "Die Konkurrenz der Ursprünge in der fränkischen Historiographie," in Walter Pohl, ed., *Die Suche nach den Ursprüngen: Von der Bedeutung des frühen Mittelalters*,

Forschungen zur Geschichte des Mittelalters 8: Österreichische Akademie der Wissenschaften, phil.-hist. Klasse, Denkschriften 322 (Vienna, 2004), pp. 191–210.

Reuter, Timothy. "Assembly Politics in Western Europe from the Eighth Century to the Twelfth," in Peter Linehan and Janet L. Nelson, eds., *The Medieval World* (London, 2002), pp. 432–50.

———. "Charlemagne and the World Beyond the Rhine," in Joanna Story, ed., *Charlemagne: Empire and Society* (Manchester, 2005), pp. 183–94.

Reynolds, Leighton D. *Texts and Transmission: A Survey of the Latin Classics* (Oxford, 1983).

Richter, Michael. *The Formation of the Medieval West: Studies in the Oral Culture of the Barbarians* (Dublin, 1994).

Robbins, Frank E. "The Hexaemeral Literature: A Study of the Greek and Latin Commentaries on Genesis" (Ph.D. dissertation, University of Chicago, 1912) and Ann Arbor micrograph, 1966.

Roberts, Michael. *Biblical Epic and Rhetorical Paraphrase in Late Antiquity* (Liverpool, 1985).

Röckelein, Hedwig. "Über Hagio-Geo-Graphien: Mirakel in Translationsberichten des 8. und 9. Jahrhunderts," in Martin Heinzelmann, Klaus Herbers, and Dieter R. Bauer, eds., *Mirakel im Mittelalter: Konzeptionen, Erscheinungsformen, Deutungen*, Beiträge zur Hagiographie 3 (Stuttgart, 2002), pp. 166–79.

———. *Reliquientranslationen nach Sachsen im 9. Jahrhundert: Über Kommunikationen, Mobilität und Öffentlichkeit im Frühmittelalter* (Stuttgart, 2002).

Roma fra oriente e occidente. Settimane di studio del Centro Italiano di studi sull'alto medioevo 49 (Spoleto, 2002).

Rossi, Giovanni B. de. *Roma sotteranea christiana*, vol. 1 (Rome, 1964).

Sæbo, Magne, ed. *Hebrew Bible/Old Testament: The History of Its Interpretation*, vol. 1.1 (Göttingen, 1996).

Sághy, Marianne. "*Scinditur in partes populus:* Pope Damasus and the Martyrs of Rome," in Kate Cooper, ed., *The Roman Martyrs and the Politics of Memory*, special issue of *Early Medieval Europe* 9 (2000), pp. 273–87.

Santangeli Valenzani, Riccardo. "Profanes Bauwesen in Rom um das Jahr 800," in Christoph Stiegemann and Matthias Wemhoff, eds., *799, Kunst und Kultur der Karolingerzeit: Karl der Große und Papst Leo III. in Paderborn* (Mainz, 1999), vol. 3, pp. 550–57.

Scharff, Thomas. *Die Kämpfe der Herrscher und der Heiligen: Krieg und historische Erinnerung in der Karolingerzeit* (Darmstadt, 2002).

Schieffer, Rudolf. *Die Entstehung von Domkapiteln in Deutschland* (Bonn, 1976).

———. "Reliquientranslationen nach Sachsen," in Christoph Stiegemann and Matthias Wemhoff, eds., *799, Kunst und Kultur der Karolingerzeit: Karl der Große und Papst Leo III. in Paderborn* (Mainz, 1999), vol. 3, pp. 484–93.

———. "Karolingische Herrscher in Rom," in *Roma fra oriente e occidente*, Settimane di Studio del Centro Italiano di studi sull'alto medioevo 49 (Spoleto, 2002), vol. 1, pp. 101–28.

Schleidgen, Wolf-Rüdiger. *Die Überlieferungsgeschichte der Chronik des Regino von Prüm*, Quellen und Abhandlungen zur mittelrheinischen Kirchengeschichte 31 (Mainz, 1977).

Schmale, Franz-Josef. *Funktion und Formen mittelalterlicher Geschichtsschreibung: Eine Einführung* (Darmstadt, 1985).

Schmidinger, Heinrich. "Das Papsttum und die Salzburger Kirche im 8. Jahrhundert," in Eberhard Zwink, ed., *Frühes Mönchtum in Salzburg,* Salzburg Diskussionen (Salzburg, 1983), pp. 145–55.

Schröer, Norbert. *Die Annales S. Amandi und ihre Verwandten: Untersuchungen zu einer Gruppe karolingischer Annalen des 8. und frühen 9. Jahrhunderts,* Göppinger Akademische Beiträge 85 (Göppingen, 1975).

Schulz, Paul. *Die Chronik des Regino vom Jahre 813 an* (Halle, 1888).

Seeliger, Hans Reinhard. "Einhards römische Reliquien: Zur Übertragung der heiligen Marzellinus und Petrus ins Frankenreich," *Römische Quartalschrift* 83 (1988), pp. 58–75.

Simson, Bernhard von. "Der überarbeitete und bis zum Jahre 741 fortgesetze Chronik des Bedas," *Forschungen zur Deutschen Geschichte* 19 (1879), pp. 97–138.

Smith, E. Baldwin. *Architectural Symbolism of Imperial Rome and the Middle Ages* (Princeton, 1956).

Smith, Julia M. H., ed. *Early Medieval Rome and the Christian West: Essays in Honour of Donald A. Bullough* (Leiden, 2000).

———. "Old Saints, New Cults: Roman Relics in Carolingian Francia," and "Appendix: Relic Translations from Rome to Francia, 750–900," in Julia M. H. Smith, ed., *Early Medieval Rome and the Christian West: Essays in Honour of Donald A. Bullough* (Leiden, 2000), pp. 317–40.

———. " 'Emending Evil Ways and Praising God's Omnipotence': Einhard and the Uses of Roman Martyrs," in Kenneth Mills and Anthony Grafton, eds., *Conversion in Late Antiquity and the Early Middle Ages: Seeing and Believing* (Rochester, 2003), pp. 189–223.

Sot, Michel. *Un Historien et son église au Xe siècle: Flodoard de Reims* (Paris, 1993).

———. "La Rome antique dans l'historiographie épiscopale de Gaule," Settimane di Studio del Centro Italiano di studi sull'alto medioevo, La Mendola, 1998, Milan (Spoleto, 2001), pp. 163–88.

———. "Local and Institutional History (300–1000)," in Deborah Mauskopf Deliyannis, ed., *Historiography in the Middle Ages* (Leiden, 2003), pp. 89–114.

———. "Autorité du passé lointain, autorité du passé proche dans l'historiographie épiscopale (VIII–XI siècles): Les Cas de Metz, Auxerre et Reims," in Jean-Marie Sansterre, ed., *L'Autorité du passé dans les sociétés médiévales,* Collection de l'École française de Rome 333 (Rome, 2004), pp. 139–62.

Spiegel, Gabriele. *The Past as Text: The Theory and Practice of Medieval Historiography* (Baltimore, 1997).

Staab, Franz. "Die Königin Fastrada," in Rainer Berndt, ed., *Das Frankfurter Konzil von 794: Kristallisationspunkt karolingischer Kultur,* Quellen und Abhandlungen zur mittelrheinischen Kirchengeschichte 80 (Mainz, 1997), pp. 183–218.

Staubach, Nikolaus. "Christiana tempora: Augustin und das Ende der alten Geschichte in der Weltchronik Fredulphs von Lisieux," *Fruhmittelalterliche Studien* 29 (1995), pp. 167–206.

Steffens, Franz. *Lateinische Paläographie*, 2nd ed. (Trier, 1909); French trans. Rémi Coulon, *Paléographie Latine* (Paris, 1910).

Stevens, Wesley. *Bede's Scientific Achievement*, Jarrow Lecture, 1985 (Jarrow, 1986).

———. "A Present Sense of Things Past: *Quid est enim tempus?*" in Gerhard Jaritz and Gerson Moreno-Riaño, eds., *Time and Eternity: The Medieval Discourse*, International Medieval Research 9 (Turnhout, 2003), pp. 9–28.

Stiegemann, Christoph, and Matthias Wemhoff, eds. *799, Kunst und Kultur der Karolingerzeit: Karl der Große und Papst Leo III. in Paderborn* (Mainz, 1999).

Story, Joanna, ed. *Charlemagne: Empire and Society* (Manchester, 2005).

———. "The Frankish Annals of Lindisfarne and Kent," *Anglo-Saxon England* 34 (2005), pp. 59–109.

Thacker, Alan. "In Search of Saints: The English Church and the Cult of Roman Apostles and Martyrs in the Seventh and Eighth Centuries," in Julia M. H. Smith, ed., *Early Medieval Rome and the Christian West: Essays in Honour of Donald A. Bullough* (Leiden, 2000), pp. 247–78.

———. *Charlemagne and Rome: The Epitaph of Pope Hadrian I*, Medieval History and Archaeology (Oxford, forthcoming).

———. "*Loca sanctorum*: The significance of place in the study of the saints," in Alan Thacker and Richard Sharpe, eds., *Local Saints and Local Churches in the Medieval West* (Oxford, 2002), pp. 1–43.

Vessey, Mark, Karla Pollmann, and Allan D. Fitzgerald, eds. *History, Apocalypse, and the Secular Imagination: New Essays on Augustine's "City of God"* (Bowling Green, OH, 1999).

Vidier, Alexandre. *L'Historiographie à Saint-Benoît-sur-Loire et les miracles de saint Benoît* (Paris, 1965).

Viret, Jacques. "La Réforme liturgique carolingienne et les deux traditions du chant romain," in Pierre Riché, Carol Heitz, and François Héber-Suffrin, eds., *Autour de la reine Hildegarde*, Paris Nanterre Études 5 (Paris, 1987), pp. 117–27.

Vogel, Cyrille. *Medieval Liturgy: An Introduction to the Sources*, revised trans. William Storey and Niels Rasmussen (Washington, D.C., 1986).

Vry, Volker de. *Liborius. Brückenbauer Europas: Die mittelalterlichen Viten und Translationsberichte* (Paderborn, 1997).

Waitz, Georg. "Zur Geschichtsschreibung der Karolingischer Zeit," *Neues Archiv* 5 (1880), pp. 475–91.

Wallace-Hadrill, David. "The Eusebian Chronicle: The Extent and Date of Composition of Its Early Editions," *Journal of Theological Studies*, new series, 6 (1955), pp. 248–53.

Walser, Gerold. *Die Einsiedler Inschriftensammlung und der Pilgerführer durch Rom (Codex Einsidlensis 326)* (Stuttgart, 1987).

Wattenbach, Wilhelm, Wilhelm Levison, and Heinz Löwe. *Deutsche Geschichtsquellen im Mittelalter: Vorzeit und Karolinger*, bk. 2, *Die Karolinger vom Anfang des 8. Jahrhunderts bis zum Tode Karls des Großen* (Weimar, 1953); bk. 3, *Die Karolinger vom Tode Karls des Großen bis zum Vertrag von Verdun* (Weimar, 1957).

Webb, Matilda. *The Churches and Catacombs of Early Christian Rome* (Brighton, 2001).

Werner, Karl-Ferdinand. "Zur Arbeitsweise des Regino von Prüm," *Die Welt als Geschichte* 2 (1959), pp. 96–116, reprinted in Karl-Ferdinand Werner, *Einheit der Geschichte: Studien zur Historiographie* (Sigmaringen, 1999), pp. 136–56.

Werra, Joseph. *Über den Continuator Reginonis* (Leipzig, 1883).

White, Hayden. *The Content of the Form: Narrative Discourse and Historical Representation* (Baltimore, 1987).

Wickham, Chris. "Gossip and Resistance among the Medieval Peasantry," *Past and Present* 160 (1998), pp. 3–24.

Wickham, Chris. "Ninth-Century Byzantium through Western Eyes," in Leslie Brubaker, ed., *Byzantium in the Ninth Century: Dead or Alive?* (Birmingham, 1998), pp. 246–56.

Wilmart, André. "Reliques réunies à Jouarre," in *Analecta reginensia*, Studi e testi 59 (Vatican City, 1933), pp. 9–17.

Witherington III, Ben, ed. *History, Society and Literature in the Book of Acts* (Cambridge, 1996).

Wolfram, Herwig. *Salzburg, Bayern, Österreich: Die Conversio Bagoariorum et Carantanorum und die Quellen ihrer Zeit*, Mitteilungen des Instituts für Österreichische Geschichtsforschung, Ergänzungsband 31 (Vienna and Munich, 1995).

Wolfram, Herwig, and Maximilian Diesenberger. "Arn und Alkuin bis 804: Zwei Freunde und ihre Schriften," in Meta Niederkorn-Bruck and Anton Scharer, eds., *Erzbischof Arn von Salzburg*, Veröffentlichungen des Instituts für Österreichische Geschichtsforschung (Vienna and Munich, 2004), pp. 81–106.

Wood, Diana, ed. *Martyrs and Martyrologies*, Studies in Church History 30 (Oxford, 1993).

Wood, Ian. "Defining the Franks: Frankish Origins in Early Medieval Historiography," in Simon Forde, ed., *Concepts of National Identity in the Early Middle Ages*, Leeds Texts and Monographs, new series, 14 (Leeds, 1995), pp. 47–58.

Woodman, A. J. "Velleius Paterculus," in Thomas A. Dorey, ed., *Empire and Aftermath* (London, 1975), pp. 1–25.

Wormald, Patrick. *The Making of English Law: King Alfred to the Twelfth Century*, vol. 1, *Legislation and Its Limits* (Oxford, 2000).

Zeller, Bernhard. "Liudolfinger als fränkische Könige? Überlegungen zur sogenannten Continuatio Reginonis," in Richard Corradini, Christina Pössel, Rob Meens, and Philip Shaw, eds., *Texts and Identities in the Early Middle Ages* (Vienna, 2006), pp. 205–24.

Ziolkowski, Jan M., and Michael C. J. Putnam, eds. *The Virgilian Tradition: The First Fifteen Hundred Years* (New Haven, CT, and London, 2006).

Index

Manuscripts are indexed under the place name of the library

ROSAMOND McKITTERICK is professor of medieval history at the University of Cambridge. She is the author and editor of over twenty books, including *History and Memory in the Carolingian World.*